THE PRISON INDUSTRY

THE PRISON INDUSTRY

HOW IT WORKS AND WHO PROFITS

BIANCA TYLEK AND
WORTH RISES

THE
NEW
PRESS

NEW YORK
LONDON

Requests for permission to reproduce selections from this book should be made through our website: https://thenewpress.com/contact.

Published in the United States by The New Press, New York, 2025
Distributed by Two Rivers Distribution

LIBRARY OF CONGRESS CATALOGING-IN-PUBLICATION DATA

Names: Tylek, Bianca, author. | Worth Rises (Organization), issuing body.
Title: The prison industry : how it works and who profits / Bianca Tylek &
    Worth Rises.
Description: New York : The New Press, [2025] | Includes bibliographical
    references and index. | Summary: "An exposé of who profits from mass
    incarceration, culminating in a compelling case for abolition"--
    Provided by publisher.
Identifiers: LCCN 2024015298 | ISBN 9781620978399 (paperback) | ISBN
    9781620978689 (ebook)
Subjects: LCSH: Prison industrial complex--United States.
Classification: LCC HV9471 .T98 2025 | DDC 365--dc23/eng/20241120
LC record available at https://lccn.loc.gov/2024015298

The New Press publishes books that promote and enrich public discussion and understanding of the issues vital to our democracy and to a more equitable world. These books are made possible by the enthusiasm of our readers; the support of a committed group of donors, large and small; the collaboration of our many partners in the independent media and the not-for-profit sector; booksellers, who often hand-sell New Press books; librarians; and above all by our authors.

www.thenewpress.com

Book design and composition by Bookbright Media
This book was set in Noto Sans and Avenir Next

Printed in the United States of America
10 9 8 7 6 5 4 3 2 1

CONTENTS

WORTH RISES

Worth Rises is a nonprofit organization dismantling the prison industry and ending the exploitation of those it touches. We work to expose the commercialization of the legal system and advocate and organize to protect and return the economic resources extracted from impacted communities.

We envision a society in which no entity or individual relies on human caging or control for their wealth, operation, or livelihood. Through our work, we strive to help pave the road toward a world without police and prisons.

As part of our public education strategy, we conduct research, collect data, and perform innovative analyses aimed at unmasking the harm caused by the prison industry. Understanding the mobilizing power of knowledge, we transform our analyses into accessible and compelling content designed to increase awareness and shift discourse around the commercialization of the criminal legal system.

ACKNOWLEDGMENTS

The authors graciously acknowledge everyone whose time, energy, and passion went into the publication of this book. We thank current and former Worth Rises staff who contributed to its content, including Tommaso Bardelli, Taylor Campbell, Megan French-Marcelin, Martin Garcia, Tolu Lawal, Connor McCleskey, Luke Noel, and Dana Rasso. We also thank Hannah Ambinder, Tamar Davis, Ekemini Ekpo, Benjamin Finegan, the Harvard Prison Legal Assistance Project, and the Yale Undergraduate Prison Project for their writing contributions, editing assistance, and research support. We thank all the people impacted by the carceral system who lent their stories to this book, namely Matthew Carrier, Jasma Credle, Joseph Delaluz, Sheron Edwards, Vidal Guzman, Sarah Faye Hanna, Larry Hardy, Jesse Krimes, Diane Lewis, Johnny Perez, Jorge Renaud, and Talib Williams. Finally, we thank Jan Combopiano and Adobe—more specifically, Jon Rogers, Jen Alleman, Mark Apker, Julie Carvalho, Josh Felt, Michael Fielding, Prashant S G, Benjamin Hillyard, Charlie Hunt, Nathan Metcalf, Mike Niedert, Nate Priday, Jamie Robinson, Aaron Sadock, and Tyson Young—for their citation assistance.

INTRODUCTION

We are living in a watershed moment created by generations of principled struggle led by Black, brown, and Indigenous people. Outrage about brutal police killings and neglect and abuse in prisons and jails has finally bubbled over and led to calls for the abolition of the carceral state. To those of us who have done this work for years, it is remarkable to hear abolition—a concept far from mainstream not too long ago—discussed in boardrooms, classrooms, conferences, academic journals, and media. But if we are truly to abolish prisons, we must understand the systems that uphold them.

The prison industry is comprised of a vast matrix of public-private partnerships that undergird the nation's commitment to human caging and control. It is a seemingly amorphous system of more than 4,000 corporations, and their government conspirators, that profit from the incarceration of grandparents, parents, children, siblings, and cousins. It relies on starvcommunities of economic, social, and political capital to exploiting their devastation.

This book maps the 12 sectors of the prison industry and details the extraction of wealth from the people who have been most disproportionately brutalized by overpolicing, mass criminalization, mass incarceration, and mass surveillance. It explains how the carceral state has metastasized across our economy and evolved to maintain systems of oppression in the face of shifting public opinion for the benefit of a privileged few.

With this book, we offer a blueprint for the constantly evolving prison industry. In each chapter, we share the origin story of privatization for that sector, what corporations are involved, how much money is at stake, what methods they use to extract resources from public coffers and communities, and what harm they cause people, families, and communities. While focused largely on the private sector's immersion into the carceral state, the book also highlights the government's complicity, facilitation, and even collaboration in these corporate abuses. We also share powerful first-person narratives that are critical to understanding the impact the prison industry has had on real people.

We must know where we are coming from to change the course of where we are going, especially as corporations and their government partners pivot to new forms of shackling, such as electronic monitoring and other forms of community surveillance, to profit from mass human control. We hope this book serves as a tool in the dismantling of the prison industry and destruction of the wholly oppressive carceral state, and that readers can imagine and design a better world built on care, not cages.

ARCHITECTURE
+ CONSTRUCTION

This [layout] improves security and floods the facility with natural light, making the white-painted cells feel more spacious.

— HOK, architecture and engineering firm[1]

Following the civil rights movement of the 1960s, state-sponsored deindustrialization and suburbanization supported white flight and hollowed out urban centers. In 1971, President Richard Nixon launched the war on drugs to intentionally disrupt urban Black communities.[6] Incarceration quickly swelled, and prisons and jails began popping up all over the country, particularly in rural areas that were struggling to replace jobs in waning industries like farming and mining.[7]

By the 1990s, the racist war on drugs and rising crime rates stemming from increased structural inequities had spurred the vilification of Black people

Description: Government agencies contract with corporate architects, designers, engineers, and contractors to design, construct, renovate, and maintain prisons, jails, immigration detention centers, and youth facilities.

$4.6 billion
Annual spending on correctional construction[2]

6,000+
Corrections facilities[3]

277%
Jail capacity growth 1970–2017[4]

in the media and bipartisan consen-
sus on "tough-on-crime" policies. The
1994 Omnibus Crime Bill represented
the culmination of these ideologies,

916,000
Jail beds[5]

dramatically escalating prison and jail expansion by offering states federal
subsidies—totaling $9 billion—to enact harsh sentencing laws, including man-
datory minimums that mandate certain prison sentences regardless of individual circumstances.[8] Consequently, between 1984 and 2005, a new prison
or jail was built every 8.5 days in the United States[9]—70 percent of which
were in rural communities continuing to suffer job loss that eagerly bought
into exaggerated promises of economic prosperity.[10] All the while, prison and
jail architects, engineers, and contractors raked in billions of dollars.

CORRECTIONS FACILITIES IN THE UNITED STATES

1970   2000

While corrections facilities are no longer being built with such haste,
there is still plenty of business for those who build them. Despite bipartisan efforts to drive down carceral populations in recent years, old
and decaying facilities continue to be restored or replaced with larger,
modern structures.

Across the country, law enforcement and policy makers alike have
extolled the notion of modernization as a means to make prisons and jails
more humane, sinking millions or sometimes billions of dollars into projects
that do nothing to address the harm caused by the institutions themselves.

Architecture, engineering, and construction firms are chomping at the bit to design and build this next iteration of cells, boasting of innovations like window slats that allow natural light to pass through. These architects, engineers, and contractors lay the foundation and framework for mass incarceration, literally.

HOW MUCH MONEY IS AT STAKE?

Federal, state, and local governments pour billions of dollars into correctional construction every year. Government spending on correctional construction peaked at $8 billion in 2008 and then fell to $4.6 billion by 2018 as public spending constricted after the market crash and the carceral population began to decrease.[11] Though some players exited the market amid concerns that it would never bounce back to pre-2008 recession levels, many firms consolidated operations to capitalize on economies of scale and pressed on.[12]

Current spending is enough to grow bed capacity every year,[13] especially in rural areas, where debunked arguments that prisons spur local economic growth still control the expansion narrative, and local communities, where architecture, engineering, and construction firms fund sheriff races. In fact, between 2009 and 2019, while the jail population declined by roughly 40,000 across the country, the number of jail beds climbed by more than 86,000.[14] Many of the largest correctional construction projects today are new jails, ranging from $130 million for a county jail in Land O' Lakes, Florida,[15] to $8.7 billion for the plan to close the Rikers Island jail complex in New York City and build four community-based jails in its stead.[16]

WHAT CORPORATIONS ARE INVOLVED?

Architecture, engineering, and construction firms work hand in hand to design and build corrections facilities. The largest architecture players in the market are also some of the nation's largest firms: HDR and HOK.

HDR has designed over 275 corrections facilities[17] and HOK has designed more than 100,000 correctional beds.[18]

MARKET SHARE

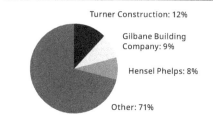

Source: IBIS World.

While there are similarly dominant construction firms, construction contracts are often split among large national corporations and regional firms in order to meet local job creation goals. Still, the largest players in the correctional market include Turner Construction Company, Gilbane Building Company, and Hensel Phelps, which together hold roughly 30 percent of the market.[19]

Turner, a subsidiary of HOCHTIEF, the German corporation that built public infrastructure for the Nazi party using forced labor,[20] generated $1.4 billion in revenue on prison and jail construction between 2007 and 2012.[21] Gilbane boasts of being one of the top five correctional builders for over a decade now.[22] Hensel Phelps has built nearly 100 million square feet of correctional space.[23] Other major players in the field include the Clark Construction Group, which has completed over $4.5 billion in correctional and judicial projects around the country,[24] and McCarthy Building Companies, which was contracted by Los Angeles County in 2019 to build a $2.2 billion new jail until activists forced the county to cancel the project.[25]

INHUMANE DESIGN

A well-designed, humane prison is a perverse fallacy. No number of architectural bells and whistles can change the fact that a more modern cage is still a cage.

The average size of a correctional cell—the closest thing to personal space an incarcerated person has and must, at times, still share with one or two others—is not much larger than the size of a parking space. Walls, floors, doors, and gates are constructed with the coldest building materials, an assortment of stone, cement, cinder, iron, and steel.[26] Natural light is limited to what passes through barred windows even in facilities with no outdoor spaces.[27] Toilet and shower stalls are built without doors or curtains. Visit rooms are designed to prohibit contact with loved ones. And all these indignities are explained away with one claim: security.

The worst manifestation of this torture architecture is a solitary confinement cell, a box often the size of an elevator in which people are confined for 22 to 24 hours a day.[28] These cells are designed to remove human contact; a single slot in a metal door serves as the pass-through for food, mail, sound, and even light.[29] On any given day, over 122,000 people nationwide

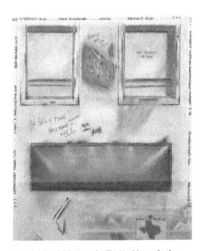

Gabriel (b. 1986), Laredo, TX, No Mercy Is the Best Business. "Here is the inside view of my solitary cell door. Two windows look onto the tier where staff escort other prisoners. But the real show happens in the slot below them. Everything passes through the slot: mail, clothes, commissary, food, light."

(Left) Source: Vox.

are tortured in solitary,[30] and many will spend weeks, months, years, and even decades there.[31] The use of solitary confinement in the United States has been condemned by the United Nations and human rights organizations for its severe psychological effects, and yet architects, engineers, and contractors continue to design and build these spaces.[32]

In recent years, architecture, engineering, and construction firms have changed the narrative around their role in prison construction, moving from silence to hyperbolic claims that they design facilities that minimize dehumanization and promote rehabilitation.[33] They gloat about wall murals of naturescapes and floor glazing that extends the reach of natural light as they design expansion projects meant to facilitate incarceration.[34]

JOHNNY'S STORY

During the 13 years I was incarcerated, I spent three years in solitary confinement in increments of anywhere from three to ten months—all for minor infractions. Solitary is devoid of human contact, and so much more: light, sound, and color. My gray cells had just one interior-facing window with frosted glass. It was the same window through which guards served me the meals that helped me assess whether it was morning or night—breakfast was at 7 a.m. and dinner at 4 p.m.

Johnny Perez
New York

In solitary, it was quiet—so quiet that you could hear small animals outside in the yard, your heartbeat, and even your thoughts. I found inspiration any way I could. I read the Bible—the only text I was allowed—at least ten times over the course of my sentence. Other times, I read the ingredients on my toothpaste and the few other products I could have. Desperate for human connection, I shouted through vents to others in my solitary units, forging deep bonds with people whose faces I never saw.

When I was younger, I sat in solitary blaming myself with a sense of hostility. As I grew older, those thoughts morphed into anger, and I questioned how such a space could even exist. Who conceived of it? Who designed it? Who built it? Who condemned me to it?

I am home now, but years later, I am still acclimating to life outside. Small spaces like public bathrooms trigger memories of solitary. Nightmares about being incarcerated again sometimes creep into my sleep. Despite it all, hope drives my dedication to criminal justice advocacy. As the National Director of U.S. Prison Programs at the National Religious Campaign Against Torture, today, I advocate for an end to solitary confinement and train other solitary survivors to do the same.

ENVIRONMENTAL HAZARDS

Nearly 600 prisons have been built on or in close proximity to Superfund sites, contaminated land zones identified by the U.S. Environmental Protection Agency as toxic to human and environmental health and requiring the sustained removal of hazardous materials.[35] The toxins in these locations have been linked to cancer, heart disease, pulmonary disease, birth defects, depression, and tooth decay.[36] Despite decades of environmental justice advocacy originating from inside prisons with the Black Liberation Political Prisoners in the late

[Contractors] extract all the good stuff from the land, then they sell it to waste companies that contaminate the land, and then they sell it to prisons. Then they start shipping inmates there, and people start getting sick.

— Richard Mosley, former incarcerated advocate in Pennsylvania[37]

1980s,[38] government agencies and complicit architects, engineers, and con-tractors continue to build prisons and jails on Superfund sites and in other environmentally hazardous areas with blatant disregard for the health and well-being of incarcerated people and corrections staff.

However, fights for environmental safety are starting to see modest returns. In 2015, Escambia County, Florida, sought to build a jail on a Super-fund site in Pensacola. Advocates successfully demanded a different site, though the county went on to build the jail in a hazardous flood zone.[39] In 2016, the Federal Bureau of Prisons (BOP) planned to build a $444 million facility in Whitesburg, Kentucky, located atop an old mine, next to a coal processing plant and sludge pond.[40] After vigorous challenges by incarcer-ated people and allied advocates, the BOP withdrew its plan for the new facility.[41] While the environmental justice efforts of advocates in these two instances proved successful, many are not.

For instance, people incarcerated at the Pennsylvania State Correctional Institution–Fayette have been exposed to hazardous pollution for decades due to the dumping of millions of tons of coal ash near the prison.[42] Toxic dust filled with mercury, lead, and arsenic runs off into the prison water. Advocates have wrestled for years with the Pennsylvania Department of Corrections for legal relief but have repeatedly been told that exposure lev-els are safe, an assertion plainly contradicted by the stories of the ailing people inside.[43]

Architecture, engineering, and construction firms are not just complicit in the building of prisons and jails on toxic land; they also often introduce health hazards through their design and construction. For example, in Texas, where temperatures routinely exceed 100°F, architects, engineers, and contractors designed and built state prisons without air-conditioning, where 23 people have since died from overheating.[44] In California, an incar-cerated person died in a corrections medical facility from Legionnaires' disease caused by bacteria in the building's water system.[45] The facility was built by McCarthy Building Companies in 2010, and by 2016, it was receiving failing grades from the state inspector general.[46] Through their indifference to and exacerbation of environmental hazards in corrections facilities, architects, engineers, and contractors have devalued the lives of incarcerated people.

LATE AND OVER BUDGET

Government agencies typically consider several factors when deciding whether to build a new or replacement facility: overcrowding, dilapidation, need for specialized services, economic impact, job creation, and revenue opportunities.[47] However, prison and jail construction has not always panned out as expected. In fact, in many cases, it has been a financial sinkhole for taxpayers—and windfall for architects, engineers, and contractors—with projects running over time and cost estimates even when using the grossly underpaid labor of incarcerated people.

For instance, a recent prison project in Salt Lake City, Utah—a joint venture between Layton Construction and Oakland Construction[48]—ran 18 months behind schedule and 20 percent over its original $650 million budget.[49] In Santa Barbara, California, a new jail build that was originally

Source: The Salt Lake Tribune. *Government officials break ground at location of new Utah prison.*

estimated to cost $77 million and slated for completion in the spring of 2019 culminated in a lawsuit against contractor Rosser International after it went out of business in the summer of 2019 and abandoned the project, which was only 80 percent complete and nearly 40 percent over budget.[50] And in Eureka, California, the construction of a youth jail was due to be completed in 2018, but a year past the due date, the county was forced to release the contractor, Hal Hays Construction, for failure to make adequate progress and go after its bond agent, Western Surety Company, to demand the project be completed.[51]

These projects only scratch the surface of the fiscal waste in the construction of carceral cages that has diverted billions of tax dollars from community investments in education, mental healthcare, substance use treatment, affordable housing, and restorative justice.

MAINTENANCE

Construction firms are not just contracted for new construction, but also for renovations and simple maintenance. While the firms contracted by government agencies for these projects are often smaller, local firms, their role is nevertheless critical to the upkeep of facilities, which is often questionable at best. The staff at these corporations regularly see the atrocity of conditions in our nation's prisons and jails, and yet they do little more than the bare minimum to keep their walls upright. Notably, much like they do with new construction projects, these corporations often use prison labor to complete contracted work, allowing them to save on staffing costs and increase their profit margins. Incarcerated people are also employed directly by facilities to do everyday grounds maintenance, from painting walls to mowing the grass. Maintenance jobs are the most common jobs held by incarcerated people without whom facilities simply could not operate.

While some architects, engineers, and contractors masquerade as reformists claiming to be designing better and more humane facilities, human rights advocates have seen through their guises. No matter how much natural light reflects off a polyurethane floor or how many beautiful naturescapes are painted on visit room walls, a building designed to cage and hide people will not address the divestment from Black, brown, and Indigenous communities that feeds mass incarceration or heal the mass trauma further perpetuated by it.

As social justice architect Raphael Sperry has said for years, communities do not need better prison design, but better community design.[52]

LEARN MORE

- *Debunking Four Myths About the Prison Building Boom Supporting Mass Incarceration*, Urban Institute (2023)
- *Broken Ground: Why America Keeps Building More Jails and What It Can Do Instead*, Vera Institute of Justice (2019)
- "Deadly Delays in Jail Construction Cost Lives and Dollars Across California," *ProPublica* (2019)
- "We Need to Rethink the Rikers Island Replacement Jails," *Architect's Newspaper* (2019)
- "County Failures, Not State Reforms, Are Killing People in California Jails," The Appeal (2019)
- "How Prisons Are Poisoning Their Inmates," *The Outline* (2018)
- "Can the Rural Prison Economy Survive Decarceration Era?" *Associated Press* (2018)
- "Is There Such Thing as 'Good' Prison Design?" *Architectural Digest* (2018)
- *Big House on the Prairie: Rise of the Rural Ghetto and Prison Proliferation*, John M. Eason (2017)
- *Prisons as Panacea or Pariah? The Countervailing Consequences of the Prison Boom on the Political Economy of Rural Towns*, Bryan L. Sykes (2016)
- "Is 'Justice Architecture' Just?" *Aggregate* (2014)
- "Architects Are Part of the Prison Industrial Complex, Too," *City Lab* (2013)
- "Should Architects Design Prisons?" *Architect Magazine* (2012)

OPERATIONS + MANAGEMENT

You just sell [prison beds] like you were selling cars or real estate or hamburgers.

— Thomas W. Beasley, founder of CoreCivic[1]

The first private prison corporation, CoreCivic (then known as Corrections Corporation of America), was founded in 1983. The founding executives included a former chairman of the Tennessee Republican Party and a former warden of the Ramsey Prison Farm in Texas who had used incarcerated Black men as personal servants on his plantation.[6] The new corporation hastily signed its first contract to build and operate a federal immigration detention center in Texas, but things did not start smoothly.[7] When construction took longer than expected, executives rented a motel, put up barbed wire, and opened the nation's first private immigration detention center.[8] CoreCivic's largest competitor, the GEO

Description: Corrections agencies contract with private prison corporations to lease and operate prisons, jails, youth detention facilities, and immigration detention centers.

$5.8 billion
Private prison market size[2]

96,700
People with criminal convictions incarcerated in private prisons[3]

90%
Immigrants detained in private prisons[4]

58
Fewer training hours for corrections officers in a private prisons[5]

Group (GEO), then known as Wackenhut, got its start the following year with a federal contract for an immigration detention center in Colorado.[9]

Through the 1990s and 2000s, the industry built up its business by pushing draconian criminal laws that drove incarceration across the country. Until 2010, CoreCivic played a prominent role in the American Legislative Exchange Council (ALEC),[10] a conservative trade organization through which lawmakers and corporate executives work together to draft model legislation.[11] As an active member, and at times even corporate chair of ALEC's Criminal Justice Task Force in the early 1990s, CoreCivic executives helped draft and champion model legislation for mandatory minimum, "three strikes," and "truth-in-sentencing" laws.[12]

The notorious 1994 Omnibus Crime Bill codified these and other severe sentencing laws at the federal level, and included billions of dollars in prison construction grants for states that passed similar legislation.[13] Within a year, 25 states passed "truth-in-sentencing" laws, which require people serve a substantial portion of their sentence before they can be eligible for parole.[14] In 1995, ALEC members drafted the Private Correctional Facilities Act to expand the use of private prisons state by state[15] and the Prison Industries Act to expand the private sector's access to prison labor.[16] And the following year, thanks to a proposed amendment and testimony by executives at GEO, the Appropriations Act of 1996 amended the original crime bill, which was silent on private prisons, to authorize states to use federal grants issued under the bill to privatize prisons.[17]

Banking on the quick uptake of all this new legislation, CoreCivic began borrowing huge sums to build prisons before even securing contracts to fill them.[18] When the growth rate of incarceration temporarily slowed in the late 1990s, the corporation struggled to fill its new prisons and make interest payments on the debt it used to build them.[19] Making matters worse for the corporation, a federal investigation in 1998 sparked public outrage when it revealed brutal conditions in one of its facilities.[20] The corporation's costly speculative construction and poor financial management as well as public uproar about facility conditions came to a head in 1999, causing its stock price to plummet to mere pennies per share and putting it on the verge of bankruptcy.[21] Marred by CoreCivic's performance and general concerns about the industry, investors in GEO's stock suit followed and its survival was similarly compromised.[22]

Working with its creditors to restructure its debt, CoreCivic staved off bankruptcy just in time.[23] A few years prior, in 1996, the U.S. Congress passed the Illegal Immigration Reform and Immigrant Responsibility Act, which significantly expanded the demand for immigrant detention and deportation.[24] The Federal Bureau of Prisons (BOP) responded with requests for proposals that CoreCivic and GEO quickly jumped at.[25] Doling out several contracts in the early 2000s, the federal government gave the private prison industry the lifeline it needed to survive.[26]

The industry thrived again until 2016, when the Obama administration announced it would phase out private prison contracts with the BOP after a study revealed that privately run facilities were less safe than publicly run facilities.[27] The Department of Homeland Security followed by announcing a review of immigration detention centers,[28] but eventually decided it would continue its use of private prisons, citing a lack of alternative options.[29] Still, overnight, the stock price of the largest two private prison operators, CoreCivic and GEO, tanked 40 percent and 35 percent, respectively.[30]

Panicked executives moved to pay their way to survival. Within days, GEO contributed $250,000 to pro-Trump super political action committees.[31] After Trump's election, CoreCivic and GEO curried favor with the incoming administration by donating an additional $250,000 each to the Trump inauguration fund.[32] As a further sign of support, GEO also moved its annual meeting to a Trump resort.[33]

This patronage paid off: the Trump administration rescinded the phase-out policy just weeks after taking office, going as far as to instruct BOP officials to identify incarcerated people for transfer to private facilities.[34] GEO's donations forced campaign finance watchdogs to sue the Federal Election Committee for allowing the corporation to circumvent the ban on contributions from federal contractors, a claim still being investigated by regulators.[35] But the administration continued its support of the industry with passage of the First Step Act, which while responsible for the release of tens of thousands of people from federal prisons funneled millions into new reentry services provided by private prison operators, among other things.[36]

Then, in January 2021, the new Biden administration issued an executive order reverting back to the Obama-era directive barring new contracts with private prison corporations for the operation of federal prisons. The executive order similarly excluded immigration detention centers.[37] Since then, the number of detained immigrants housed in private facilities has continued to increase.[38]

Despite policy volatility, the industry remains stubbornly entrenched in the federal system today with more than half of its revenues each year coming from federal contracts.[39] But in recent decades, CoreCivic and GEO spent billions diversifying their business lines to ensure their survival.

HOW MUCH MONEY IS AT STAKE?

Private prisons hold about 96,000 people in the corrections system, or roughly 8 percent of the total U.S. prison and jail population.[40] The immigration detention system is significantly more reliant on private prisons with more than 30,000 people, or 90 percent of detained immigrants, in private facilities as of 2023—up from 72 percent in 2017.[41] And, altogether, private prisons bring in $5.8 billion annually.[42]

Private prison corporations are paid a fixed daily rate for each person they incarcerate, also known as a "man-day" in the industry.[43] In this compensation structure, every empty bed represents lost revenue. However, private prison corporations have insulated themselves from oscillating occupancy rates by including occupancy guarantees in their contracts typically ranging from 80 percent to 90 percent. This means that if a facility falls below the guaranteed occupancy rate, the contracting agency is still required to pay for unused beds needed to fulfill the guaranteed occupancy rate. In 2022, CoreCivic and GEO were paid for 18.8 million and 17.9 million man-days, respectively.[44]

Since their start, private prison corporations have faced significant volatility at the hands of political swings. And again, their industry is under threat as the criminal justice movement gains traction to decarcerate prisons and jails and end mass incarceration. While these corporations are spending hundreds of millions of dollars to protect their current business, they are also diversifying their business by turning to community corrections and other correctional services that open up new market opportunities for them.[45]

WHAT CORPORATIONS ARE INVOLVED?

Two corporations dominate the private prison and immigration detention industry: CoreCivic and GEO. Based on revenue, these two corporations control more than half of the U.S. private prison market,[46] but they hold the vast majority of people in private facilities.[47]

As the nation's oldest private prison corporation, CoreCivic brings in $1.8 billion in annual revenues.[48] It remains heavily dependent on the federal government with roughly 54 percent of its revenue coming from federal contracts, including 30 percent from U.S. Immigration and Customs Enforcement (ICE).[49] In the 1990s, CoreCivic acquired many of its smaller competitors in the industry. In recent years, it has focused its acquisition activity in the community corrections space with the hopes of diversifying its business lines. In 2015, it acquired Avalon Correctional Services for $158 million to build out its residential reentry and day reporting business.[50]

Competing neck and neck for contracted beds in the United States, GEO is the largest private prison corporation in the world, with additional operations in the U.K., Australia, and South Africa[51] and $2.4 billion in global revenues.[52] In recent years the corporation has aggressively pursued acquisition growth. In 2010, it purchased Cornell Companies, then the third-largest private prison operator in the country, for $685 million.[53] GEO has also spent $1 billion diversifying beyond prison management into transportation, residential reentry facilities, day reporting centers, and electronic monitoring.[54]

Management and Training Corporation (MTC) is a smaller operator that still has a significant presence in both the criminal and immigration systems. Unlike CoreCivic and GEO, MTC is not publicly traded and thus its financials are not available, but industry estimates put the corporation's annual revenues at roughly $840 million, though only about half is expected to come from the operation of U.S. prisons and jails.[55] While its competitors use acquisitions in community corrections to protect their bottom lines from decarceration, MTC is expanding its existing workforce training programs.[56]

	The GEO Group[57]	CoreCivic[58]	Management & Training Corp[59]
Annual Global Revenue	$2.4 Bn	$1.8 Bn	$841 Mn
Annual U.S. Revenue	$2.2 Bn	$1.8 Bn	~$450 Mn
U.S. Prisons	50	44	20
U.S. Prison Beds	64,828	66,000	25,224
U.S. Residential Reentry Centers	42	23	—
U.S. Residential Reentry Beds	10,207	5,000	—
U.S. Electronic Monitors	200,000+	—	—

With CoreCivic, GEO, and MTC essentially swallowing up the field, the remaining private prison operators are regional outfits that operate only a handful of facilities each. These include LaSalle Corrections, a family-run operation that manages prisons in Louisiana, Texas, and Georgia,[60] and Akima Global Services, a defense contractor that staffs and operates immigration detention centers.[61]

There is also a handful of large private prison corporations operating facilities in other countries with a limited presence in the United States. G4S, one of the world's largest employers, operates private prisons in the U.K. and staffs immigration detention facilities and transports detained immigrants in the United States.[62] Sodexo, a French multinational conglomerate, operates private prisons in Australia and the U.K.,[63] which it bought from CoreCivic, and provides food services in U.S. prisons.[64]

CORRECTIONS

Compensated for each day a person spends in one of their beds, private prison corporations drive profitability in just two ways: by increasing the number of people in their facilities or cutting costs related to their care. Since their start, these corporations have done both with dire consequences.

For decades now, private prison corporations have spent hundreds of millions of dollars on campaign contributions and lobbying to advance policies that put more people in prison for longer and promote the unregulated use of private prisons.[65] It is a story that has been written about often.

Less known is the way in which they expand their market share by maintaining a revolving door of informal influence with departments of corrections, regularly hiring former correctional administrators into high-paying roles—often just days after leaving their government posts.[66] These new corporate executives use their government experience and relationships to usher in and negotiate lucrative contracts for their new employers.

But these corporations also have even more direct ways to increase prison stays in their facilities or further extract value from incarcerated people, and they exercise them liberally. Disciplinary infractions are just one example. Corrections officers in private prisons, like those in public prisons, can issue disciplinary infractions, hold review hearings, determine guilt or innocence, and hand down punitive sentences. In private prisons, these sentences often involve the loss of good-time credit, lengthening a person's stay and padding their bottom lines.[67] Unsurprisingly, the rate of guilty findings in disciplinary review hearings is quite high—easily over 95 percent in many private prisons.[68] In one such disciplinary hearing in a CoreCivic facility, a man lost 30 days of good-time credit because he used a broom to sweep the area in front of his cell without permission, which generated an extra $2,000 for the corporation.[69]

Yet, the easiest way that private prison corporations stretch their profit is by lowering operational costs, particularly staff pay, their largest expense. Offering below-market wages and limited benefits, they attract underqualified staff.[71] Making matters worse, they spend, on aver-

People say a lot of negative things about [CoreCivic]. That we'll hire anybody. That we are scraping the bottom of the barrel. Which is not really true, but if you come here and you breathing . . . then we're willing to hire you.

– CoreCivic training officer[70]

Source: New York Times. Cell in a prison operated by MTC in Mississippi.

age, 58 fewer hours training staff than publicly run facilities, and what little training they offer emphasizes use of force—rather than de-escalation—as a response to every situation, including mental health crises.[72] The outcomes are frustrating for officers set up to fail and detrimental for incarcerated people at their whim. At one CoreCivic facility in Tennessee, for instance, poorly trained officers pepper-sprayed a man who had attempted suicide before trying to help him.[73]

Unsurprisingly, private prisons have high staff turnover,[74] but this constant churn of employees exacerbates another common cost-cutting measure: understaffing. In Idaho, for example, CoreCivic did not just routinely understaff its facilities, but it also then falsified records to make critical positions appear filled. In 2012, the corporation paid $1 million to the state to settle fraud claims.[75] Audits of federal and state prisons have revealed similar understaffing levels at private prisons around the country operated by CoreCivic, GEO, and MTC alike.[76]

Understaffed with corrections officers ill-suited or unprepared to perform their duties effectively, let alone safely, private prisons have created breeding grounds for flagrant human rights violations against those in their custody. In Mississippi, for instance, the average hourly wage for corrections officers in public prisons is $14.83 per hour, the lowest in the country. And yet, MTC, which operates three prisons in the state, pays its officers as little as $9.50 per hour, amounting to an annualized salary of just $19,760.[77] Predictably, MTC regularly reports vacancies as high as 31 percent in its facilities.[78] Unable to effectively manage its prisons, MTC prison administrators often lock down entire facilities, sometimes for months at a time, trapping people in their cells, prohibiting family visits and phone calls, preventing doctor visits, and more.[79] Unable to go to commissary, people go without soap, blankets, and even food.[80] This has led to understandable tensions at these facilities that have erupted violently time and time again.

Efforts to minimize costs and pad profits also leave facilities to deteriorate. Private prison corporations have little interest in maintaining existing facilities and often let them fall into disrepair. In 2018, MTC was sued by the Southern Poverty Law Center and ACLU for the deplorable conditions in its Mississippi prisons that included incidents of cells with no lights and rats crawling out of toilets.[81]

MATTHEW'S STORY

Matthew Carter
Pennsylvania

I spent seven months incarcerated at George W. Hill Correctional Facility, a local jail in Pennsylvania privately operated by the GEO Group at the time. The day I arrived, they charged me a $100 process-ing fee—I'd never heard of such a thing, a fee to be booked. I didn't have it, so they took 50 cents out of every dollar my family put in my commis-sary account until it was paid.

The jail had a history of death—a lot of suicides—and when I walked in, it made sense. The facility was understaffed and misman-aged, and the conditions were filthy and unsanitary. Imagine what crawls in and what seeps out of a commercial kitchen with doors left wide open all day. Almost every morning, I went without breakfast. What they served was inedible. Wednesdays were the worst—they served grits that smelled and tasted like vomit.

A health inspector once stopped by my cell during a facility inspec-tion. I shared my concerns with her about the cruelty and neglect I had experienced at the jail—all to profit a few executives sitting in Florida. She was unfazed.

But it wasn't just the conditions; it was also how they were prepar-ing people for release, or not. While the facility held primarily people who were awaiting trial, there were no resources or programs for people inside who had not been sentenced. The limited resources and programs that existed were available only to the small number of sentenced individuals.

For my part, I longed for substance abuse treatment. I wanted to be sober, and I was willing to fight for my sobriety, but I couldn't do it alone. Against all odds, despite my incarceration, I made it. Today, out of jail, I'm finally sober. Among other things, I spend my time speaking with local elected officials and the public about the harm caused by private prisons. And thankfully, they've started to listen. The most recently elected county council has finally deprivatized the jail.

IMMIGRATION DETENTION

The private prison model does not differ much from the corrections system to the immigration detention system. Business is still driven by more bodies, longer stays, and low costs. So, much like it does in the corrections system, the private prison industry pushes for harsh immigration policies intended to drive up immigration detention. And private immigration detention centers suffer from many of the same problems as private prisons and jails, but the people held in them have even fewer rights and thus, at times, can suffer even more abuse.

As they do in their prisons and jails, private prison corporations cut corners on staffing and training in immigration detention centers. In fact, given the lower-risk population, they can drive costs down even more significantly and produce even greater human rights violations. For instance, in 2017, Omar Rivera, an

Dear. Mr. Priminster haper
I don't like to stay in this jail. I'm only nine years old. I want to go to my school in Canada. I'm sleeping beside the wall. Please Mr. Priminster haper give visa for my family. This place is not good for me. I want to get out of the cell. Just please give visa for my family. My home land is in canada. My life is over there. I'm also sleeping in washroom. Mr. Priminster haper Please bring me and my family to Canada. Thank you so much.

Source: ACLU. Card written by child in GEO detention center.

asylum-seeker from El Salvador, led a hunger strike to protest poor conditions at the Adelanto Detention Center run by GEO. In response, staff beat
him, pepper-sprayed him, and placed him in solitary confinement for nearly
two weeks, according to a lawsuit filed by Rivera and seven others who were
detained at the facility.[82] The lawsuit, which was settled for an undisclosed
amount, is one of several against GEO involving assaults and deaths at the
Adelanto facility.[83]

Importantly, the privatization of the Adelanto facility is itself an impro-
priety, but a common one in the space.[84] Looking to circumvent rigorous
federal procurement procedures, ICE and its private prison contractors
often look to intergovernmental service agreements (IGSAs) to indirectly
contract through counties.[85] In these agreements, ICE contracts with counties for beds for detained immigrants, and the county in turn subcontracts
the operation of its facility to a private prison corporation.[86] The county and
private prison corporation then split the per diem ICE pays for each person
held in the facility.[87] Interested in seeing more money flow into their dis-
tricts, county officials have joined the corporations in pushing for harsher
immigration laws.[88] IGSAs represent a win, win, win for ICE, counties, and
private prison corporations all at the expense of the people detained.

COMMUNITY CORRECTIONS

Amid growing backlash, private prison corporations have tried to both
whitewash the narrative around their industry and diversify beyond traditional facility operations.

With profit on their minds and the criminal justice movement on their
heels, in 2013, executives at both CoreCivic and GEO restructured their corporations as real estate investment trusts (REITs).[89] In exchange for keeping
their assets primarily in real estate, or in this case corrections and immigration detention facilities, and paying out most of their earnings to investors, REITs pay significantly lower taxes.[90] But the move also had important

brand implications for the corporations, which were trying to reframe themselves as merely government "landlords," as one CoreCivic executive put it.[91] But the marketing ploy failed and had an unintended consequence: illiquidity—which activists quickly exposed.

After years of advocacy, public opinion has finally synonymized private prisons with corporate greed and amorality. In recent years, nearly all major banks withdrew their financial support for private prisons,[92] credit agencies downgraded their ratings,[93] and lawmakers passed laws intended to ban private prisons in their states.[94] As a result, CoreCivic and GEO have experienced considerable market volatility and suffered financially.

In a last-ditch effort to discredit public protest, the industry banded together to spread misinformation in support of its practices. In 2020, Core-Civic, GEO, and MTC created the Day 1 Alliance, an industry trade group that claims to educate the public on the "valued role" private prisons play in the United States.[95] After recruiting veterans from far-right political organizations, the group launched an offensive that supported weak reforms like the First Step Act that funneled money into its coffers while trying to veil the industry's history of abuse.[96]

But it's too late; the corporations' access to capital has dried up. Past debt has begun to mature, and the corporations are finding themselves having to take out more expensive new debt to pay off cheaper old debt. They also have no capital for growth projects and their operations are shrinking. The predicament forced both CoreCivic and GEO to reinvest earnings and drop their REIT status.[97]

However, there is still another strategy that private prison corporations have been deploying to save their business and it seems to be working out better: expanding into community corrections, or the growing industry of community-based control mechanisms like halfway houses, day reporting centers, and electronic monitoring. Since 2004, both CoreCivic and GEO have spent billions acquiring smaller competitors in this space and marketing it as the solution to mass incarceration.[98] While many have unfortunately bought into these so-called "alternatives to incarceration," criminal justice advocates are actively rejecting the transformation of communities into carceral analogues.[99] At the very least, certainly those who helped to create our carceral crisis should not be trusted to solve it.

Private prisons are a uniquely U.S. export, which emerged in the 1980s as the perfect encapsulation of the decade's embrace of Reagan-era privatization and greed. Prisons had always been used to generate revenue, but this was something new: the complete outsourcing of the criminal legal system to the highest bidder. And the corruption of money in politics allowed them to help decimate families in disproportionately Black, brown, and Indigenous communities.

Since then, private prisons have embedded themselves in every facet of the criminal and immigration systems. While people have begun to challenge private prison corporations, there must be vigilant attention paid to the industry's attempt to change its toxic image and expand into adjacent business lines. After all, whether walls are built out of concrete, wire, or WiFi, a prison is still a prison, and a private prison still needs more bodies to grow. No matter their form, private prison corporations have no place in any system that claims to be about justice.

LEARN MORE

- *Private Prisons in the United States*, The Sentencing Project (2023)
- *Are Private Prisons in Trouble?* The Brennan Center (2019)
- "Who Makes Money from Private Prisons?" CNBC (2019)
- "'These People Are Profitable': Under Trump, Private Prisons Are Cashing In on ICE Detainees," *USA Today* (2019)
- *An Examination of Private Financing for Correctional and Immigration Detention Facilities*, In the Public Interest (2018)

- *Capitalizing on Mass Incarceration: U.S. Growth in Private Prisons*, The Sentencing Project (2018)
- "Today, It Locks Up Immigrants. But CoreCivic's Roots Lie in the Brutal Past of America's Prisons," *Mother Jones* (2018)
- "Private Prisons, Explained," *The Conversation* (2017)
- *The Banks That Finance Private Prison Companies*, In the Public Interest (2016)
- A Brief History of America's Private Prison Industry, *Mother Jones* (2016)
- *Community Cages: Profitizing Community Corrections and Alternatives to Incarceration*, American Friends Service Committee (2016)

PERSONNEL

If they don't fit the criteria, put them there anyway and we will weed them out and fire them later.

— *Former manager at a third-party staffing firm*[1]

Private security corporations were the first to enter the third-party staffing market in corrections facilities. These corporations began as private detective agencies at the turn of the 20th century, often hired by factory owners to forcibly end labor disputes.[2] When the private prison industry emerged in the 1980s, multinational security corporations like G4S, or its predecessors Group 4 Falck and Securicor, began acquiring these private detective agencies as an entryway into the U.S. market.[3] Arming a large fleet of its staff with firearms, G4S took contracts that its major competitors would not, including contracts to staff youth detention centers and drive prison transportation vans.[4] Other security conglomerates followed suit with their own acquisitions—Securitas, for example, acquired the notorious strikebreaking Pinkerton National Detective Agency in 1999[5]—and

Description: Corrections agencies contract with personnel corporations to hire and train staff and implement workforce management systems. Third-party staffing firms are often tapped to fill vacancies in security, medical services, and transportation.

quickly, third-party security corporations established a foothold in the carceral system.

As prisons began to pop up across the country in the 1990s, there were also legal developments in staff training. In 1989, in *City of Canton v. Harris*, the U.S. Supreme Court held that a government agency could be held liable for providing inadequate training to an employee that results in the deprivation of a person's constitutional rights, so long as the failure to train amounted to deliberate indifference.[6] The holding was applied to correctional agencies by several federal courts in the decade that followed.[7] This led agencies to reconsider not just their training programs but also how participation was documented, making standardized training curricula attractive.

In 2003, Lexipol emerged as the leading provider of training resources. And with the broad adoption of internet services in the years that followed, the corporation began pushing online training instead of in-person training to officials trying to cut costs.[8] Enticed by the increase in corrections bureaucracy, technology corporations entered the space with specialized workforce software intended to help officials track everything from attendance to trainings.

Still, today, most correctional agencies prefer to at least employ their own staff directly, particularly in security positions. But with correctional agencies now struggling to recruit and retain staff, many do not see that as an option. Prisons and jails are facing dire staff shortages, with the number of people working in corrections at a 20-year low even as the incarcerated population bounces back from COVID-19 lows.[9] More are turning to private security personnel to fill vacancies that otherwise leave shifts significantly below expected staffing levels.[10]

Third-party staffing has also spilled over into non-security roles with some critical implications. For example, staff shortages in medical positions are uniquely detrimental as the incarcerated population has aged and incarcerated elders require more care.[11] Correctional officials stretch budgets by turning to part-time and temporary healthcare workers,[12] at times even to fill gaps left by their own private correctional healthcare providers.[13]

HOW MUCH MONEY IS AT STAKE?

The U.S. private security industry generates about $9 billion per year from government contracts, but what portion of that the corrections and immigration detention systems are each responsible for is unclear.[14] Security corporations have contracts to patrol borders, shuttle people between facilities, and even staff facilities and detention centers themselves.[15]

G4S alone has been awarded hundreds of federal contracts related to immigration detention, at times for providing violent border security and at others for operating deadly transport services.[16] In 2019, there was a record 510,854 admissions to detention resulting from U.S. Immigration and Customs Enforcement (ICE) and U.S. Customs and Border Patrol (CBP) arrests, with 50,922 people detained at the end of the year.[17] Not only were both figures up substantially year-over-year, but the breakdown between the two agencies showed disproportionate spikes in arrests and detention by CBP,[18] which awarded a noncompetitive contract to G4S at the beginning of the year for border security among other things.[19] Under the Biden administration, arrests and detentions dropped significantly but were still disproportionately driven by CBP.[20]

Still, data is scarce about third-party staffing in the corrections and immigration detention landscapes, but the understaffing of critical positions across prisons and jails, including their medical units, suggests demand is strong. And while there is also no information about the size of the market for private correctional training or workforce management systems, the nation's roughly 400,000 corrections officers represent a sizable and stable market.[21] In North Carolina, for instance, a vacancy rate of nearly 40 percent led the state to hire 400 private security personnel to patrol prison perimeters.[22]

EMPLOYMENT OF CORRECTIONS OFFICERS AND JAILERS

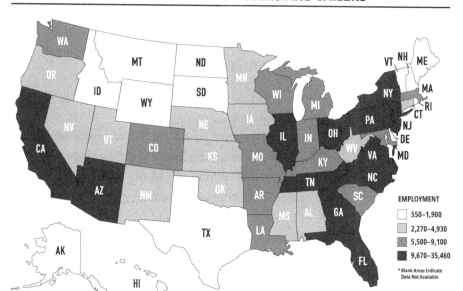

EMPLOYMENT

☐ 550–1,900
▨ 2,270–4,930
▧ 5,500–9,100
■ 9,670–35,460

* Blank Areas Indicate
Data Not Available

Source: U.S. Bureau of Labor Statistics

WHAT CORPORATIONS ARE INVOLVED?

▪ THIRD-PARTY STAFFING

A handful of mega–multinational corporations dominate the market for outsourced security in corrections and immigration detention. G4S is the world's largest private security staffer in prisons, jails, youth detention centers, and immigration detention centers, and one of the world's largest private employers.[23] In just the past ten years, G4S has had lucrative federal contracts for guards and transportation services valued at nearly $600 million, earning on average almost $60 million per year.[24] Security behemoth Securitas, which for years competed with G4S for these contracts, has since shifted its focus in the space to security technology.[25]

Unable to compete with G4S in security staffing, smaller third-party staffing firms have specialized in other correctional roles. Many focus on staffing medical positions. For example, Supplemental Health Care provides short-term and temporary nurses to corrections facilities across the country but, like its competitors, does not report how many contracts it has or how many facilities it serves.[26] There is simply no reliable market data.

▪ STAFF TRAINING

While corrections agencies manage much of their own physical and hands-on training, they often rely on private corporations such as Lexipol for classroom and online courses. Through its training brand Corrections-One Academy, Lexipol boasted of 1.9 million completed courses in 2017.[27] National trade associations like the American Correctional Association and the National Institute of Corrections, which evaluate and accredit facilities, also provide training resources.[28] Niche corporations, such as Mock Prison Riots, offer violent tactical and situational training.[29] Notably, these corporations do not just train correctional staff—they also establish the policies that govern their behavior. Lexipol has drafted staff policies for 3,400 police, fire, and correctional agencies.[30]

▪ WORKFORCE MANAGEMENT SYSTEMS

Workforce management services in corrections is dominated by broader workforce management corporations that serve a host of industries. For example, Kronos, which brings in $1.4 billion annually from its workforce management services,[31] provides payroll management for government agencies, including corrections agencies.[32] Other big players include Orion, which has a tailored corrections product,[33] and InTime, which works only in the law enforcement space.[34]

THIRD-PARTY STAFFING

Third-party staffing firms provide contracted labor to public and private corrections and immigration detention facilities as well as correctional vendors, often on a temporary basis to fill vacancies. Driven to cut costs, these corporations have a history of lax hiring standards and related poor results. They often hire people without diligently reviewing their employment histories or hire candidates who are clearly unqualified to fill vacancies.[35] From security staff to medical practitioners, unqualified and untrained staff can present a significant threat to the lives of the incarcerated people entrusted to their care.

For example, in 2006, the Georgia Department of Corrections hired Dr. Yvon Nazaire as a temporary physician, relying on the vetting of Physician Providers, a third-party staffing firm. However, Physician Providers failed to uncover that, in New York, Nazaire had admitted to gross negligence in the treatment of five emergency room patients, was the subject of four malpractice death claims, and was on probation, though the information was widely available online.[37] Nazaire stayed with the agency until 2015, when he was terminated after a media investigation exposed the painful deaths of nine incarcerated women under his care; at least three died from substandard medical treatment.[38]

> In my 16 years, I don't have enough fingers and toes to count the bad outcomes I've seen. And I've never seen one physician disciplined.
>
> – Dr. Timothy Young,
>   former medical director at
>   Georgia's Augusta State
>   Medical Prison[36]

STAFF TRAINING

While most corrections agencies, particularly state prison systems, still manage their own officer training programs, many use private training resources and some entirely outsource officer training to private corporations. The largest correctional training corporation, Lexipol, markets online training courses comprised of videos and quizzes under the brand CorrectionsOne Academy.[39] Designed to be cheap for corrections agencies and easy for officers, Lexipol's online courses are increasingly replacing in-person training.[40]

Lexipol claims that officers can learn complex tasks, like negotiating a hostage standoff or deciding whether to use deadly force, by watching a series of short videos.[41] But, quite obviously, an online course cannot adequately prepare officers to deal with such crises. The corporation is setting officers up for failure in such situations and threatening the lives of the incarcerated people in their custody. And Lexipol is not the only private corporation teaching critical coursework online. The National Institute of Corrections lists "Inmate Suicide Prevention" and "Responding to Sexual Abuse" as popular online courses.[42]

Lexipol also drafts policies for correctional agencies—at times the very policies that govern officer training and proper protocols. Unsurprisingly, their boilerplate policies are very popular. They prioritize the interests of their customer, the corrections agency, focusing more on protecting correctional administrators from civil liability than on protecting the civil rights of incarcerated people. Putting litigation risk above humane policy, Lexipol

Source: Al Jazeera. *Officer raiding a school bus during a mock prison riot.*

claims to save agencies money in settlement payouts. But should things go awry, Lexipol disclaims any liability for the impact of its policies.[43]

Still, the most bizarre spectacle in correctional training is the West Virginia Mock Prison Riot. Held at a vacant prison, this yearly exhibition brings together hundreds of officers for a series of combat competitions. The organizers bill it as a training program for corrections officers but sell it to arms manufacturers as an opportunity to market weapons. The conference is so lucrative that corporations pay up to $25,000 to be sponsors and even more for exhibit booths. Some even hand out free samples of chemical weapons like pepper spray and tear gas. Filmmakers also sell footage of the riot to corporations seeking "intense, realistic footage" to use in their correctional advertisements.[44]

The event encourages corrections officers to view people as targets. Egged on by arms manufacturers, officers practice using tear gas on protesters, subduing mentally ill people using pepper spray, and raiding school buses with shotguns.[45] There is no discussion of when to use force—only which weapons to use. Events like these demonstrate how corporations selling staff training encourage, perpetuate, and commodify the violence that people face behind bars every day.

TALIB'S STORY

It was 3 a.m. early one morning when I was violently snatched from the top bunk of my cell at Soledad Correctional Training Facility in California and slammed headfirst into the wall by a corrections officer. I thought I was dreaming.

They zip-tied my hands and dragged me from my cell by my throat. I could see my cellmate, a

Talib Williams
California

diabetic 55-year-old man with degenerative spine disease and a chronic shoulder injury, crying out as he was also dragged from his bunk, head-slammed and zip-tied. I remember two men, equipped with night-vision goggles, helmets, and fatigues, and black masks covering their faces.

Wearing nothing but boxer briefs, I and the others were forced to walk on the filthy floor down the central corridor toward the dining hall. Along the way, I witnessed the same thing happening in every unit we passed. Officers yelled "Drag him!" as men were ripped suddenly from their sleep.

I arrived at the dining hall to find 200 other incarcerated men looking as shocked as me. I've been in prison for nearly 20 years, and our cells had never been raided like this before. As I looked around, I realized that every person sitting in the dining hall—from their early 20s to late 70s—was Black.

Zip-tied, sitting practically naked in a freezing kitchen during the worst pandemic to hit the world in more than a 100 years, we realized that we were sitting next to each other without masks. We began to demand face masks, but we were ignored. One officer yelled, "I hope you motherfuckers get COVID!" Another shouted, "Black lives don't matter!"

A week after the raid, during which nothing notable was found, the department released a statement denying the injuries and claiming officers followed proper protocol. Well, if proper protocol calls for dragging Black men by their necks out of bed, who wrote the protocol? Who trained the officers on it? Who made them hate Black people? And who unleashed them on us?

This story was adapted, with the author's permission, from an article originally published September 2, 2020, in the San Francisco Bay View.

WORKFORCE MANAGEMENT SYSTEMS

Personnel corporations also provide specially designed workforce management systems for the correctional environment. The largest, Kronos, sells cloud-based workforce technology that makes administrative tasks easier. Their corrections product helps administrators, corrections officers, civilian staff, and contractors manage absences, schedule time off, track attendance, process payroll, and run reports to make data-driven decisions. Importantly, Kronos is keen to recognize that the workforce in prisons and jails is not limited to those who go home to their families every day, but also includes incarcerated workers. Kronos' software allows prisons to use prison labor more efficiently by maximizing the productivity and minimizing the downtime of incarcerated workers making just pennies an hour.[46]

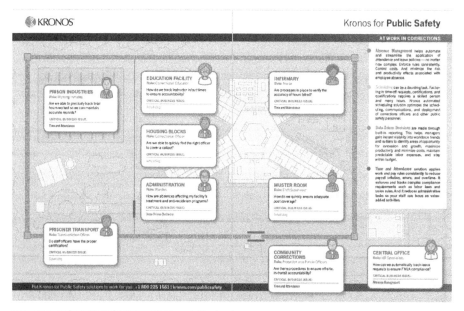

Source: Kronos for Public Safety: Corrections, marketing brochure.

Personnel corporations supplement, train, and manage the workforce behind the prison industry. They deploy modern-day mercenaries, fill vacancies with unqualified staff, train for violence, reduce institutional liability, and facilitate the abuse of prison labor. The true cost of their involvement—in labor exploited, people abused, and lives lost—is devastating.

LEARN MORE

- "Dangerous Guards, Low-Cost Security," *USA Today* (2019)
- "Police Policy for Sale," The Appeal (2019)
- "State Official Failed to Delve into Prison Doctor's Troubled Past," *Atlanta Journal Constitution* (2018)
- "The Mock Prison Riot: Where Guards Play Jail," *Al Jazeera* (2014)
- "Can Privatization Kill?" *New York Times* (2012)

LABOR + PROGRAMS

> We need to keep some out there, that's the ones that you can work, that pick up trash, the work release program. But guess what? Those are the ones that they are releasing. . . . They are releasing the good ones, that we use every day to wash cars, change oil in our cars, to cook in the kitchen, to do all that, where we save money. . . . Well, they are gonna let them out.
>
> — *Sheriff Steve Prator of Caddo Parish, Louisiana*[1]

When the U.S. Congress moved to abolish slavery in 1865 with the Thirteenth Amendment, the members agreed to an important exception, designed to retain control over the Black labor force, that allowed slavery as punishment for crime. As Black people sought economic autonomy during the Reconstruction Era, politicians and their monied allies raced to rebuild their well of cheap, forced labor. They passed Black Codes to restrict the ability of Black people to move freely, criminalizing so-called

Description: Corrections agencies contract with private corporations for access to the labor of incarcerated people. They also buy raw materials from private corporations for use in their own correctional industries, though notably governments use prison labor the most. Corrections agencies also contract with private corporations to provide rehabilitative and educational programs and course materials to incarcerated people.

acts of "vagrancy" such as unemployment.[2] States filled prisons with newly freed Black people[3] and ushered in the most brutal era of "convict leasing," whereby wardens leased out incarcerated people to local business owners and individuals.[4] Quickly, the practice became a huge source of revenue for Southern states. By 1898, it generated 73 percent of Alabama's annual revenue.[5] To justify the use of this forced labor, states recycled pro-slavery arguments that it benefited Black people who needed to be rehabilitated and learn civilized obedience.[6]

800,000
Incarcerated people working[14]

$0.14–$0.63
Average hourly wage range for incarcerated workers in facility operations maintenance and jobs[15]

7
States that do not pay incarcerated workers for the majority of jobs[16]

$15.5 billion
Wages stolen from incarcerated workers annually[17]

By the early 20th century, a recession had lowered the cost of labor and progressive reformers soured the public opinion on "convict leasing," leading states to pass laws banning the practice.[7] In 1935, Congress passed the Ashurst-Sumners Act to prohibit the sale of products made using prison labor in interstate commerce,[8] though it notably excluded agriculture and services from its prohibition.[9] Nevertheless, correctional administrators adapted, forcing incarcerated people into chain gangs to build public infrastructure instead.[10] By the 1950s, public outcry over the brutal treatment of people on chain gangs led many states to ban the practice,[11] though some still exist today.[12] And administrators nevertheless continued to use prison labor to maintain facilities and produce goods in government-run correctional industries.[13]

By the 1960s, the concept of rehabilitation expanded beyond labor to also include education, and the federal government introduced educational funding for incarcerated people through Pell Grants. Within a few years, nearly 10 percent of the prison population was participating in Pell-funded programming.[18] As the prison population boomed over the next few decades, the private sector lobbied to regain access to the labor of incarcerated people under the guise of vocational training.[19]

In 1979, Congress created the Prison Industry Enhancement Certification Program (PIECP), which renewed the private sector's access to prison labor, but at prevailing wages that corrections systems could garnish for room and board, among other things.[20] But even at prevailing wages, this labor remained very attractive to corporations that would otherwise have to pay benefits and other payroll costs to retain a dedicated workforce. Notably, consistent with the Ashurst-Sumners Act, the legislation governing the program omitted services and agriculture jobs, which continue to be a corporate mainstay in prisons.

But, in the midst of the "tough on crime" era that followed, politicians reversed course and began pulling educational and other rehabilitative programs from prisons and jails, including those funded by Pell Grants, relying on now-debunked studies to argue that these rehabilitative programs did not work.[21] Some correctional administrators went so far as to declare the entire concept of rehabilitation "dead."[22] Incarcerated people were then responsible for paying for their own education, often buying materials by mail order.[23]

Things pivoted again in recent years when new research showed that, in fact, education profoundly improves reentry success.[25] Despite the clear evidence in favor of education, programs remained woefully underfunded in most states into the early 2010s,[26] and were deprioritized as compared to work, keeping the private marketplace for education services and materials small for many years. But, in 2023, thanks to the tremendous advocacy efforts led by college prison programs, legislators reinstated Pell Grant eligibility for incarcerated people, increasing funding for educational programs in prisons and jails.[27] Unfortunately, predatory prison technology corporations have answered the call with substandard education technology, which is now quickly expanding in facilities across the country.[28]

But perhaps the most significant shift in this space has come with a new movement to end the exception in the Thirteenth Amendment that is at the root of the exploitation of prison labor and much more in our carceral system. In 2018, Colorado became the first state in the modern day to end the exception in its state constitution.[29] Since then, six other states of varied political ideologies have followed, from Alabama to Vermont.[30] Building on these growing state efforts, there is now also a federal campaign to amend the U.S. Constitution to end the Thirteenth Amendment's exception.[31] And litigation is starting to follow these legislative wins to bring prison slavery to its practical end.[32] These efforts have the chance to radically transform our carceral system.

HOW MUCH MONEY IS AT STAKE?

Nearly all of the 1.2 million people in federal and state prisons[33] are required to participate in some combination of work, rehabilitative, and educational programming during their sentences.[34] In most systems, the only limiting factors are the scarcity of jobs or programs or a medical condition that prevents participation.

▪ LABOR

Work programs are the most pervasive type of correctional programming required across prisons. In fact, in most prison systems, people are forced to work often under the threat of punishment, including solitary confinement.[35] Currently, roughly two-thirds of incarcerated people work for pennies an hour, if anything. Most job assignments fall into one of three categories: roughly 3 percent of people manufacture goods or provide services for private corporations, 15 percent work in government-run businesses and public works projects, and 80 percent work in facility operations and maintenance.[36] The remaining 2 percent work in agriculture,[37] which can involve private and public sector applications. While cheap for private corporations, government-run businesses, and the carceral system itself, incarcerated labor is estimated to be valued at $16.3 billion annually based on applicable minimum and prevailing wages, though incarcerated people are estimated to make just $847 million today.[38]

■ PROGRAMS

Despite routine underfunding, the growth of the carceral population and evolution of correctional theory have created a small market for rehabilitative and educational programs that cater to people behind bars. Most prison systems require people to complete rehabilitative coursework such as cognitive thinking, anger management, or life skills.[39] The majority also offer some type of educational programming, and 22 states require people to take education classes.[40] Funding for higher education comes almost entirely through government grants for partnerships with local colleges, who supply faculty instructors.[41] People in facilities that do not offer higher education can at times pay for their own correspondence courses taught by a variety of nonprofit and for-profit colleges.[42]

With more transitive populations, jails tend to have fewer jobs or programs, but the exponential growth of the pretrial population over recent decades has expanded their prevalence.

WHAT CORPORATIONS ARE INVOLVED?

■ LABOR

The deepest financial opportunity for government agencies and corporations is in exploiting labor. While few recognizable corporations report directly employing incarcerated people, many do or support the exploitation of prison labor through their product sales and supply chains.[43] Some corporations even support the use of prison labor in multiple ways. And notably, when corporations do directly employ incarcerated people at higher wages, government agencies siphon a tremendous amount from their checks, creating a system largely akin to "convict leasing."

For example, 3M, the conglomerate behind brands like Post-it and Scotch, uses the labor of incarcerated people directly and helps others exploit it. In Minnesota, where 3M is headquartered, the corporation utilizes incarcerated people to manufacture shipping containers for its industrial paper products.[44] It also sells raw materials to government-run correctional industries that are used to manufacture products like license plates.[45] In fact, the corporation even has a team dedicated to supporting correctional agencies in building and growing their license plate manufacturing businesses.[46]

3M is a premium member of the National Correctional Industries Association, a trade group that protects the interests of corporations using prison labor. Among the other 26 premium members is VF Workwear, which ironically has an explicit policy barring the use of forced labor.[47] Another 60 corporations are standard members.[48] While many of these corporations are required to abide by PIECP regulations, many are not because, as noted, the program does not regulate services and agriculture.

Accordingly, a 2024 investigation by the Associated Press revealed that hundreds of food corporations have prison labor in their supply chains. From grains to eggs to cattle, incarcerated people help harvest, raise, and process a wide variety of agricultural commodities that are then sold to some of the biggest brands and by the largest retailers, including Cargill, Tyson, and Target, among many others.[49] Some of these corporations have even banned prison labor in their supply chains, with good intentions, but its ubiquitous prevalence has made it hard to circumvent without diligent audits and compliance measures.[50]

Many corporations also use prison labor to run their businesses outside of PIECP. Fast food corporations like Burger King use incarcerated people on work release to staff their restaurants.[51] Political campaign consultants, like the one used by former presidential candidate Michael Bloomberg, use incarcerated people to make campaign calls.[52] Third-party customer service firms like Televerde use incarcerated labor to field customer calls.[53] All claim to pay incarcerated people fairly while boasting of huge returns for their clients but ignore the massive deductions that send their incarcerated workers home with far less than what they earned.[54]

Finally, corporations that contract with prisons and jails to provide services inside also bank on the labor of incarcerated people to pad their bottom line. Consider private prison operators like CoreCivic and the GEO Group or food service and commissary providers like Aramark and Trinity Services Group that use prison labor to fulfill their service contracts. It is often incarcerated people who are cleaning CoreCivic and GEO facilities or managing Aramark and Trinity kitchens and commissaries. Their ability to rely on free or cheap prison labor reduces their expenses and increases their profits.

▪ PROGRAMS

Government agencies, nonprofits, and corporations all produce materials for rehabilitative programs. The National Institute of Corrections, a division of the U.S. Department of Justice, developed "Thinking for a Change," one of the most widely taught courses in prisons and jails.[55] The federal government distributes these materials freely and funds pilot programs for new approaches.[56] Private researchers, like those at Correctional Counseling, also develop and sell program materials to corrections facilities and train instructors to teach their courses, which run $500 each.[57] Publishers catering to adult education produce classroom materials. Publishing giant McGraw-Hill has test preparation tools designed specifically for use in corrections facilities and other institutions that lack internet access.[58] Smaller players like Paxen Publishing, which acquired the continuing education arm of Houghton-Mifflin in 2018, specialize in GED course materials for use in corrections facilities.[59]

Though over two-thirds of all educational programs are provided by community and other colleges,[60] technology is beginning to change the programming landscape in prisons and jails. The first to enter this market were smaller technology start-ups that positioned themselves as ethical alternatives to the prison telecom behemoths. Most prominent are Orijin (formerly American Prison Data Systems),[61] which directly charges agencies for its tablet-based educational programs, and Edovo, which perhaps counterintuitively shifted recently to deploying its educational software through tablets distributed by the major prison telecoms.[62] Both offered telecom services but deprioritized those services in favor of their educational offerings. Since their emergence, correctional telecom corporations like Aventiv Technologies (formerly Securus) and ViaPath (formerly Global Tel Link) have started providing their own rehabilitative and educational programs over their tablets.[63] Both corporations underwent recent rebrands to highlight their educational products and distract from the exploitative communications and media products that still dominate their businesses.

LABOR

In most facilities, the only vocational training someone can receive comes in the form of forced labor.[64] Almost every incarcerated person is required to work. Those who refuse can be denied parole, put in solitary confinement, or lose access to basic necessities, like family visits, care packages, and recreation.[65]

■ PRIVATE SECTOR

About 5,000 incarcerated people work for corporations through the federal PIECP,[66] which allows corporations to use prison labor to manufacture goods intended for interstate commerce.[67] While few high-profile corporations use PIECP workers, some include 3M, Avery Dennison, and Burlington Industries.[68] PIECP workers are required to receive prevailing wages for the manufacturing of goods, but corrections agencies are allowed to garnish the cost of "room and board" and make other deductions.[70] Many states further cut into people's income by requiring them to pay into mandatory savings accounts, paternalistically dictating what people can do with their meager earnings.[71] As a result, people are left with a tiny fraction of what they actually earn and less money to purchase necessities at commissary, support their families, and prepare for release, while corporations and agencies capitalize off their labor.

> We would receive services from an onshore agent—a U.S. citizen—but at offshore prices.
>
> — Anonymous CEO of corporation that used federal incarcerated workers[69]

THE BEST KEPT SECRET IN **CONTACT CENTERS**

OVERVIEW   ■   CASE STUDY #1   ■   CASE STUDY #2

Source: UNICOR advertisement for call center services.

In Nebraska, for instance, PIECP workers manufacture cleaning and janitorial equipment for CleanCore Solutions in exchange for a local prevailing wage—about $53 per day.[72] After deductions for taxes, room and board, and crime victims funds, workers are left with just half of their actual paycheck.[73] The state's mandatory savings program further requires them to save 63 percent of their pay after deductions, reducing their take-home pay to a little more than $9 for a full day's work, or $1.50 an hour—far less than the "prevailing wage" that the program advertises.[74] And still, the pay for a PIECP job is better than nearly every other prison job.

Despite the shortcomings of PIECP, those working for corporations in the program are better served than those working for corporations in jobs not regulated by PIECP, namely jobs in services or agriculture.[76] These jobs, including those that are part of work-release programs, fill out the roughly 3 percent of incarcerated people working for corporations.[77]

> We established this partnership with [Colorado Correctional Industries] in 2007, just as our need for goat milk was growing. . . . CCI had the means (the farmland, equipment, and strong-willed human power and spirit) to get a Colorado dairy up and running, and the results have been incredible.
>
> – Haystack Mountain Cheese[75]

Corporations use incarcerated workers in service jobs that do not fall under PIECP regulation, both inside and outside of prisons. Some corporations operate factories, call centers, and other businesses out of prisons while others transport incarcerated people to and from their businesses in the community through work-release programs that can run the gamut. In some cases, incarcerated people have even been leased out to private individuals for work assignments.[78] Incarcerated people in these service jobs are not required to be paid prevailing wages, though they face many of the same wage garnishments as those in PIECP jobs. Work release can even come with additional fees, like a transportation fee for being taken to and from work.[79]

Finally, there are agriculture jobs that actually teeter between the private and public sectors. While the importance of prison labor in private sector farming was highlighted in 2018 when the Trump administration rolled out its zero-tolerance immigration policy, and many farms that relied on undocumented workers turned to prisons for cheap labor,[80] most farms with incarcerated workers are run by corrections agencies. Still, the fruits of their labor—hundreds of millions of dollars' worth of grain, fruits, vegetables, dairy, and livestock—feed into the supply chain of some of the world's largest food and retail corporations, both in the United States and overseas. Some purchase their harvests and livestock as commodities while others sell products made from them.[81] In the end, through these agriculture jobs, prison labor touches so much of the food we consume that it would be imprudent not to reflect on its relationship to the private sector.

Since the formal end of chattel slavery, and its obvious omission from the Ashurst-Sumners Act in 1935, prison labor has been used in farming. In fact, many prisons sit on former plantations, including the nation's largest maximum-security facility: the Louisiana State Penitentiary, commonly referred to as Angola after the ancestry of the people previously enslaved there.[82] These plantation prisons still grow some of the same crops grown during antebellum slavery in similarly unsafe conditions.[83] In 2023, a 35-year-old man died while mowing the fields at a Texas prison from a heart attack triggered by the excruciating heat of the sun.[84]

Source: People's World. Incarcerated workers at Angola prison, Louisiana.

The extent to which corporations and their agency partners will go to make prison labor available to farms was exposed during the pandemic. A 2023 investigation published by *Cosmopolitan* revealed the dangerous and inhumane treatment of incarcerated women at an egg farm run by Hickman's Family Farms. One of the largest corporate clients of the Arizona Department of Corrections, Hickman's employed hundreds of incarcerated women—a quarter of its workforce. When the pandemic hit and prisons shuttered, Arizona moved women employed at Hickman's farms to a warehouse that had been repurposed as a dormitory. For months, they lived on top of each other in squalor and worked on skeleton crews with dangerous conditions. At least one woman suffered an injury that left her permanently disfigured. The women took home just a few dollars an hour after the agency took its cut, though they were not even housed at a state facility.[85]

▪ GOVERNMENT-RUN BUSINESSES AND PUBLIC WORKS PROJECTS

About 51,500 incarcerated people work for government-run businesses called correctional industries and another 64,000 for public works projects, which are typically out in the community.[86] These businesses manufacture goods primarily for government use such as school furniture, street signs, and military equipment, and provide services that include staffing call centers, conducting asbestos abatements, and cleaning roads. Through these jobs, states subsidize their budgets by offsetting correctional costs and creating savings for other state agencies.[87] Many states even have laws that make their correctional industries preferred vendors, requiring their state and local agencies to procure products and services from them, if available, before going to the public market.[88]

However, governments have used prison labor not only to save money, but also to generate revenue more broadly when facing budget gaps. For example, in 2019, New York Governor Andrew Cuomo announced a revenue plan that required car owners to purchase new license plates.[89] The plan was dependent on the cheap labor of the state's incarcerated workers, who make as little as $0.16 per hour manufacturing plates.[90] Thankfully the plan failed.

But, notably, plans like these do not just emerge from and solely benefit the governments that propose them. Corporations knowingly sell billions of dollars in raw materials to correctional industries.[91] In New York, as in many states, license plates manufactured by incarcerated workers are made using raw materials and machinery sold by 3M.[92] And the corporation gets creative in devising ways to expand this business line. In Washington, 3M lobbied elected officials to pass legislation requiring car owners to replace their license plates every five years, creating a continual need for their products and $10 million in annual revenue for the state.[93]

Incarcerated people are also often tapped to respond to state emergencies in dangerous conditions for little or no pay. For example, in California in 2019, state officials used 200 incarcerated firefighters to combat the deadliest forest fires in state history. They paid them just $2.90 to $5.12 per day, a sharp difference from the average $91,000 salary that non-incarcerated firefighters were paid to do the same job.[94] Though two incarcerated

Source: Fortune: Incarcerated firefighters in California.

firefighters died fighting fires in 2017,[95] the job remains highly coveted because it pays significantly more than other prison jobs.[96] As they risk their lives, incarcerated firefighters save California over $100 million each year.[97] And until recently, incarcerated firefighters were barred from working as firefighters after release due to their criminal record.[98]

In a similar vein, nearly every state tapped incarcerated workers to respond to the pandemic in 2020. Governor after governor grossly underpaid incarcerated workers to produce personal protective equipment like masks and gowns for first responders, as well as hand sanitizer for the public.[99] New York's governor Andrew Cuomo publicly bragged about the state's mass production of hand sanitizer and joked about illegally selling it in the public market to compete with commercial brands.[100] He failed to ever mention the incarcerated workers producing the hand sanitizer or the $0.65 per hour they were earning on average. The New York City Department of Corrections reached a low when it went as far as to announce plans to use incarcerated workers to dig mass graves for those who succumbed to the disease and whose bodies went unclaimed. Under public pressure, the city canceled its plan.[101]

▪ FACILITY OPERATIONS AND MAINTENANCE

The vast majority, or roughly 80 percent, of incarcerated people work to support the operation and upkeep of the facilities in which they are held. They prepare food, deliver commissary, do laundry, clean units, perform maintenance, serve as clerks, and more.[102] Outwardly insignificant and ostensibly simple, these jobs are critical to the basic operations of corrections facilities. Without incarcerated workers in facility operations and maintenance jobs, prisons and jails simply would not run. There are not

> It was pretty much slave labor, but there was nothing I could do about that. I needed stamps to write to my child. I needed hygiene products.
>
> — Laurie Hazen, incarcerated kitchen worker in Massachusetts[103]

enough corrections officers and staff to fulfill the tasks they do. In fact, in 2018, when incarcerated people across the country went on strike,[104] some prisons and jails locked down without the staff to keep running as normal.

Yet, facility operations and maintenance jobs pay the least, often as little as $0.05 per hour.[105] There are seven states—Alabama, Arkansas, Florida, Georgia, Mississippi, South Carolina, and Texas—that do not pay incarcerated people in facility operations and maintenance jobs anything.[106] Accordingly, it is nearly impossible for the majority of incarcerated people to afford basic necessities such as hygiene products from commissary or phone calls with loved ones.[107] Instead, the cost of these essentials is forced onto their families, and disproportionately Black, brown, and Indigenous women.

By using grossly underpaid labor, elected officials and correctional administrators are able to disguise the real financial cost of mass incarceration. An incarcerated person working a custodial job that pays $0.14 per hour makes as little as $221 for an entire year's work. If they were instead paid at least the federal minimum wage, or $7.25 per hour, that custodian would make $11,484 per year, or 52 times more. Depressing the wages of incarcerated people reduces the cost of our carceral system by roughly 16 percent.[110] While seemingly appealing, these savings are shortsighted.

As a society, we have a lot to gain from paying incarcerated workers fair wages, besides moral amends. A 2024 study estimated that ending slavery and mandating fair wages for incarcerated workers would not just generate $11.6 billion to $18.8 billion in wages for incarcerated workers, but

> For 12 years, I worked at the prison infirmary as a nurse's aide. I was part of the BERT, Blood Emergency Response Team. I would clean blood, feces, and bodily fluids throughout the facility. For cleaning a blood spill, I would be paid 75 cents. During every incident, I would be forced to play "Russian Roulette" with my health for these wages. If I would refuse, I was liable to receive a disciplinary infraction.
>
> — Gonzalo Aguilar, incarcerated person in New York[109]

also improve the quality of jobs and with it increase reentry success and future earning potential. The study concluded that this policy change would result in net economic benefits of $18.3 billion to $20.3 billion per year.[111]

JORGE'S STORY

I spent decades working fields, tending crops, and paving the grounds of Texas prisons. I never earned a penny. Texas doesn't compensate incarcerated people for their work.

Jorge Renaud
Texas

Field labor was ugly. We were forced to perform physically demanding tasks in the grueling heat of Texas summers. Mounted on horseback and armed with guns, officers watched over us to drive productivity. They often incited fights for fun, while the administration claimed that the exploitative, brutal work was good for us—that it built up our work ethic and skill sets. It's an argument recycled from plantation owners in the antebellum South, whose plantations are now prisons, in many cases.

Eventually, I was allowed to move inside—out of the 100-degree heat—to work in kitchen commissaries, clerking positions, and the furniture factory, where most furniture in the state capitol building is built. But if I ever argued with an officer, they would threaten to put me back in the fields.

The state's free labor scheme forces incarcerated people to develop "side hustles." How else can you afford deodorant from commissary or a phone call home? I got paid for writing for folks—writing poetry, grievances, and appeals. Those who didn't have a unique skill set had to take bigger risks. If you worked in the kitchen, for example, you stole meat, sugar, or whatever you could, and risked discipline to sell it in the underground prison economy. Taking from the master's house could result in the loss of one's job or even solitary confinement.

The bottom line is that slavery is alive and well right here in Texas. Incarcerated people—majority Black and Latinx like me due to racist policies—work full days in backbreaking conditions without pay and under the threat of punishment. After each of my three bids of 3, 7½, and 17 years, I walked out of prison with only $50—after nearly 50,000 hours of work altogether.

Today, I'm committed to transforming the narrative around prisons and the policies that fill them. As an abolitionist, I want to do more than reform our system. I want to replace it with a vision that truly rehabilitates lives and supports communities. There's no iteration of slavery that does that.

REHABILITATIVE AND EDUCATIONAL PROGRAMS

Nearly every correctional facility requires people to complete some form of rehabilitative programming,[112] such as cognitive behavioral therapy, chemical dependency recovery, domestic violence prevention, anger management, and treatment for people convicted of sex offenses.[113] But these courses rarely provide people with the tools they actually need to succeed.

The most popular rehabilitative program is cognitive behavioral therapy, which claims to teach improved decision-making skills.[114] But rather than rigorous coursework, correctional rehabilitation corporations design and sell prepackaged therapy programs that often consist of merely a booklet titled *Thinking for a Change* or *Rules Are Made to Be Followed*.[115] Many of these programs were developed by federal researchers for classrooms and are freely available online,[116] but corporations repackage cheap versions and sell them to the correctional market.

One of the most prominent distributors is Correctional Counseling, which sells the "Moral Reconation Therapy" program and holds trainings for instructors.[117] Avoiding any discussion about the systemic causes of crime, these courses teach people that they are incarcerated because they lack self-control or social skills.[118] Many of these programs are so misguided that researchers now refer to them as "correctional quackery."[119] Nevertheless, correctional administrators continue to purchase these program materials, insincerely claiming to prepare people for release.[120]

The situation is even bleaker for educational programming. Constantly under the threat of funding cuts, educational programs recently celebrated the restoration of Pell Grant eligibility for incarcerated people. However, college programs are still limited in most prisons and many incarcerated people do not qualify based on their prior educational attainment. With few other choices, many opt to educate themselves using the limited resources in prison libraries.

But both these formal and informal educational options are now being threatened by correctional telecom providers and their tablets. Advertised as innovative tools for education, entertainment, and communication, tablets are replacing critical educational resources to extract money from corrections systems and incarcerated people. Correctional telecom providers, notorious for once charging as much as a dollar a minute for phone calls, use tablets to bring their predatory business practices to prison education.

To start, they sought to replace physical books and law libraries with sparse digital alternatives.[121] In West Virginia, which contracts with ViaPath, incarcerated people must pay $0.03 per minute to read books on their tablets that are free in the public domain online.[122] This scheme turns reading into a luxury that many cannot afford. At ViaPath's prices, the average reader would have to pay $18—potentially months of wages for an incarcerated person—to read a 300-page book. Many corrections agencies allow this predatory behavior because they earn kickbacks from purchases made on tablets.[123]

Next, they developed a suite of digital education tools to replace in-person educational programming, including a fully remote college program.[124] They convinced at least some correctional administrators to make the shift. In 2022, the Massachusetts Department of Corrections, for example, chose not to reapply for state educational funding for prison programs, opting instead for tablet-based education.[125]

Finally, when Pell Grant eligibility was restored for incarcerated people, tablet providers quickly got to developing ways to charge college programs, which had gone wildly underfunded for years, to use their tablets.[126] JPay, for example, developed a three-tiered sales package with gold, silver, and bronze options. Around the same time, ViaPath claimed to be pivoting its focus to reintegration services, namely education and training content for its tablets.[127]

In prisons and jails across the country, rehabilitative and educational programs have routinely been deprioritized in favor of work programs that are more profitable for both the private and public sectors. The public's comfort with using prison labor is especially disturbing given our nation's history with slavery and the racial disparities in our carceral population. But the prioritization and exploitation of prison labor will persist until the nefarious exception in the Thirteenth Amendment allowing slavery as the punishment for a crime is addressed and all people are seen as deserving of labor rights.

LEARN MORE

- *A Cost-Benefit Analysis: The Impact of Ending Slavery and Involuntary Servitude as Criminal Punishment and Paying Incarcerated Workers Fair Wages*, Edgeworth Economics (2024)
- *Captive Labor: Exploitation of Incarcerated Workers*, ACLU (2022)
- "Coronavirus Limits California Efforts to Fight Fires with Prison Labor," *New York Times* (2020)

- "The Free Prison Tablets That Aren't Free," *The Outline* (2019)
- *Environmental Injustice Behind Bars: Toxic Imprisonment in America*, The Global Environmental Justice Project (2018)
- "The True History of America's Private Prison Industry," *Time* (2018)
- "Slavery in the U.S. Prison System," *Al Jazeera* (2017)
- "Prison Labour Is a Billion-Dollar Industry, with Uncertain Returns for Inmates," *The Economist* (2017)
- *What Are Inmates Learning in Prison? Not Much*, The Marshall Project (2017)
- *How Much Do Incarcerated People Earn in Each State?* Prison Policy Initiative (2017)
- *State and Federal Prison Wage Policies and Sourcing Information*, Prison Policy Initiative (2017)

EQUIPMENT

Business is very good. Because crime is crazy and there are lots of inmates. We are happy, the number [of customers] is increasing every day.

— *Ahmad Afzal, director of Fine Cotton Textiles, a uniform manufacturer*[1]

As the prison population soared in the 1970s and 1980s, equipment and supplies corporations that had previously served other institutional settings, such as hospitals and schools, saw an opportunity.[2] Appealing to the burgeoning correctional market, these corporations began manufacturing products specifically designed for punitive settings, like triple-stacked bunks that allow correctional administrators to pack people in small cells and shackle restraints for people experiencing mental health crises. When population growth began to strain correctional budgets, manufacturers and suppliers of even basic consumer goods entered the market by producing cheap knockoff supplies that barely served their intended use.

Description: Equipment and supplies corporations furnish nearly everything used in prisons and jails, from desks and uniforms to restraint jackets and tear gas. The products they sell can be organized into four categories: furnishings and hardware, supplies, security equipment, and security technology.

At the same time, defense contrac- tors and arms manufacturers were expanding into the correctional mar- ket. The demand for weapons surged after the 1971 Attica prison uprising, when incarcerated men took control of Attica Correctional Facility in New York to demand better living condi- tions and an end to racial assaults common at the prison. State officials

1,300+
Correctional equipment and supplies corporations[3]
$10.7 million
Federal Bureau of Prisons spending on weapons, 2014–2023[4]
104
Taser deaths in prisons and jails[5]

responded with militarized violence, killing 39 people.[6] Ultimately, rather than addressing or even acknowledging the injustices raised by organiz- ers, correctional administrators concluded that the uprising was a result of a lack of security equipment. State officials immediately allocated $4 mil- lion in emergency funds—then equal to 5 percent of the state's correctional budget—to the purchase of "the latest things in mob control."[7] Other states quickly followed suit,[8] and military-style weapons became commonplace behind bars.

As technology evolved over the years, corporations also started to sell security technology like electronic locks and surveillance systems. Although these products were traditionally sold by specialized correctional manufac- turers, mega consumer brands have also expanded into the correctional market through technology like facial recognition software.

HOW MUCH MONEY IS AT STAKE?

The ubiquity of fear and prioritization of security above all else in pris- ons and jails has led correctional administrators to spend excessively on equipment. Corrections agencies spend as much as 10 percent of their annual budget on equipment, with the largest expenditures coming from one-time purchases of costly items like surveillance systems.[8] Together, law enforcement and corrections agencies spend $1.2 billion annually on security equipment and technology alone.[9] That figure is expected to grow with the cost of new technology.[10]

When short on funds for equipment and supplies, agencies find creative funding sources. Many supplement their legislatively appropriated equipment and supplies budgets with money extracted from incarcerated people and their families through commissions on commissary and communication sales. These funds are, in some cases, placed in so-called "inmate welfare funds," intended to support educational programs, reentry services, and improvements to quality of life for people behind bars. But instead, correctional administrators often use them to purchase equipment and supplies for corrections officers, including weapons.[11]

For instance, California penal code requires that "inmate welfare funds" be used "primarily for the benefit, education, and welfare" of incarcerated people.[12] However, between 2011 and 2013, the Los Angeles County Sheriff's Department used 87 percent of the money in its "inmate welfare fund," or $1.3 million, for capital improvements, equipment for the medical dispensary, security camera monitoring, the repainting and upkeep of jail facilities, and, finally, televisions for entertainment.[13]

While officials quickly allocate money for their own equipment and supplies, supplies for incarcerated people remain under-resourced. Still, the sheer size of the incarcerated population drives even those sales. But in the end, the true size of the correctional equipment and supplies market is unknown.

WHAT CORPORATIONS ARE INVOLVED?

The steady demand for correctional equipment and supplies has created a highly fragmented ecosystem of manufacturers and suppliers, from multinational conglomerates to "mom and pop" operations. Over 1,300 corporations sell correctional equipment and supplies, making it the largest sector in the prison industry.[14] Though there are a handful of corporations that sell a variety of products, most corporations in the space specialize in a single type of equipment or supplies, whether it be furnishings, hardware, technology, weaponry, or consumer goods.

In recent years, some of these niche areas have gone through a process of consolidation as more established players acquire smaller competitors. For instance, Cornerstone Detention, a large correctional equipment corporation that manufacturers and installs correctional furnishings and hardware, has acquired ten equipment manufacturers.[15] Other major players in furnishings and hardware include Stanley Black & Decker, Assa Abloy, Kane Innovations, Southern Folger, Accurate Controls, and Norix.

One of the largest suppliers of correctional equipment and supplies is the Bob Barker Company, a family-run business that sells over 5,000 different products for corrections facilities and collects an estimated $67 million in revenue annually. Founded in 1972 as a restaurant supply company, Bob Barker entered the correctional market by selling kitchen equipment before expanding to sell uniforms and mattresses.[16] The corporation cemented its

	Cornerstone Detention Products[19]	Stanley Black & Decker Corrections Security[20]	The Bob Barker Company[21]	Southern Folger[22]	Kane Innovations[23]
Annual Prison Revenue	$155 Mn	Unknown	$67 Mn	$49 Mn	$37 Mn
Employees	288	Unknown	175	160	160
Products	Reinforced windows, doors, cells	Hardware, electronic systems, locks	Furniture, uniforms, security equipment, consumer goods (e.g., hygiene products)	Hardware, electronic systems	Security barriers, furniture

dominance in the industry in 2006 by merging with Leslee Scott, another manufacturer and supplier in the space.[17] Today, Bob Barker sells nearly every type of equipment and supplies used behind bars, from shampoo packets for incarcerated people to weapons for officers.

Investors have also emerged to provide financing to equipment manufacturers and suppliers seeking to expand into the correctional market. These financiers require new entrants to maintain a gross profit margin of 15 percent, encouraging aggressive pricing and cost cutting.[18]

FURNISHINGS AND HARDWARE

Equipment corporations that manufacture and supply furnishings and hardware have created a niche market in the correctional space by playing on trumped-up safety and security concerns to sell specially designed, costly products that facilitate the abuse of people behind bars. By fear-mongering and dehumanizing incarcerated people, furnishings and hardware manufacturers and suppliers encourage facilities to use more extreme methods of confinement that call for expensive products.

Examples of their products include:

- "Therapeutic modules," or human pens, used to cage people during programs.[24]
- Benches with loops designed for handcuffs typical in booking areas.[25]
- Stackable, plastic sleeping platforms intended for temporary use in overcrowded facilities.[26]
- Basic plastic storage containers assigned individually to store and move property.[27]
- Hinged slots used to pass through food for people in solitary confinement.[28]

SUPPLIES

While equipment corporations invest in reinforced furnishings and hardware for facilities to justify higher pricing, those that manufacture supplies distributed to incarcerated people cut corners. Their cheap, knockoff consumer products claim to protect facility security but create serious health risks for incarcerated people.

Source: Bob Barker Company catalog. "Areas of the body that have or are only even suspected of having come in contact with the product should be rinsed immediately with plenty of running water and possibly soap."

For instance, Bob Barker emphasizes both contraband prevention and cost-efficiency in selling its Maximum Security® & Clear All-in-One Shaving Cream, Soap, and Shampoo. However, the company takes cost cutting a step further by replacing typical soap ingredients with dangerous preservatives not found in free-world consumer brands that irritate skin and may even cause birth defects.[29] Unbelievably, the corporation's own safety warning advises people to avoid skin contact with the soap.[30] Yet, at just $0.14 per ounce[31]—compared to $0.62 per ounce for name-brand products like Pert Plus[32]—it remains attractive for corrections agencies. As a result, to protect their health, incarcerated people often purchase soap in commissary.

SECURITY EQUIPMENT

Correctional equipment corporations enable and encourage some of the most brutal practices behind bars. They sell correctional administrators the tools needed to force people into obedience, using advertising that

> I can count on one hand when [a Taser] was used appropriately.
>
> — Steve Martin, former general counsel for Texas Department of Criminal Justice[33]

either obscures or downplays the harm they inflict. Some corporations go as far as to sell security equipment that resembles medieval torture devices. For example, Humane Restraint—whose name alone appears to make light of its cruel products—sells leg weights, restraint beds, and wrist shackles with inappropriately kitschy marketing.[34] These restraints can cause severe physical and mental harm.[35] Though federal, state, and local regulations often restrict the use of restraints, corrections officers frequently turn to them to punish minor infractions.[36] In fact, in some facilities, these restraints have become the default response to someone suffering a mental health crisis.[37]

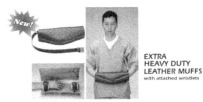

Source: Humane Restraints, Wholesale catalog.

With little regard for those on the receiving end of their equipment, these corporations also deceptively market dangerous weapons as "less lethal," spreading military-grade weaponry across prisons and jails while avoiding liability for the consequences of their use.[38] These weapons include batons, stun guns, rubber bullets, tear gas, and pepper spray.[39]

For instance, stun guns are extremely dangerous, but equipment corporations continue to sell them without consequence. Axon, which sells Tasers, previously advertised its products as "non-lethal" and "safe" before adopting the term "less lethal" to avoid lawsuits by people who suffered cardiac arrest after being struck with their products.[40] Axon even

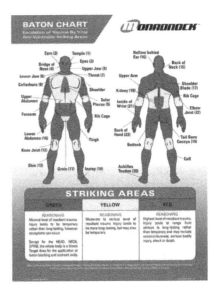

Source: Defense Technology. Poster instructing corrections officers how to use a baton to inflict pain without causing lasting damage.

warns that a stun gun is more likely to kill someone if they have a mental illness, history of drug use, or heart disease,[41] conditions that are disproportionately common among incarcerated people due to failures in social support. Still, corrections agencies purchase and use Tasers in large quantities, endangering people behind bars.[42] Since roughly 2000, over a 100 incarcerated people have died in incidents involving Tasers, a third of whom were already restrained when the Taser was used.[43]

SECURITY TECHNOLOGY

For years, facilities have purchased cameras and powered locks from security technology corporations. Major security technology firm Securitas Technologies, for instance, offers security management systems that monitor all aspects of corrections facilities, from perimeter control to the spread of viruses.[44] However, these corporations are increasingly developing and marketing new Orwellian technology to surveil people using biometric data, including their fingerprints, retinas, and, in some cases, even the way they walk.[45] Familiar consumer technology corporations like Microsoft and Amazon are entering the space. Both have developed facial recognition technology being implemented in corrections facilities.[46]

However, these new security technologies raise serious concerns. For instance, existing facial recognition technology struggles to identify people of color accurately, which creates a significant risk of false identification for the Black, brown, and Indigenous prison population.[47] These identifications are often used in prison disciplinary hearings, where a false positive can lead to severe consequences: the denial of visits and calls, solitary confinement, or even the denial of parole—often without any legal representation or recourse. While local municipalities have begun to pass legislation prohibiting this technology in the free world,[48] correctional administrators continue to implement it across prisons and jails without transparency or accountability.[49]

But these types of false identifications are not limited to the analysis of biometric data. Security technology includes forensic equipment—like drug tests used to detect contraband narcotics—that also often produce false positives with many of the same dire consequences for incarcerated people. In New York, for example, leaked documents confirmed an abundance of false positives in both urinalysis tests conducted using Thermo Fisher Scientific tests and field tests conducted directly on suspected substances using Sirchie tests.[50] This faulty testing equipment caused many people to suffer for months in solitary confinement, and some were even refused early release.[51] Notably, these tests are not just used in New York, but across the country in law enforcement, correctional, and even employment environments.

LARRY'S STORY

On a hot July day in 2019, corrections officers dragged me out of my cell and put me in handcuffs, with their batons at their waists silently threatening violence. They threw me in solitary confinement without explanation and left me there for hours without anything as much as toilet paper. The next morning, I received a misbehavior report that stated I had tested positive for drug use. It was impossible; I knew I had not used anything.

Larry Hardy
New York

As it turns out, I was among more than 2,000 incarcerated people who falsely tested positive for drugs in 2019 as a result of faulty testing equipment manufactured by Microgenics, a subsidiary of Thermo Fisher Scientific.

Despite my pleas of innocence, I was sanctioned with 90 days in solitary confinement, loss of all privileges, including regular and family reunification visits, and removal from all activities. Through the summer heat, I was confined to a closet-sized cell with no ventilation, stripped of any personal belongings, and limited to two showers a week. I was devastated, traumatized. My character, reputation, and credibility were defamed. I went into a hopeless state of depression, feeling like there was no chance that I would be vindicated. I questioned my faith.

Then, on my 67th day in solitary confinement, now late September, the reversal came down from prison administrators. Just like that, my false positive had been reversed, my sanctions ended, and I was returned to my cell in general population. It was as if nothing had happened—but a lot happened.

Months later, hundreds of formerly and currently incarcerated people, who suffered the loss of calls and visits, solitary confinement, and even extended prison stays, filed a lawsuit against the New York Department of Corrections and Community Supervision and Thermo Fisher Scientific. While there has been momentum in the case and increased media coverage over the year since, my life and the lives of thousands of others just in New York have been irreparably damaged. But I wonder how many other state and local agencies have used Thermo Fisher Scientific's faulty drug tests to destroy lives?

TRADE ASSOCIATIONS

Trade shows are the most important marketing tool for correctional equipment and supplies corporations. The American Correctional Association (ACA), an influential industry trade group with over 20,000 members, holds the country's largest annual trade show, known as the "Congress of Corrections."[52] An astounding 81 percent of sales made by the correctional

Source: American Correctional Association, Orlando Program Book. Advertisement from annual conference program.

equipment and supplies sector occur at these trade shows.[53] The American Jail Association and National Sheriffs' Association also host large trade shows each year.

> This is a great opportunity to meet face-to-face with thousands of decision makers who have the need and budgets for your products. . . . We wish you a profitable 2018.
>
> — American Correctional Association[54]

Manufacturing and supplying inherently violent equipment and supplies, corporations facilitate the traumatization and abuse of people behind bars. Worse yet, their products are often purchased using public funds and money siphoned from the families of incarcerated people. By selling the tools that allow correctional administrators to run facilities by brutal force, these corporations are responsible for some of the worst abuses in the prison industry.

LEARN MORE

- National Police Funding Database, LDF's Thurgood Marshall Institute (2023)
- "Police Equipment," The Marshall Project (2018)
- "Shock Tactics: Inmate Deaths Reveal 'Torturous' Use of Tasers," *Reuters* (2017)

- Video: "Person in an Alabama Jail Pepper Sprayed While in a Restraint Chair," *Washington Post* (2017)
- "Prisons Are Using Military-Grade Tear Gas to Punish People," *The Nation* (2016)
- "Making Profits on the Captive Prison Market," *New Yorker* (2016)
- "Welcome to Jail Inc.: How Private Companies Make Money Off U.S. Prisons," *The Guardian* (2016)
- "Prison Vendors See Continued Signs of a Captive Market," *New York Times* (2015)

DATA
+ INFORMATION

Laws have to determine what's legal, but you can't ban technology. Sure, that might lead to a dystopian future or something, but you can't ban it.

— David Scalzo, founder and Managing Partner at Kirenaga Partners[1]

Since the turn of the 20th century, racist ideologies have been enshrined in crime statistics. Touted as objective, statistical discourse ascribed criminal traits to Black people as innate and even biological. Using early risk assessment tools and biometric programs, Progressive Era social scientists rationalized racially disparate rates of arrest and punishment to propel forward predictive policing and new tools aimed at measuring criminal risk.[2]

Description: Law enforcement, courts, and corrections agencies contract with private corporations for data and information systems that track people through the criminal legal system. These corporations also provide decision-making tools that can determine one's experience in the system. These systems and tools include prison and jail management systems, risk and needs assessment tools, and biometrics.

■ PRISON AND JAIL
MANAGEMENT SYSTEMS

It was not until the prison and jail population began to explode in the 1970s that correctional administrators began to introduce more robust information management and classification practices. They sought to manage growing populations, improve efficiency, and, most importantly,

$4.8 billion
Global prison and jail management system market size[3]

88%
Projected global market growth by 2033[4]

rebut litigation.[5] By the 1980s, technology had become readily accessible and corrections agencies were eager to find more sophisticated tools and systems that would make facility management easier.[6] Private software corporations responded to their calls with increasingly sophisticated information management tools that rely on invasive biometric data.

■ RISK AND NEEDS
ASSESSMENT TOOLS

States introduced risk assessments in the 1920s to inform parole decisions, relying on clinical evaluations of psychologists, social workers, and criminal legal system actors.[9] Courts

150+
Risk and needs assessment tools[7]

77%
Increased likelihood of "high risk" flag for Black versus white defendant[8]

expanded their use in the 1960s into the pretrial context to predict whether an accused person would return to court to face trial.[10] In the 1970s, as the carceral population began to balloon, risk assessments shifted from being a matter of professional opinion to algorithmic calculations.[11] Soon, actors across the criminal legal system started to use risk and needs assessment tools to help set bail, determine sentences, assign security levels, assess programming needs, make parole decisions, and establish supervision conditions.[12] Some developed tools in-house while others looked to private corporations and foundations, resulting in the release of more than 150 new risk and needs assessment tools over the next two decades.[13]

▪ BIOMETRICS

Biometrics—the automated identification of a person based on physical or behavioral traits—started well before modern technology.[17] The New York prison system began using fingerprinting to identify people as early as 1902, and the Federal Bureau of Investigation followed in 1924.[18] Between the 1930s and the 1990s, advances in face, eye, and hand recognition technology significantly expanded law enforcement's use of biometrics, which often helped reinforce racist policing.[19] In 2000, the National Institute of Justice began testing emerging biometric technologies in military prisons for broader correctional uses.[20]

117 million
Faces stored by law enforcement[14]

200,000+
Incarcerated voice prints collected by correctional telecom corporations[15]

290 million
Identities stored by the U.S. Department of Homeland Security[16]

In fact, some of the most sophisticated biometric tools were developed for the military and later adapted for law enforcement and correctional settings.[21] For example, in the 2000s, the U.S. Department of Defense awarded the Massachusetts Institute of Technology a $50 million grant to develop voice recognition technology that it intended to use to combat terrorism.[22] In 2010, JLG, now a subsidiary of correctional telecom giant Aventiv Technologies (formerly Securus Technologies), licensed the technology to monitor prison and jail phone calls.[23]

Around the world, advocates and lawmakers have sounded the alarm about the dangers of biometrics, and at least some geographies have heeded these warnings. The European Union, for instance, passed laws protecting personal biometric data,[24] but in the United States, this technology remains almost largely unregulated.[25] Thus, unsurprisingly, a growing number of private corporations are entering the market eager to sell biometric data collected in prisons and jails to everyone from big tech to law enforcement.

HOW MUCH MONEY IS AT STAKE?

▪ PRISON AND JAIL MANAGEMENT SYSTEMS

In 2017, the global prison and jail management systems market was valued at roughly $1.8 billion.[26] It reached $4.8 billion in 2023, and by 2033, it is projected to reach $9 billion.[27] North America, and the United States in particular, is expected to dominate the market and drive much of its growth as it continues to the lead the world in incarceration and increase the use of mobile and cloud technologies to store and share data across government agencies.[28]

▪ RISK AND NEEDS ASSESSMENT TOOLS

The federal system and nearly every state system use risk and needs assessment tools in the pretrial context and correctional settings, and both are growing at the county level.[29] However, the market opportunity for assessment tools is bigger than merely geographic expansion. Courts and correctional agencies are increasingly using risk assessment tools at new decision points in the criminal legal system—from bail to sentencing to classification to parole.[30] There are now hundreds of different risk and needs assessment tools used across the country.[31] The use of these tools has increased most dramatically in recent years. In 2013, just 10 percent of the United States lived in a jurisdiction that used a pretrial risk assessment tool. By 2017, that number had risen to 25 percent.[32]

PRETRIAL RISK ASSESSMENT TOOLS USED IN JURISDICTIONS ACROSS THE UNITED STATES

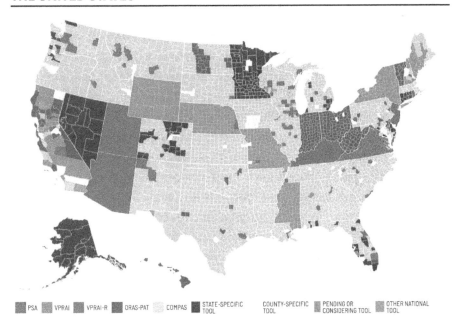

PSA · VPRAI · VPRAI-R · ORAS-PAT · COMPAS · STATE-SPECIFIC TOOL · COUNTY-SPECIFIC TOOL · PENDING OR CONSIDERING TOOL · OTHER NATIONAL TOOL

Source: Movement Alliance Project and MediaJustice, Mapping Pretrial Injustice.

■ BIOMETRICS

The global biometrics market is projected to grow from $30.8 billion in 2022 to $76.7 billion by 2029.[33] While the use of biometrics is beginning to expand, its primary users remain law enforcement, corrections, military, and border control.[34] Two of the leading drivers of its expected growth are surveillance and security—from street corners to borders to cyberspace.[35] In the United States alone, there are 1,049 corporations that scan biometric data[36] and, consequently, have access to over billions of pieces of identifying human information.[37] However, there is no market data related to the use of biometrics specifically in corrections.

WHAT CORPORATIONS ARE INVOLVED?

■ PRISON AND JAIL MANAGEMENT SYSTEMS

The prison and jail management systems market is dominated by a few large players and filled out with dozens of smaller players. Among the oldest and most prominent is Syscon, which launched its first prison and jail management system in 1985,[38] and now also tracks financial information, integrates biometric data, and supports mobile devices and cloud storage.[39] Another major player promoting a shift to cloud-based solutions is publicly traded information technology giant DXC Technology.[40] Equivant (formerly Northpointe), which is best known for developing one of the most widely used risk and needs assessment tools,[41] is also a leading provider of prison and jail management systems, its original core business.[42] But the field of management systems is quickly evolving beyond these traditional software products due to major technology conglomerates like Amazon and Microsoft that are now providing cloud-based data services to power advanced management systems for government agencies like U.S. Immigration and Customs Enforcement (ICE).[43]

■ RISK AND NEEDS ASSESSMENT TOOLS

The three most widely used risk and needs assessment tools are Level of Service Inventory Revised (LSI-R), Correctional Offender Management Profiling for Alternative Sanctions (COMPAS), and the Public Safety Assessment (PSA).[44] The first two were developed by private corporations while the last was developed by a private foundation. Multi-Health Systems Assessments developed LSI-R in 1995.[45] Since, LSI-R and adapted versions have been adopted widely in states like California and Washington.[46] Created by Equivant in 1998, COMPAS is currently thought to be the most widely used assessment tool, with over 500 court systems and 100 corrections agencies, including seven state prison systems, using the tool.[47] That is in large part because COMPAS has the broadest adaptations. Arnold Ventures, backed by philanthropists Laura and John Arnold, spent $1.2 million to develop PSA in 2013,[48] which has now been adopted by 5 state systems and 59 counties across 20 states.[49]

Some jurisdictions have also developed their own risk assessment tools, often using modified versions of existing algorithms.[50] Virginia, for instance, developed its own tool, variations of which are now used in at least nine counties across 18 other states.[51] In 2019, in response to the federal First Step Act, the Department of Justice developed and released its Prisoner Assessment Tool Targeting Estimated Risk and Needs (PATTERN), which it used to decide who would be released under the Act and later as part of COVID-19 response efforts.[52]

▪ BIOMETRIC DATABASES

The top players in the biometric data market are a combination of large technology conglomerates and smaller correctional vendors, and their products vary widely.[53] Some focus on a few biometrics with a variety of applications while others cover a variety of biometrics but focus narrowly on law enforcement applications. For instance, Google, Gemalto, Academia, Meta, Microsoft, and Amazon lead the charge on facial recognition across markets[54] while DataWorks Plus provides everything from fingerprint identification to facial recognition just to law enforcement and corrections agencies—over 1,000 agencies across the country.[55] Idemia is a major player that covers a wide array of both biometrics and markets, specifically helping law enforcement use facial recognition in investigations.[56] Finally, some players spill over from other prison industry sectors like correctional telecom giant Aventiv, which dominates the nascent voice printing market, recording and tracking people across more than 240 corrections agencies.[57]

PRISON AND JAIL MANAGEMENT SYSTEMS

Prison and jail management systems are massive repositories of personal information used to track people as they move through the criminal legal system. In the correctional setting, this information includes a person's

security level, perceived gang affiliations, programming progress, administrative sanctions, medical records, cell assignments, property inventory,
and more.[58]

Although portrayed as seemingly innocuous information systems, prison
and jail management systems are yet another tool correctional administrators use to surveil, profile, target, and control incarcerated people. The
use of gang databases is just one example. Up to 67 percent of prisons and
jails use restrictive housing to target people labeled as gang members,[59]
meaning that a gang designation often further restricts a person's already
limited movement while incarcerated.

And gang affiliations are not tracked just in prisons and jails; law enforcement in the criminal and immigration context use these opaque databases
to target Black, brown, and Indigenous communities. The criteria for inclu-
sion can be simply wearing a certain color or congregating in a particular
neighborhood. Children as young as six years old have been added to gang
databases.[60] In one 2019 case, law enforcement jailed an El Salvadoran man
seeking asylum for six months, took away his children, and delayed his asylum after he was erroneously put in a gang database.[61]

In recent years, technology has
expanded the capabilities of traditional prison and jail management systems. Corporations have developed
coded identification cards and wristbands that allow correctional administrators to track every move made by

> GUARDIAN RFID helps
> corrections soldiers com-
> mand, control, and gain
> operational dominance
> without compromise.
>
> — Guardian RFID[62]

a person in their custody. Scanners placed around facilities log each time
someone passes a checkpoint and interface with prison and jail management systems to create a real-time record of movement.[63] The result is a
surveillance panopticon whereby all movement is tracked and frequently
penalized. And the cost of this monitoring is often passed on to incarcerated people, who are charged as much as $25 to replace identification cards
and bands.[64]

Cloud technology is further changing the landscape. As corrections facilities increasingly depend on networked devices, security and technology corporations have developed products to store and protect data online.[65] These tools give officers ready access to personal information and records using smartphones or tablets.[66] In the immigration system, ICE spent nearly $600 million to build new information infrastructures in 2019.[67] Partnering with Amazon and Palantir, ICE collects, stores, and analyzes vast amounts of personal information that agents use to profile and surveil immigrants as well as their friends and family. Although information about the system is largely hidden from public view, it is suspected to have enabled ICE agents to track and detain people in their homes, courthouses, and even hospitals.[68]

VIDAL'S STORY

Vidal Guzman
New York

I came up in the streets, and I am still in the streets. I am one of the few activists who can organize among a unique diversity of people: the Bloods, Crips, and Latin Kings gangs. And that's because I once was a gang member.

As a young person, my gang protected me. But I didn't know that I was being tracked by the police as a gang member until the moment I was standing in a courtroom at just 16 years old.

While I was a gang member, that's not why I was put into a gang database. People are put in gang databases based on their neighborhood, friends, clothing, and tattoos. Children as young as 12 years old are put in gang databases for wearing certain colors in certain neighborhoods or just saying "hi" to particular people on the block.

Gang databases are Stop and Frisk 2.0, a secret weapon that gives law enforcement almost unregulated authority to stop and harass Black and brown youth without reason. People in gang databases, like me, are subject to constant surveillance and invasions of privacy: our movements are tracked, and our social media is watched. And gang databases follow you for life.

When I came home from prison, I had "gang" parole, which meant I wasn't eligible for early termination like others and that the consequences for any violation would be exponentially worse. After years of studying as an organizer, I have learned that gang databases aim to enforce social control and disrupt our ability to organize. I see them now for what they are: racist, coercive systems of surveillance.

Today, I help educate my people about gang databases and all forms of oppression as we work to create our own systems of justice. I know we will get free.

RISK AND NEEDS ASSESSMENT TOOLS

Risk and needs assessment tools use algorithms to determine whether a person should be detained pretrial, whether they qualify for diversion or reduced sentencing, which facility they should be assigned to, what their treatment needs are during incarceration, and whether they should be granted parole. While some jurisdictions have developed their own tools, many have turned to private corporations.[69]

In the pretrial context, risk assessment tools are purported to objectively measure risk of flight and risk of rearrest, which in turn determine whether someone charged with a crime should be released, granted bail, or detained pretrial. Proponents assert that risk assessment tools can reduce pretrial incarceration or racial disparities in pretrial outcomes, but there is little evidence they do either; there is even evidence to the contrary.[70] Their mere use seeks to justify pretrial detention and exaggerate the risk of flight.[71] Charitable bail funds have shown that with some basic help getting to court, even without a financial obligation to do so, people appear for their court dates 95 percent of the time.[72]

Risk assessment tools rely on bias factors that reflect the overpolicing of Black and brown neighborhoods and inequalities that undergird mass criminalization. And yet these tools are dangerously painted as objective. For example, risk assessment tools consider one's arrest history, often including uncharged arrests and dismissed cases, ignoring the disproportionate targeting of Black and brown communities by police. Most also rely on housing and employment status, which further reflect racial and economic biases.[73] And some even consider the ZIP code in which a person lives, the clearest proxy for race after decades of entrenched residential segregation.[74] In the end, risk assessment tools only further legitimize existing racial and structural disparities.

In sentencing and correctional contexts, risk and needs assessment tools are used to measure risk of violence and "criminogenic" needs. They rely on many of the same bias factors, and thus also produce biased outcomes. For sentencing, these assessments often determine eligibility for diversion, meaning they can be the difference between someone going home and someone going to prison. Once in prison, correctional administrators use assessment tools to determine a person's security classification, programming needs, and facility assignment,[76] factors that considerably affect a person's experience while incarcerated.

> I don't like the idea myself of COMPAS being the sole evidence that a decision would be based upon.
>
> — Tim Brennan, COMPAS developer[75]

Despite their dramatic impact, the corporations behind proprietary risk and needs assessment tools often refuse to turn over their algorithms, obscuring remarkably important information about how decisions are made. Corporations like Equivant are entrusted with critical decisions about whether to incarcerate or free people but claim their formulas are trade secrets and must be shielded to protect their competitive advantage.[77] This lack of public accountability has come at a deep cost. In 2016, a study showed that COMPAS scored Black people charged with crimes more punitively than similarly situated white people: Black people were twice as likely as white people to be labeled high risk but not reoffend.[78]

Nevertheless, government agencies and foundations continue to invest in risk and needs assessment tools. In 2019, the National Institute of Justice spent $2 million on research using electronic monitoring data to enhance risk assessment capabilities,[79] layering one problematic tool on top of another and multiplying the concerns they raise, all under the guise of evidence-based practices.

BIOMETRICS

Every year, law enforcement and corrections agencies increase their use of biometrics to expand their surveillance and enforcement operations. Corporations help agencies collect data; they also sell data to agencies that they collect from other clients or the public market.[80]

For example, correctional telecom corporations like Aventiv Technologies (formerly Securus Technologies) collect, analyze, and sell the voiceprints of incarcerated people and their loved ones. With the enforcement power of its correctional partners, Aven-

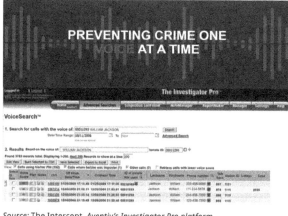

Source: The Intercept. *Aventiv's Investigator Pro platform.*

tiv requires incarcerated people to read preselected phrases and creates a voiceprint for each person. Those who refuse are barred from calling their loved ones.[81] The voices of their loved ones outside are separately printed through phone call recordings, and often flagged if recognized speaking to more than one person in the same system.[82] This raises privacy, censorship, and retaliation concerns for families with more than one incarcerated loved one and service providers, advocates, and media who are often in contact with many people in one system. The corporation then packages these voiceprints into databases, which it sells to federal, state, and local law enforcement agencies.[83] Consequently, a person's voiceprint lives long beyond incarceration.

Corporations claim that these tools are objective, but biometrics are disproportionately used to target Black, brown, and Indigenous people. Jurisdictions that use this technology rarely monitor its use or release information about its accuracy, so it is impossible to even know the true scope of this issue.[84]

> Unless Securus or the sheriff's office receives an expunction order, that information is still able to be resided in the system and utilized. Unless we get that [order], it doesn't get deleted.
>
> — Jail administrator in Fort Bend County, Texas[85]

Facial recognition, for example, has a significant risk of false identification, but specifically for people of color. In fact, the darker someone's skin, the more likely a system is to produce a false positive.[86] In one study, researchers found that facial recognition tools could identify a white man correctly 99 percent of the time compared to 65 percent for women with darker skin.[87] Despite this grave disparity, law enforcement agencies are increasingly connecting this technology to footage captured by police body cameras and other surveillance sources,[88] putting overpoliced Black, brown, and Indigenous communities at an even greater risk of harassment and violence. In a 2019 lawsuit, facial recognition technology used on store surveillance footage misidentified and erroneously linked a Black teenager to a string of thefts in Apple stores, leading to his wrongful arrest.[89]

Immigration agents have also started to use this technology around the country. In at least three states that allow undocumented people to get driver's licenses, agents have used facial recognition technology to analyze driver's license photos and identify immigrants suspected of being undocumented.[90] This technology enables racial profiling and forces undocumented immigrants to put themselves and their families at risk of arrest and deportation for a driver's license—often an employment necessity.

Technology corporations have provided the computer software needed to further weaponize biometrics. Launched in 2011, the federal Cloud First program pushed for increased partnership between governments and private developers of cloud technology.[91] The program allocated $20 billion for cloud computing solutions.[92] Today, the U.S. Department of Homeland Security stores the biometric data of over 290 million people.[93] Amazon Web Services provides the digital infrastructure needed to host such a massive data trove.[94]

Over the past few decades, corporations have moved the collection, storage, analysis, and sale of personal information from science fiction to daily reality. But while these data and information systems may seem innocuous enough in movies, these tools can mean the difference between life and death in the hands of law enforcement and corrections agencies.

For Black, brown, and Indigenous people, prison and jail management systems, risk and needs assessment tools, and biometrics make their personal information perpetually accessible to the law enforcement agencies that target them. The technology corporations that develop these systems and tools put Black, brown, and Indigenous people under a constant threat of false predictions and identification, setting the stage for a never-ending cycle of harassment and violence.

LEARN MORE

- *Police Surveillance and Facial Recognition: Why Data Privacy Is Imperative for Communities of Color*, Brookings (2022)

- *Mapping Pretrial Injustice: A Community-Driven Database*, Media Mobilizing Project and MediaJustice (2020)

- "The Secret History of Facial Recognition," *WIRED* (2020)

- *An Organizer's Guide to Confronting Pretrial Risk Assessment Tools in Decarceration Campaigns*, Community Justice Exchange (2019)

- "Risk Assessment: Explained," The Appeal (2019)

- *Fact Sheet: Electronic Monitoring Devices as Alternatives to Detention*, National Immigration Forum (2019)

- *Who's Behind ICE? The Tech and Data Companies Fueling Deportations*, National Immigration Project, Immigrant Defense Project, and Mijente (2018)

- "Recidivism Risk Assessments Won't Fix the Criminal Justice System," Electronic Frontier Foundation (2018)

- "NYPD Gang Database Can Turn Unsuspecting New Yorkers into Instant Felons," *The Intercept* (2018)

- "Making Sense of Pretrial Risk Assessments," National Association of Criminal Defense Lawyers (2018)

- "Machine Bias," ProPublica (2016)

- "The Perpetual Line-Up: Unregulated Police Face Recognition in America," Georgetown Law Center on Privacy & Technology (2016)

- "The New Science of Sentencing," The Marshall Project (2015)

TELECOM

The reason that we are in this mess right now, on my side, [is that] my industry has abused the public and I'm willing to admit that. We have abused the public.

— *Vincent Townsend, Chief Executive Officer of Pay-Tel Communications*[1]

The modern correctional telecom industry emerged in the 1970s just as legislators began passing dog whistle "tough-on-crime" laws that sent the prison population surging. Initially, AT&T controlled almost the entire correctional telecom market much like the broader telecom market. Though expensive, the costs of collect calls from prisons and jails at the time were comparable to the cost of collect calls outside. But, in 1984, when federal regulators broke up the AT&T monopoly, new providers like MCI and Sprint entered the correctional market, and other niche competitors that had previously marketed surveillance services quickly followed. The niche players would eventually corner the market by agreeing to shift the cost of their surveillance services to incarcerated people

Description: Correctional telecom corporations contract with corrections agencies to provide communications services, including phone calls, video calls, and electronic messaging, to incarcerated people and their support networks. Layered on these services are surveillance tools.

and their families while sharing revenue from the calls with prison and jail administrators. By the mid-1990s, 90 percent of corrections agencies nationwide had contracted with a for-profit provider.[5]

In the early 2000s, private equity firms began to buy in to the prison telecom market and drive consolidation. In 2004, H.I.G. Capital formed Securus Technologies—now one of

$1.5 billion
Correctional telecom market size[2]

$11.25
Example cost of a 15-minute jail phone call[3]

1 in 3
Families with an incarcerated loved one that go into debt trying to stay in touch[4]

the country's largest correctional telecom corporations—through The acquisition and merger of two smaller niche providers.[6] That same year, The Gores Group bought correctional telecom provider Global Tel*Link (GTL),[7] and two years later, in 2006, it acquired and merged with Verizon's correctional telecom division to create the country's largest correctional telecom business at the time.[8] Since then, the two corporations have traded hands among private equity investors several times. Today, GTL is owned by American Securities[10] and Securus is owned by Platinum Equity.[11] Notably, The Gores Group and Platinum Equity were founded and are run by brothers Alec and Tom Gores, respectively.[12] With their financial backing, GTL and Securus have acquired nearly every major competitor in the industry, creating a virtual duopoly.[9]

These correctional telecom corporations quickly became notorious for their high rates and exploitative practices. In response, families litigated and advocated for change.[13] Perhaps the most persistent was Martha Wright-Reed, a grandmother fed up with paying the high cost of calls with her incarcerated grandson whose 2001 lawsuit would eventually come before the Federal Communications Commission (FCC).[14] After more than a decade, the FCC started rulemaking in 2012 and instituted rate caps in 2015, but the industry challenged the agency's regulations in court.[15]

After the 2016 election, Ajit Pai, an attorney who formerly represented

Securus, was appointed chairman of the FCC and announced that the agency would no longer defend its rate caps in court.[16] The decision doomed the regulation, most notably its rate caps for in-state calls—those that originate and end within a state and make up 80 percent of all prison and jail calls.[17] They were struck down by a federal court in 2017, which concluded that in-state rates were a state matter and not for the FCC to regulate.[18]

In 2020 and 2022, Securus and GTL, respectively, restructured in efforts to create distance from the negative press associated with their brands and prepare for future financial challenges. Platinum Equity created Aventiv Technologies and separated out Securus and JPay, its new tablet business, as subsidiaries.[19] American Securities created ViaPath and similarly separated out GTL from recent acquisitions like Telmate.[20]

As the industry continued its corporate maneuvering, advocates persisted on their agenda. By 2023, advocates successfully passed legislation in Congress, named after Martha Wright-Reed, restoring the FCC's regulatory authority over in-state calls[21] and in five states making prison calls entirely free.[22] These wins have begun to revolutionize the correctional telecom space.

As their profit margins have been squeezed, correctional telecom providers have moved to diversify their businesses, introducing new communication products and services to the correctional landscape, such as video calling, electronic messaging, and tablets. They have also developed and embedded new surveillance technologies and services, such as voiceprinting and mail digitization, to entice correctional administrators. These burgeoning products and services raise new challenges that necessitate new advocacy efforts.

HOW MUCH MONEY IS AT STAKE?

Correctional telecom is quite a saturated and mature market. Nearly every single corrections agency in the country at the federal, state, and local levels contracts with a private telecom provider for communications services. They sign exclusive contracts granting providers monopoly control over communications services in their facilities. These contracts cover a suite of telecom and sometimes even other services. Altogether, correctional telecom rakes in $1.5 billion annually in just communications revenue, and three corporations control 86 percent of the market.[23]

These contracts also often include profit-sharing clauses that establish what portion of call revenue the corporation will pay to the contracting agency, often referred to as commissions. To further sweeten the pot, at times providers offer to prepay these commissions, make technology grants, and even pay signing bonuses. Corporations then charge incarcerated people and their loved ones egregious rates for their products and services to cover these government kickbacks, baking in their own profit margin.

Rates vary widely across the market based on federal, state, and local regulations, or lack thereof, and the negotiating intentions and aptitude of each contracting agency. While the FCC has capped the cost of interstate phone calls from both prisons and jails at $0.21 per minute for prepaid calls and $0.25 for collect calls, for the moment, in-state calls—which make up over 80 percent of all calls—remain unregulated at the federal level and inconsistently regulated at the state level.[24] As a result, in-state call rates can run as high as $0.75 a minute in some places.[25] The highest rates are most commonly charged in local jails, which are often more reliant on and interested in kickbacks and receive less scrutiny.[26]

However, thanks to decades of advocacy and recent wins, call rates are declining. In just the five years between 2018 and 2023, the weighted average cost of a 15-minute prison call dropped 51 percent from $1.83 to $0.89.[27] And these rates are expected to drop further when the FCC releases its new rate regulations in 2024 as required by the Martha Wright-Reed Just and Reasonable Communication Act, which established the FCC's regulatory authority over in-state calls among other things.

Moreover, several federal, state, and county systems are now taking on the cost of correctional communication services directly rather than passing it through to incarcerated people and their families.[28] One county, San Francisco, has even abandoned the industry's antiquated, but standard, per-minute pricing model, instead implementing a per-line pricing model that better aligns with the pricing structure of the broader telecom market in the free world.[29] The state of Connecticut went a different direction, implementing a per-person pricing model, similar to a subscription.[30] Reforms like these are drastically changing the sector and how it makes money.

With phone revenues on the decline, telecom corporations are introducing new products and services to diversify and grow their businesses, often bundling them into existing contracts to justify increased costs and avoid procurement.[31] It started with video calling, which first emerged in 1995 but did not reach critical mass until the 2010s.[32] As of 2016, over 600 facilities had introduced some form of video calling and,[33] as was often required contractually by the corporations, 74 percent of agencies scaled back or eliminated visits after implementation to drive up usage.[34] While corporations in the space have stopped contractually mandating that facilities eliminate visits, they continue to benefit from these prior practices since few facilities have reinstated visits. Still, video calling did not really pan out to be the new cash cow the sector had hoped, even after corporations made sizable infrastructure investments.

Since then, the sector has shifted its focus to tablets and all the communication and entertainment services that can be sold through them, from electronic messaging to movies and music. In many facilities, providers charge incarcerated people to purchase tablets. For instance, in Pennsylvania, ViaPath charges people $147 per tablet.[35] In other facilities, tablets are provided to incarcerated people for free, but they are then charged either a subscription to use it or fees for each product or service on it, or sometimes both.[36] In New York, for example, the state's five-year contract with JPay, which included free tablets, was expected to generate $8.8 million over the contract term.[37]

Among the most popular services on these tablets is electronic messaging. Often marketed as "email," electronic messaging is rapidly expanding in prisons and jails.[38] Corporations charge incarcerated people and their loved ones for "stamps" to exchange electronic messages, sometimes as much as real stamps.[39] Each stamp comes with a limited character count, and attachments like photos require additional stamps. While market data about electronic messaging services in the correctional landscape is not available, in 2014, early adopter JPay brought in $8.5 million on its electronic messaging product, a 77 percent increase over the year before.[40]

Importantly, the rollout of these new consumer-facing products and services has been accompanied by the rollout of new security and surveillance technologies and tools for correctional agencies, such as the biometric scanning of call recordings. These technologies and tools are used largely to justify the egregious costs of the consumer products and services as they are still rarely charged to the agencies directly, though the FCC is currently considering shifting that cost burden back.

WHAT CORPORATIONS ARE INVOLVED?

Correctional telecom is essentially a duopoly, with Aventiv and ViaPath controlling roughly 80 percent of the market.[41] In 2020, ViaPath was the largest prison telecom provider in the country, contracting with 479 counties and 23 prison systems that together held roughly 960,000 people, giving it control of 43 percent of the market by population served.[42] As of 2024, it maintained contracts with 23 prison systems, including the federal system, that alone hold over 620,000 incarcerated people.[43]

Founded in 1980, ViaPath, then GTL, was first acquired by conglomerate Schlumberger Technologies in 1993.[44] In 2004, The Gores Group acquired GTL for an undisclosed amount. The Gores Group then sold the corporation to Veritas Capital and Goldman Sachs in 2009 for $345 million.[45] Just two years later, the joint venture put the business back up for sale, hoping to collect $800 million for it.[46] The winning bid came in at $1 billion from American Securities, which continues to own the corporation after rebranding and restructuring it as ViaPath in 2022.[47] Today, ViaPath and all its subsidiaries generate $588 million in revenue from their broad suite of communications, and other services, down from $654 million in 2019.[48]

In 2020, Aventiv, the other major player in the market, contracted with 692 counties and 18 prison systems that together held about 860,000 people, or 39 percent of the market.[49] As of 2024, Aventiv had contracts with 20 prison systems that together hold 480,000 incarcerated people. However, due to the recent diversification of its products and services, Aventiv rakes in roughly $700 million annually.[50]

MARKET SHARE

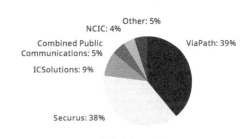

Other: 5%
NCIC: 4%
Combined Public Communications: 5%
ViaPath: 39%
ICSolutions: 9%
Securus: 38%

Source: Worth Rises unpublished data model

Aventiv, then Securus, was formed in 2004 from the acquisition and merger of two smaller correctional telecom corporations by H.I.G. Capital.[51] In 2011, Castle Harlan acquired Securus for $440 million.[52] Abry Partners joined Castle Harlan in 2013 when it acquired a 67 percent stake in the corporation at an estimated valuation of $700 million.[53] Within four years, the corporation more than doubled in value, selling for $1.6 billion in 2017 to Platinum Equity,[54] a firm founded by Tom Gores, the brother of Alec Gores, founder of The Gores Group.

However, in 2019, Securus' valuation dropped hundreds of millions of dollars as the leveraged loan debt propping up the corporation plummeted under activist pressure.[55] In response, Platinum Equity rebranded and restructured the corporation, separating all its business lines under a new holding company: Aventiv Technologies.[56] With the rebrand and restructuring, Platinum Equity tried to distance itself from Securus while investing in a public relations campaign to clean up the corporation's image.[57] So far, the efforts have proven largely unsuccessful. In 2023, Aventiv struggled to refinance almost $1.4 billion of debt maturing between August and November 2024, which compelled credit agencies to slash its credit rating to distressed levels.[58]

In recent years, ViaPath and Aventiv have bitterly competed for market dominance through corporate acquisitions fueled largely by their private equity backers and costly patent litigation.[59] Since 2012 alone, Aventiv has spent almost $600 million acquiring competitors and new business lines,[60] including its 2015 acquisition of JPay that helped it break into tablets and financial services.[61] ViaPath has also made sizable acquisitions, including its 2017 purchase of Telmate, the fifth-largest correctional telecom provider in the market at the time.[62] In 2019, their acquisition race came to a halt when advocates blocked Aventiv's attempt to acquire Inmate Calling Solutions (ICSolutions), the last independent player that could compete on a national scale. They argued that the deal created antitrust concerns and would lead to higher prices for incarcerated people and their families. The FCC agreed, rejecting the deal after determining that it was not "in the public interest."[63] Rather than appeal, Aventiv pulled the merger applications, and consolidation in the space has slowed since.

ViaPath and Aventiv have also pressured smaller competitors into signing licensing agreements that allow them to expand their reach without attracting the attention of regulators,[64] obscuring the true nature of the market landscape. Aventiv, for instance, used the threat of litigation to bully dozens of smaller competitors into signing patent licensing agreements to achieve what it called "patent peace."[65]

But the corporate melding does not end there. Historically, ViaPath and Aventiv have both served as the customer-facing partner for competitors providing only back-end telecom infrastructure, often major telecom corporations sensitive to public headlines. For instance, publicly traded CenturyLink stayed out of the limelight for years by providing only the back-end telecom infrastructure and partnering with Aventiv and ICSolutions for its customer-facing needs, namely payment collection.[66] In fact, up until 2020, when it sold most of its correctional telecom business to ICSolutions, CenturyLink held the third largest foothold in the market.[67] ViaPath has played a similar role for Unisys, a publicly traded global technology corporation.[68]

ICSolutions is the third largest correctional telecom provider, earning $137 million annually.[69] The corporation accounts for roughly 12 to 15 percent of TKC,[70] a prison services conglomerate owned by H.I.G. Capital that provides financial, com-

> People don't call home. . . . It's just too expensive. I feel like this is separating families.
>
> – Casey Cormani, incarcerated person in Millard County, Utah[71]

missary, food, laundry, and maintenance services across the correctional landscape.[72] After its sale to Securus failed, H.I.G. Capital made a desperate attempt to offload ICSolutions to management with a $280 million loan, $60 million of which was interest-free.[73] But with roughly half of its business wrapped up in a contract held by CenturyLink at the time, the deal could not secure additional financing. To create a viable standalone asset, H.I.G. Capital was forced instead to buy out CenturyLink's correctional telecom business—except its contract with the Texas prison system, one of the nation's largest, which it sold to its longstanding partner there, Securus.[74]

The rest of the market is split among smaller providers like Combined Public Communications, NCIC, and Paytel. These smaller players compete largely for jail contracts, which tend to have fewer requirements.[75]

TOP MARKET PLAYERS

	Aventiv[76]	ViaPath[77]	ICSolutions[78]
Annual Revenues	$700 Mn	$588 Mn	$147 Mn
State Prison Systems	20	22	8
Local Jail Systems	555	276	183
Max 15-Minute Call	$3.15	$9.95	$3.25

PHONE CALLS

Connecting with others, especially loved ones, is a core human need. For families with incarcerated loved ones, travel time and costs as well as arbitrary visit restrictions often impede their ability to connect in person. Consequently, in many cases, phone calls are the primary way that incarcerated people stay in regular contact with their support systems in the outside world.

Still, communication for incarcerated people is about more than simply maintaining interpersonal relationships. Regular communication between incarcerated people and their loved ones is the easiest, cheapest, and most effective way to reduce hopelessness and promote positive behavior during incarceration and improve reentry success upon release.[79] It is also critical to mitigating the trauma that children with incarcerated parents face.[80]

Despite the undeniable personal, familial, and public benefits of providing incarcerated people with regular access to communication with their support systems, correctional administrators and their corporate vendors have spent decades conspiring to exploit this most basic need by charging exorbitant rates for simple communication services like phone calls. Correctional administrators often negotiate against the interests of those in their custody, and the public, to collect hefty kickbacks on calls. An estimated 85 percent of state correctional systems collect kickbacks on prison phone calls,[81] with some kickback commitments topping 90 percent of call rates.[82] In exchange for these kickbacks, administrators sign exclusive contracts with providers,[83] which then build in their own generous profit margins. Incarcerated people and their families are left with no alternative to their costly calls.

While interstate calls, also known as long-distance calls, have been regulated federally, in-state, or local, calls—which make up 80 percent of prison and jail calls—were deemed a state matter by courts until the passage of the Martha Wright-Reed Act.[84] Unfortunately, not all states have a government agency with the authority to regulate prison and jail calls, especially as providers begin using cheaper but often unregulated internet protocols,[85] and of those with the proper regulatory authority, few use it, allowing providers to charge what they wished in most jurisdictions. And they do. New regulations expected in 2024 will soon change that.

Today, call rates range from $0.009 per minute to $0.75 per minute across all providers.[86] While rates have come down meaningfully over the last decade, the relief has not been felt equally across the country. The highest rates continue to be charged in jails, where regulation and advocacy is limited. As recently as 2020, Aventiv was still charging nearly $25 for a 15-minute call in some jails. Later that year, under pressure from advocates, the corporation reduced rates in what it called its "outlier" facilities, or those where a 15-minute call ran over $15, reducing 44 out of 53 of these to a cost between $10 and $15 for the same call—hardly a cause for celebration.[87] However, continued advocacy and public pressure has forced the corporation to further lower rates. Today, its maximum rate is $3.15 for a 15-minute call, 87 percent lower than its peak rates.[88]

However, these rate reductions have not been easy to come by. When challenged on their egregious rates, telecom providers use kickbacks as a political tool. They build the dependency of corrections agencies on kickbacks in part to incentivize them to help fight advocacy efforts to lower rates, and when that does not work, they just blame the corrections agencies and the contractual requirements for kickbacks for their inability to lower rates.[90] While kickbacks do dramatically increase the cost of calls, these corporations rely on them to win contracts and hide their own culpability. For instance, until 2021, when Connecticut became the first state to make all phone calls from

> We deliver on our promise to increase your revenue.
>
> – ICSolutions pitch to facilities administrators[81]

prison free, incarcerated people and their loved ones in the state were being charged as much as $0.325 per minute for a call from state prison.[91] The state collected a 68 percent commission,[92] leaving the state's prison telecom provider, Aventiv, with $0.104 per minute. The same year, in Illinois, where the state took no commission, Aventiv charged incarcerated people and their loved ones $0.009 per minute.[93] In other words, Aventiv made over ten times more in Connecticut than it did in Illinois per call minute even after kickbacks were removed from the calculus.

Still, the exploitation does not end there. Correctional telecom providers also charge a myriad of fees in addition to their per-minute call rates. For instance, for families to receive calls from their incarcerated loved ones, they are coerced to deposit funds into a prepaid account—they are threatened with additional fees and higher rates if they do not. But these deposits come at a steep cost of $3 per transaction in most jurisdictions. To further maximize their profit, the corporations often cap deposits at $50 to force more transactions and collect more fees. These fees can increase the cost of staying in touch with incarcerated loved ones by 40 percent.[94] And to top things off, the corporations often unlawfully take unused funds on accounts that have been inactive for a certain period, sometimes as little as 90 days. In 2022, ViaPath settled a lawsuit for $67 million for illegally confiscated funds from what they deemed were inactive accounts.[95]

These costs add up with detrimental consequences for incarcerated people and their loved ones. One in three families with an incarcerated loved one goes into debt trying to pay for calls and visits alone.[97] These costs are over-

> A dollar a minute strikes me as a fair price. I guess it depends what viewpoint you're coming from. The way I look at it, we've got a captive audience. If they don't like [the rates], I guess they should not have got in trouble to begin with.
>
> — Tom Maziarz, purchasing manager for St. Clair County, Illinois[96]

whelmingly borne by women, and as a result of the racist policing and the disproportionate criminalization and incarceration of Black, brown, and Indigenous communities, they are largely women of color.[98] Sadly, many families lose contact over lengthy sentences because the financial burden is untenable. Others are left struggling with the financial burden for years after their loved one's release.[99] Some have even pled guilty while awaiting trial in jail because they could not afford calls with their attorneys.[100] Still others risk new charges and long sentences to use contraband cellphones to stay in touch with loved ones and connected to a world they hope will not forget them.[101]

Diane's Story

My son was incarcerated for almost 15 years before I even realized the burden that call fees were placing on my family and me. I just hadn't thought about it. But my Securus bill was the first one I paid every month, and it often meant that I couldn't afford our gas or light bills. Yet, I knew the cost of not keeping in touch with my son would have been even higher.

Diane Lewis, Connecticut

I saw the difference between my son, who had a lot of support, and others in prison who couldn't make phone calls or never had family visits. There's a big difference, and it's why they struggle while inside and often go back after. It's the anger and depression that comes with doing time by yourself, and the lack of practical support needed when you get out.

I was constantly forced to make sacrifices to pay Securus' high prices, and those sacrifices had consequences for my family. The week my sister fell ill and ultimately passed away, I spoke to my son on the phone every day, four or five times, just to keep him posted on what was happening, so that he could still feel like he was with us. My sister was his favorite aunt; I had to help him mourn. I encouraged him to place as many calls as he wanted and had to shoulder the added financial burden alongside the emotional burden of my own grief.

Across the country, the absurd call rates and rushed nature of 15-minute conversations are a result of political decisions and corporate business practices that ignore our humanity. And it pains me when the media reinforces them. People think that just because my son committed a crime, he doesn't deserve to know his family or feel love. It burns me not just for him, but because it ignores me too. A mother is a mother regardless of where her child is or what they've done. My love shouldn't be exploited.

VIDEO CALLS

Introduced in the mid-1990s, video calling has only recently taken hold in the correctional landscape. It was marketed as a technology service that would augment family bonds by allowing for connections that are more accessible than visits and more intimate than phone calls. Instead, video calling has further separated families with incarcerated loved ones in many cases by replacing, rather than supplementing, visits at costs that top the high cost of phone calls—an intentional ploy by correctional telecom providers.

While video calling was originally introduced by two small players, VuGate and Renovo, it was not until the nation's largest correctional telecom providers, Aventiv and ViaPath, began selling video calls around the 2010s that the product really gained meaningful traction. Since few prison and jail systems were procuring video calling services, they started by tacking the new product on to existing telecom contracts and enticing correctional administrators with promises of more kickbacks.[102] In fact, 84 percent of video calling services are contractually bundled with phone, electronic messaging, or commissary services.[103]

These larger corporations also had the capital to front the cost of installing video kiosks, recouping their expenses and far more over the course of lengthy contracts. In the early years of the product rollout, they went as far as to contractually require correctional administrators to eliminate or limit visits to force the use of their costly systems. They named the new product line "video visitation" to grossly suggest that video calls were comparable to visits. Their plan worked and the term stuck. By 2016, more than 600 facilities in 46 states were using some form of video calling services.[104] Jails, which hold largely local people, were the early adopters[105] and 74 percent of them ended or significantly reduced visits after implementing the technology.[106] It is devastating to families, especially children, who can no longer look into their loved one's eyes or give them a hug during a visit. It is even worse for those who do not have access to a phone or computer and now have no way to communicate at all.[107] The corporations retired the contractual prohibitions on visits after widespread outrage,[108] but continue to benefit as few facilities have reinstated visits since.

Unlike free video calling services in the outside world like FaceTime, Zoom, or Google Hangouts, video calls in prisons and jails are quite costly. More expensive than phone calls on average, video calls run as high as a dollar per minute.[109] However, video calls are often prepaid for a set length of time—often 10, 20, or 30-minute intervals—and refunds are rarely issued when a call is interrupted or prematurely terminated, which are common occurrences. Some jails offer free on-site video conferencing, which requires families travel to the jail to use a kiosk to have a video call with their incarcerated loved one who is likely in the same building or on the same premises. In many cases, these video calling centers physically replaced visit rooms.

In addition to threatening visits and imposing high costs on families, video calls are often poor in quality. Grainy or blank video, distant or static audio, and live monitoring further frustrate efforts to connect using video conferencing.[111] Surveillance on video calls can even threaten family members in

> The majority of the company's profit comes from the inmates and their family.
>
> – Craig Diamond, director of marketing for Telmate[110]

their own homes. For example, people have been arrested after drugs were spotted in the background of a jail video call.[112]

In the end, while video calling can be a powerful supplementary tool for incarcerated people to connect with their loved ones, especially when held in distant facilities, correctional telecom providers deploy it in the most exploitative and inhumane way, significantly undermining its beneficial value. Thankfully, some relief came in 2024 when the FCC released its new rules as the Martha Wright-Reed Act mandated the regulation of video calls for the first time.

ELECTRONIC MESSAGING

Electronic messaging has been in the correctional landscape for roughly a decade. However, like many other technology products and services, it has picked up steam in recent years. For many with access to technology, electronic messaging offers an easy and effective, though costly, substitute to postal mail. But electronic messaging in prisons and jails is not all that comparable to email, though correctional telecom providers attempt to suggest it is.

In prisons and jails, these corporations require incarcerated people and their families to buy "stamps" that range from $0.05 to $1.25 and are sold both individually and in bundles to send electronic messages.[113] Each stamp is good for one message with a character or page limit—typically one page typed or 5,000 characters. An additional stamp must be added for longer messages and for each attachment. Videos require several stamps. For inexplicable reasons, outbound stamps can cost more than inbound stamps.[114]

The cost of stamps can also fluctuate, often around holidays.[115] And like other prepaid telecom services, there are also often fees for purchasing stamps that add to the overall cost of electronic messaging. When added together, these costs can quickly surpass the cost one would bear to send the same content through postal mail, let alone email, which is generally free in the outside world.

	Cost of a Typed, Two-Page Letter with Two Attached Photos
Real-World Email	$0.00
U.S. Postal Mail	$0.73
Electronic Message to New York Prison	$1.20

Again, unlike email, electronic messages are not delivered instantaneously. They are surveilled and reviewed much like postal mail in prisons and jails before they are delivered and can take days to reach the intended recipient. And it is also not always easy for incarcerated people to access their emails. While some facilities have individual tablets that incarcerated people can use to access their emails—generally at an additional one-time, subscription, or session cost—in many facilities, incarcerated people must access their emails on communal kiosks, which are often busy and have limited privacy.

TABLETS

Perhaps the fastest growing technology in prisons and jails today is the tablet, in part because it's not yet regulated. In an increasing number of systems across the country, incarcerated people are being given or allowed to purchase tablets. These devices resemble small, knockoff iPads with basic software that cannot access the internet and are used to purchase communication, education, and entertainment products and services.[116] Despite their poor quality, these tablets can cost north of $140, an enormous amount of money for incarcerated people earning pennies per hour.[117]

Telecom providers claim that tablets offer ready communication access, educational opportunities, and solutions to idleness, bringing incarcerated people closer to their families and making institutions safer.[118] However, while modern technology is welcome in prisons and jails that are generally devoid of it, these claims ignore the unprecedented exploitation that these devices facilitate.

The cost of correctional tablet products and services defies comprehension, and as is commonplace in correctional telecom, correctional administrators often get kickbacks from tablet purchases.[119] A single song on a JPay tablet can cost up to $2.50 and an album as much as $46.[120] Compare that to the price of a monthly family Apple Music subscription, which costs $17 and allows up to six users to stream over 100 million songs.[121] And incarcerated people routinely lose their purchases when correctional administrators switch providers. In Florida, for example, incarcerated users lost $11 million in music purchases after administrators switched contractors in 2018.[122]

To push back on complaints of exploitation, correctional telecom providers now offer free tablets in many jurisdictions. But this is not just an empty gesture; it is actually a doubly exploitive ploy. In negotiating free tablet contracts, providers are often successful in convincing correctional administrators that to recoup the cost of the tablets, the products and services sold on them—calls, electronic messages, music, movies, and books—must be priced higher. In other words, these contracts trade a one-time fixed cost for higher rates into perpetuity, which cost incarcerated people and their loved ones much more in the long run. Since 2016, tablet providers have executed free tablet contracts in several states, including Connecticut, Indiana, Missouri, and New York, with these types of parameters.[123]

Still, perhaps the most egregious tablet scam was exposed in 2019 when ViaPath was found charging incarcerated people to read books available for free online.[124] Worse yet, it was charging readers by the minute.[125] The $0.03 per minute rate would make reading too expensive for the average person, not to mention people who typically earn little more than pennies for a full hour's work and who are statistically more likely to have literacy limitations or learning disorders.[126]

SURVEILLANCE

Correctional communication was not always universally monitored in the way that it is today. In fact, in the 1990s, when the jail population was at its peak in New York City, phone calls were not monitored and they were free. But correctional telecom corporations now lean heavily on new surveillance technology to advertise their products and justify their high rates, raising critical concerns for not just incarcerated people, but also the loved ones they are in communication with.

Correctional telecom providers record and store every conversation completed through their systems, and even listen in live at times. They willingly share these recordings with law enforcement and prosecutors. And while privileged communication with attorneys is supposed to be excluded, they have illegally recorded and shared these calls too. In fact, Aventiv settled a lawsuit in 2016 for recording 57,000 privileged calls between incarcerated people and their attorneys,[127] and has faced several similar lawsuits since.[128]

The corporations are now layering new surveillance technologies onto their communications services. For instance, Aventiv has introduced voiceprint analysis tools—which were originally developed for the U.S. Department of Defense to identify terroristic threats—to identify and track the voices of not just incarcerated people, but also those they call on the outside.[129] As of 2018, the corporation had already captured more than 200,000 incarcerated people's voiceprints, which it would keep forever.[130] While the providers claim voice printing is designed to improve facility security, patents reveal their intention to create a market for and sell voiceprint databases to law enforcement.[131] Unsurprisingly, in some systems, incarcerated people are denied phone access if they refuse to give a voiceprint.

Aventiv, ViaPath, and others in the market also use proprietary programs, often powered by problematic artificial intelligence, to monitor recorded calls and recognize specific trigger words.[133] They boast about the ability to decipher various accents or dialects.[134] Some even claim they have trained their systems to "speak inmate,"[135] presenting serious concerns about the biases of those training the machines.

> We've taught the system how to speak inmate.
>
> – James Sexton, executive at LEO Technologies[121]

To make matters worse, these corporations, entrusted with the security of prisons and jails, have had several major data breaches that leaked recorded calls and other private information to the public.[136] In 2015, hackers concerned about the constitutional rights of incarcerated people leaked 70 million calls from Aventiv's servers, revealing 14,000 recorded privileged attorney calls.[137] A lawsuit was brought, and the corporation quietly settled in 2020,[138] never revealing how many cases were negatively impacted by the recording of those calls. In 2023, the Federal Trade Commission took an enforcement action against ViaPath after it failed to notify 650,000 customers about a data breach that leaked their sensitive personal information, including social security numbers.[139] Correctional telecom providers exploit the fundamental need for human connection.

They force families to make impossible choices, such as paying for rent or paying for a child to speak to an incarcerated parent. The situation was made materially worse by the pandemic and ensuing economic crisis that barred families from visiting incarcerated loved ones at a time when connection was more necessary and resources lower than ever.

New communication services, like video calling and electronic monitoring, have the potential to connect incarcerated people and their loved ones, but, in the hands of correctional telecom corporations, have been transformed into additional extractive tools. Behind this exploitation are some of the nation's most prominent private equity firms, passively building wealth off of overpoliced communities.

However, the tide is turning against this predatory industry. After years of advocacy, cities and states across the country are looking for change and are increasingly beginning to consider legislation to make prison and jail communication free and curb invasive surveillance technology. The FCC is also taking decisive action to increase the regulation of correctional telecom, which will create relief for incarcerated people and their families. These efforts have pushed this exploitation out into the public's view and dragged down the value of the entire sector. Although the movement is still in its early days, a growing group of prison phone justice advocates are in a promising fight to connect families and bury this predatory sector for good.

LEARN MORE

- ConnectFamiliesNow.com, Worth Rises,
- "Is This the End of Prison Phone Fees?" *Mother Jones* (2023)
- "Prisoners Are Going Viral on TikTok," Vice News (2020)
- *State of Phone Justice: Local Jails, State Prisons and Private Phone Providers,* Prison Policy Initiative (2019)
- "Tech Company Gave Two New Orleans-Area Sheriff's Offices Access to Track Cell Phones Without Warrants," The Appeal (2019)
- "How Private Equity Is Turning Public Prisons into Big Profits," *The Nation* (2019)
- "Can Screen Time Replace the Warmth of a Hug? Prisons Make a Big Push on Devices," *Fast Company* (2018)
- " 'Free' Tablets Are Costing Prison Inmates a Fortune," *Mother Jones* (2018)
- "Captive Audience: How Companies Make Millions Charging Prisoners to Send an Email," *WIRED* (2018)
- "When Prisoners Are a 'Revenue Opportunity,'" *The Atlantic* (2017)
- "The End of American Prison Visits: Jails End Face-to-Face Contact—And Families Suffer," *The Guardian* (2017)

- "'Video Visitation' Is Ending In-Person Prison Visits—and Prisons Are Going to Make a Ton of Money," *Business Insider* (2016)
- "You've Got Mail: The Promise of Cyber Communication in Prisons and the Need for Regulation," Prison Policy Initiative (2016)
- "The High Cost of Calling the Imprisoned," *New York Times* (2015)
- "Criminal Charges," *The Verge* (2015)
- "Screening Out Family Time: The For-Profit Video Visitation Industry in Prisons and Jails," Prison Policy Initiative (2015)

FINANCIAL SERVICES

> Numi's model is based on "turnover." We market to the 3,300 jails in the country. When you go to the state or federal prisons, you're in there for a while. They don't do us any good.
>
> — Richard E. Deloney Jr., Vice President of Business Development at Numi Financial[1]

People in prison and jail are not allowed to hold money. The federal prison system was the first to establish trust accounts for incarcerated people in 1930. Upon doing so, administrators banned families from bringing food and essential products into facilities, forcing them to send money to support their loved ones behind bars instead.[2] The change allowed correctional administrators to charge abusive fines and fees and easily garnish accounts. This soon became common practice across the country.

Description: Corrections agencies contract with financial services corporations to provide money transfer services and debit release cards to incarcerated people. Probation and parole agencies also contract with these corporations to process supervision and other court-imposed fees.

Historically, money transfers to incarcerated people were processed in person, often during visits, or by mail, using cash, checks, or money orders.

In some facilities, money transfers are still processed in this way. However, the invention and expansion of the internet in the 1990s revolutionized electronic payments, which date back to the 1870s, by enabling online payment processing.[3] But, as with all technology, it would be at least another decade before such modern payment processing services became available in the correctional market.[4] And when they did, they would carry steep price tags.

The federal prison system was again the first to adopt these new financial innovations. In 1998, the federal prison system contracted with JPMorgan Chase for the issuance of debit release cards—used to disburse trust account balances to people upon release. A few years later, in 2000, it contracted with Bank of America for the management of trust accounts for incarcerated people during their incarceration, which, in turn, subcontracted money transfer services largely to Western Union and MoneyGram. Both exclusive, no-bid contracts were awarded by the U.S. Treasury under the National Bank Act of 1864, which was passed to create the national banking system that helped fund the Civil War when state banks were funding the Confederate army.[5] Today, the act is used to dole out lucrative government contracts to preferred banks without competitive bidding.[6]

In 2002, tech entrepreneurs created JPay and introduced electronic money transfers to the broader correctional landscape. But adoption was slow until corporate executives offered to pay correctional administrators commissions on the fees they charged,[7] which further drove up the cost of the new online service. Soon, many facilities raced to replace free money transfer options with this costly service. By 2014, 400,000 incarcerated people were in facilities that no longer had a free money transfer option.[8]

Throughout the 2000s, competitors emerged with their own money transfer services. And over the years, JPay and these new players grew their financial services by introducing their own debit release cards and expanding into the probation and parole space, where they manage the electronic payment of community supervision and other court-imposed fees.

HOW MUCH MONEY IS AT STAKE?

▪ MONEY TRANSFERS

The families and support networks of incarcerated people transfer an estimated $1.8 billion into prisons and jails to support their loved ones every year.[9] In 2015, the correctional money transfer market was estimated to be worth $172 million—with the federal prison system contract worth $15 million, state prison contracts worth $99 million, and county jail contracts worth $58 million.[10] And while reductions in the prison population in recent years suggest that by 2018 the market opportunity had contracted by 11 percent to $153 million,[11] there is still significant growth expected for the sector, particularly at the county level. In 2015, JPay, the largest player in the field, had 71 percent of the state prison market but less than 15 percent of the county jail market,[12] an area of focus for the market's leading player.

▪ DEBIT RELEASE CARDS

Unfortunately, little is known about the size of the debit release card market. However, with about 610,000 people released from federal and state prisons and roughly 10.7 million people churned through county jails each year, the market opportunity for debit release cards appears even larger than it is for money transfers.[13] In 2014, a survey revealed that at least 14 out of 33 states had implemented debit release cards and 9 of those had adopted the new financial product between 2011 and 2014, suggesting that uptake is rapidly increasing.[14]

▪ PROBATION AND PAROLE PAYMENTS

The payment processing market for probation and parole supervision and other fees was estimated to be worth $298 million in 2015.[15] Declines in the number of people on probation and parole suggest that the market opportunity is closer to $264 million today.[16] Nevertheless, the sheer volume of people subjected to probation and parole supervision—3.7 million as of

2021—makes the probation and parole payment market not just newer but also larger than that of money transfers.[17] And the market may expand as some reformers argue for probation and parole as an "alternative to incarceration"—an argument now used by corporations in the space.

WHAT CORPORATIONS ARE INVOLVED?

The financial services sector was dominated by major banks like JPMorgan Chase and Bank of America at its inception, but by the 2000s, it was overtaken by more targeted niche players. Of the biggest players today, JPay entered in 2002, TouchPay in 2003, Numi Financial and Rapid Financial Solutions in 2005, and Access Corrections in 2007.[18]

Notably, the financial services sector has been merging with the correctional telecom and commissary sectors over recent years. In 2015, two of the largest correctional financial services corporations were acquired by the two largest correctional telecom corporations: Aventiv (then Securus) acquired JPay, and ViaPath (then Global Tel*Link or GTL) acquired TouchPay. And Access Corrections is merely a product brand of the Keefe Group, the largest correctional commissary corporation and parent company of the third largest prison telecom corporation, ICSolutions.[19]

▪ MONEY TRANSFERS

JPay is undoubtedly the largest player in the correctional money transfer space, with a virtual monopoly over the market.[20] In 2014, JPay had 71 percent of the money transfer market share across state prison systems and 46 percent across all federal, state, and county corrections agencies,[21] serving more than 1.7 million incarcerated people in 32 states, 40 percent of which had no alternative option.[22] That year, JPay transferred more than $525 million in 7.5 million transactions, generating $53.9 million in revenues for its financial services business segment.[23] By 2018, JPay's financial services business was generating $143.7 million annually—up 166 percent in just four years—with contracts in 35 states.[24]

JPay recently began serving the federal prison system, a relationship it sought for years and is dependent on a subcontract with Bank of America, which held the federal contract since 2000. For years, Bank of America limited money transfers to Western Union. But as its contract grew in scope over two decades, it has increasingly subcontracted with new vendors, many of which would not otherwise qualify for federal contracts with the U.S. Treasury. Because it is these subcontractors that typically interface with consumers, Bank of America's role in the prison industry is often hidden from public view, though this contracting structure exacerbates profiteering.[25]

▪ DEBIT RELEASE CARDS

JPay, Numi Financial, and Rapid Financial Systems are the most common debit release card vendors across the country.[26] ViaPath also now has a debit release card product.

▪ PROBATION AND PAROLE PAYMENTS

JPay and its sister corporation AllPaid (formerly GovPay), another subsidiary of Aventiv, are leaders in the probation and parole payment space.

MONEY TRANSFERS

Given the limited earning opportunities offered by prisons and jails, incarcerated people often depend on money sent to them by loved ones on the outside to pay for food, hygiene products, medical copays, phone calls, and other necessities not provided by

$1.8 billion
Money transferred to incarcerated people annually[27]

$6.95
Max money transfer fee for a $20 deposit in prison[28]

corrections facilities. Paying for these basic needs places a strain on both incarcerated people and their loved ones, and often their relationships, which is only further exacerbated by the additional fees charged by financial services corporations to merely transfer funds.

As with other service contracts in telecom or commissary, although incarcerated people and their families pay these fees, correctional administrators are generally responsible for the contracts that set them. And with just a few corporations holding the lion's share of the market, bidding for these correctional contracts is rarely competitive. Market players set predatory rates in the resulting monopolistic environment and rake in millions preying on families.[29]

Similar again to telecom and commissary, procurement in this market is often centered around generating revenue for government agencies. The industry was built on a profit-sharing model between financial services corporations and corrections agencies—the cost of which compounds money transfer fees billed to families.[30] After years of corporate grooming, some agencies now explicitly award contracts to the bidder offering the highest commission.[31] As a result, not only are contracts often awarded to the most expensive service provider, but correctional administrators are also incentivized to limit cheaper or free alternatives from which they do not profit.

Even in jurisdictions where there are still free options, these corporations use deceitful tactics to get people to use their costly services instead. For example, some states that contract with JPay require that people still be permitted to mail in a check or money order at no cost. But to make things difficult, JPay mandates that a money deposit slip accompany every deposit. The corporation then makes the slip impossible to find, and when asked, it mails the slip out to consumers to delay the deposit and push people to use their costly electronic service.

Moreover, the money deposit slip itself is laden with shameless plugs for JPay's online system: "Did you know money orders/checks can take days to mail and process? There's a more convenient way."[32] These calls are paired with misleading statements that read "Sign up for free," when, in fact, after creating an account, their electronic services are anything but free.[33] The corporation also routinely rejects slips that it claims are completed incorrectly, only to process them without incident upon receiving the same slip, unaltered, a second time. In the most egregious cases, JPay has outright lied to consumers about not being able to accept checks or money orders in states that require they do.[34]

But even if everything goes right, JPay has a policy of holding checks for ten days before depositing them.[35] All told, incarcerated people dependent on JPay can now wait as long as a month for funds deposited by free options that previously took just a few days, and all this maneuvering helps JPay force more consumers onto their expensive online platform.[36] In fact, a former marketing director for JPay bragged that he shifted 78 percent of

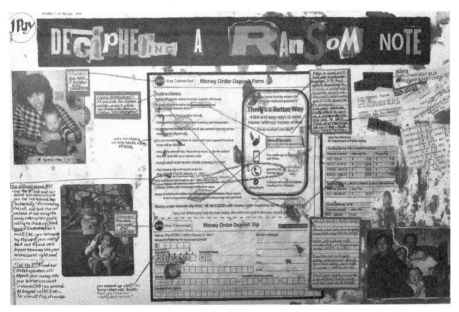

George T. Wilkerson (b. 1981), Central Prison, NC. "There's a better way! Go online or call, use the credit/debit option, and it'll be deposited in moments! Can your loved one really afford to wait on a money order? He only has 7 cents left! Think of all the things he can't buy... Think how hungry he'll be."

consumers using free money orders to online deposits, increasing annual revenue by $985,000.[37]

In the absence of regulation around money transfer fees, some have tried to advocate systems to renegotiate rates. Advocates in New York pushed the state's corrections agency to renegotiate money transfer rates with JPay, resulting in a drop of as much as 41 percent.[38] Unfortunately, these wins are limited. More must be done to systemically cure or prevent the harm caused by these predatory financial services corporations.

DEBIT RELEASE CARDS

When a person is released from prison or jail, the predation of the financial services sector does not stop. Prior to the privatization of financial services, incarcerated people who still had money in their trust accounts at the time of their release would receive it in full, at no cost, by cash or check. This might be money they came in with, they earned through work, or that was deposited by loved ones while they were incarcerated.

However, today many prisons and jails entrust financial services corporations with distributing these funds, more commonly referred to as "gate money,"[42] using debit cards that are issued upon release. Not only do these corporations ignore the challenges of being restricted to a debit card for money in the moments after release, such as paying for a taxi or bus in communities where cashless systems may not be prevalent, but they also rarely disclose the countless fees associated with the use, and mere possession, of the card.

These corporations charge exorbi-

$3.50
Example of weekly debit release card maintenance fee[39]

$30
Example of account closing fee for a debit release card[40]

17
States issuing debit release cards[41]

tant fees to access one's own money. For example, people forced to use debit release cards issued by Numi Financial, a leading player in county jails, may be charged a $2.95 fee per purchase, a $0.95 fee for declined transactions, and a weekly service fee of $2.50.[43] Across various vendors, balance inquiry fees can range from $0.50 at an ATM to $3.95 by phone.[44] Even closing an account comes at a cost: Access Corrections charges $30 to cash out and close an account.[45]

This is one of the few business models in the prison industry that distinctly profits off of the act of releasing a person from prison or jail. These corporations are dependent on the churn of people through prisons and jails, and thus they are interested in high arrest and admission rates, shorter stays, and clear pathways back into the system. Consequently, their business model profits most off low-level repeat offenses like drug possession.

The high fees charged for debit release cards have been the subject of lawsuits and consumer complaints for years.[46] The vast majority of these cases are brought under state consumer protection laws. Many of these are forced into arbitration, and only a small number have been successful. In one case, people formerly incarcerated in the federal prison system brought a class-action lawsuit against JPMorgan Chase regarding fees on its debit release cards, which settled for more than $400,000 in damages.[47]

Advocates have also called for the Consumer Financial Protection Bureau (CFPB) and state consumer protection agencies to step in and meaningfully regulate financial services, particularly debit release cards.[48] And while the CFPB has investigated some corporate practices in the space,[49] the lack of regulation has empowered corporations to brazenly charge high fees that bear little relation to the actual costs of the services provided.[50] However, in 2021, the CFPB was successful in fining JPay for its exorbitant debit release card fees: $4 million back to consumers and $2 million as a civil penalty.[51] Unfortunately, this is a drop in the bucket for a corporation bringing in hundreds of millions of dollars annually using these predatory practices.

JESSE'S STORY

I spent six years in federal prison, earning $0.40 an hour as an art instructor. For an artist, it was the best job I could have, but I didn't make enough to cover my basic needs in prison. I was fortunate to have friends and family who put money in my commissary account.

Jesse Krimes
Pennsylvania

As my release got closer, I focused on saving money so that I could survive when I came home. I worked as much as I could and limited my trips to commissary. The day I was released, I had approximately $140 in my account—not enough to get myself back on my feet, but it was something. To my surprise, my funds were put onto a prepaid debit card. I didn't get a dollar in cash, which made my first few hours out difficult. The card also had my prison photo on it—an immediate warning to anyone who saw it that I had just left prison.

But the worst part was that the card issuer, JPMorgan Chase, was charging exorbitant fees on these debit cards, which were designed specifically for people leaving prison. There were transaction fees for everything, including a $10 fee for an ATM withdrawal. There was no way to avoid the fees; Chase even charged an inactivity fee for not using the card.

I worked hard for every penny on that card. And now that I was free, Chase was taking a significant portion of it. I saved all of my documents and receipts and was lucky enough to have a friend who referred me to a lawyer. Without that support, I might never have challenged a system that's meant to take advantage of already vulnerable people.

Eventually, we filed a class-action lawsuit against Chase for charging formerly incarcerated people exorbitant fees on prepaid debit release cards. The case was so strong, the bank settled in a matter of months. Chase was required to return nearly half a million dollars to the thousands of formerly incarcerated people it stole from like me.

Today, I am a full-time artist whose work has been featured in major institutions, including the Philadelphia Museum of Art, Palais de Tokyo, and MoMA PS1. I am also the co-founder of Right of Return USA, the first national fellowship dedicated to supporting formerly incarcerated artists, and the inaugural Executive Director of the Center for Art and Advocacy, a nonprofit dedicated to mentoring justice-impacted creatives.

PROBATION AND PAROLE PAYMENTS

Correctional supervision can take many forms. Some people are placed on pretrial supervision while awaiting trial. Others are sentenced to probation supervision in lieu of incarceration. And people released from prison or jail often serve time on parole, a period of supervision after incarceration.

$264 million
Supervision payment processing market potential[52]

Over 1.1 million
People on probation and parole making payments through JPay[53]

Many states and counties now charge people for their supervision, claiming that the fees paid help offset the operating costs of supervision as well as police, prosecution, public defense, courts, and jails.[54]

People subject to supervision are often required to pay these periodic fees through a for-profit payment processor that layers on yet another fee. For those who cannot afford it, missing a payment can lead to a technical violation of their supervision conditions and jail time, amounting to what many regard as modern-day debtors' prisons.[56]

In New York, for example, people on parole must pay $30 for their supervision every month. The state has an exclusive contract with JPay, which tacks on an additional $1.99 for online payment and $2.99 for payment by phone.[57] These costs undermine reentry efforts for those on parole working to find employment and housing, especially since 45 percent already leave the state's prison system with court debt. And while the state does not consider non-payment a violation of parole, non-payment can be considered in the decision to terminate or continue parole.[58] With 16,000 people on parole, New York rakes in as much as $6 million annually on parole supervision fees and JPay an estimated $384,000.[59]

Financial services corporations showed up in the correctional landscape without an invitation and paid off administrators to take over what were free services. Now, their reach is growing faster than ever, and faster than many of the other sectors in the prison industry. Without legislative, regulatory, or litigative intervention, their predatory services will become as ubiquitous as that of the correctional telecom and commissary corporations that have bought them up.

LEARN MORE

- "How Private Equity Is Turning Public Prisons into Big Profits," *The Nation* (2019)
- "Lawsuit Reveals How Tech Companies Profit off the Prison-Industrial Complex," ThinkProgress (2018)
- "How States Can Take a Stand Against Prison Banking Profiteers," *George Washington Law Review* (2017)
- "The Multi-Million Dollar Market of Sending Money to an Incarcerated Loved One," Prison Policy Initiative (2017)

- "The Financial Firm That Cornered the Market on Jails," *The Nation* (2016)
- "How Private Bankers Cash in on Released Prisoners," Vox (2015)
- "CFPB Comment: Curb Exploitation of People Released from Custody," Prison Policy Initiative (2015)
- "Profiting from Prisoners [series]," The Center for Public Integrity (2014, 2015)

FOOD + COMMISSARY

[Aramark's food service] was a human atrocity against the inmates, in my opinion—the rotten garbage that was being served, plus the way they were allowing it to be prepared.

— Ronald Taylor, retired Michigan corrections officer[1]

Prison and jail administrators have long weaponized food—or the lack thereof—to inflict additional punishment on incarcerated people.[2] The U.S. Supreme Court responded to the most egregious of these practices in 1978 when it ruled in *Hutto v. Finney* that serving incarcerated people calorie-deficient and otherwise unhealthy diets for a prolonged period of time constituted a violation of the Eighth Amendment's protection against cruel and unusual punishment.[3] This meant that administrators could no longer force people behind bars to subsist on bread, water, and gruel. Challenged with improving food while facing rapid population growth in the late 20th century, administrators turned to the private sector that promised quality food service at lower costs.

Description: Corrections agencies outsource various types of food services to corporations, namely the operation of kitchens, commissary stores, care packages, and visit room vending machines. Agencies that manage these services in-house purchase raw ingredients and commissary products from private manufacturers and suppliers.

Since then, corporations have maintained a regular presence in the correctional food space. They manufacture and distribute raw and prepackaged ingredients as well as manage food preparation and service in prison and jail kitchens. As a former Arizona food service supervisor explained, "Though the inmates do most of the work, and the corrections officers are there to maintain order, it is civilian contractors who are often responsible for every aspect of the meal preparation: inmate training, adherence to recipes, ensuring food safety standards are met, theft prevention, portion control, and general quality of service."[7] But rather than improving nutritional value and quality, privatization exacerbated the carceral food problem. In Michigan, for example, privatized food service in state prisons has "been the source of almost continuous scandal, embarrassment, and administrative difficulty."[8] Yet few of the endless lawsuits regarding food in prisons and jails since *Hutto* have been successful.

$4.1 billion
Correctional food service market size[4]

$2.30
National average daily spending on food per person in prison[5]

6.4x
Increased likelihood of food poisoning in prison or jail[6]

Failures in food service have forced incarcerated people to depend on commissary, or on-site convenience stores first introduced in federal prisons in 1930,[9] and care packages sent by loved ones for food as well as hygiene and clothing essentials—all of which are insufficiently provided by correctional administrators. But the very corporations that commit these food service atrocities are often also entrusted with operating commissaries and care package programs, which means that providing substandard

$1.8 billion
Annual commissary sales[10]

17
States with privatized commissary operations[11]

$947
Average annual commissary spending per person[12]

food service is rewarded with increased revenue in commissary and care package sales.[13] But the food sold in commissary and care packages also fails to meet the nutritional needs of incarcerated people.

In fact, the one place where incarcerated people will, at times, find nutritional and emotional reprieve is in the vending machines of visit rooms. Understanding the power of a shared meal, corporations sign exclusive contracts to stock visit room vending machines with expensive, ready-made food—a cost that the occasion of a visit might warrant.

HOW MUCH MONEY IS AT STAKE?

▪ FOOD SERVICE

The correctional food service industry, made up of just a handful of players, is estimated to rake in $4.1 billion each year.[14] Larger prison systems can serve as many as three million meals per week and pay between $0.56 and $3.00 per meal each year.[15] The largest food service provider, Aramark, serves 380 million meals each year, bringing in $1.6 billion in revenues from prison and jail food service annually.[16] As of 2020, at least 15 corrections agencies have privatized food services.[17]

▪ COMMISSARY

The commissary market that incarcerated people rely on to supplement prison and jail food, basic hygiene, and clothing necessities was estimated to be worth $1.8 billion in 2016, but recent data suggests a more accurate estimate could run far higher.[18] A survey of commissary sales in three state prison agencies revealed that incarcerated people spend an average of $947 annually on commissary, 73 percent of which is spent on food.[19] And while only 17 states outsource the operation of prison commissaries to corporations, that figure increased 21 percent between 2013 and 2020.[20] In jails, outsourcing commissary operations to corporations is more common.[21] Importantly, commissary operators also make money charging families hefty deposit fees to transfer money into their loved ones' commissary accounts.[22]

▪ CARE PACKAGES AND VENDING MACHINES

Unfortunately, there is no aggregated data about the care package and vending machine markets specifically in correctional settings.

WHAT CORPORATIONS ARE INVOLVED?

▪ FOOD SERVICE

The carceral food industry is dominated by Aramark, which pioneered the space in 1978; Sodexo, one of the world's largest food service providers; and Trinity Services Group, which entered in 1990.[23] Today, Aramark operates in more than 600 corrections facilities[24] and serves roughly a million meals

MARKET SHARE

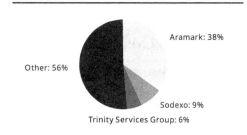

Aramark: 38%

Other: 56%

Sodexo: 9%

Trinity Services Group: 6%

Source: HTF Market Intelligence

each day[25] to bring in $1.6 billion annually on its correctional business[26]—or roughly 12 percent of its total revenues. Sodexo takes in $360 million annually on its U.S. correctional food service business.[27] And Trinity Services Group contracts with over 400 correctional facilities in 43 states to make $252 million annually on its food service business,[28] which is almost 40 percent of its total $660 million in revenues.[29] Other major prison food service providers include subsidiaries of Compass Group and the Elior Group.[30]

▪ COMMISSARY AND CARE PACKAGES

The commissary market is similarly dominated by just a few familiar corporations: Keefe Group, Trinity Services Group, Union Supply, and Aramark.[31] Keefe Group, the market's largest player, entered the business in 1975;[32] Trinity Services Group's commissary business also dates back to the 1970s through its subsidiary Swanson Services;[33] Union Supply emerged in

1991;[34] and Aramark launched its commissary brand iCare in 2006.[35] Today, Keefe Group serves 650,000 incarcerated people in 14 states[36] and brings in more than $1 billion in revenues a year across all its business lines.[37] Most commissary vendors also have a care package business line.[38]

Notably, Trinity Services Group and Keefe Group joined forces in 2016 when they were merged under TKC by its private equity owner H.I.G. Capital, which also owns correctional healthcare and telecom corporations.[39] Beyond its commissary and care package services, Keefe Group also has a subsidiary that provides correctional telecom services (ICSolutions) and a brand that provides correctional financial services (Access Corrections).[40] Altogether, TKC is estimated to bring in $1.5 billion in sales, the majority of which is derived from the carceral market.[41]

▪ VENDING MACHINES

The vending machine market is far smaller and served by small, and often local, vendors. These include corporations like Microtronic US, Three Square Market, 365 Retail Markets, Canteen Vending, Avanti Markets, and Fresh Healthy Vending.[42]

FOOD SERVICE

Correctional administrators outsource food service to corporations to reduce facility operating costs, with detrimental consequences.[44] Moreover, they allow their vendors to use incarcerated people, paid just pennies an hour, if anything, to conduct their food service from beginning to end.

> I got meal costs down to $0.40 a day per inmate. It costs $1.15 a day to feed the department's dogs. Now, I'm cutting prisoners' calories from 3,000 to 2,500 a day.
>
> — Joe Arpaio, former Maricopa County, Arizona, sheriff[43]

Few laws regulate food service in correctional facilities, so contractors set their own standards for quality and safety.[45] Considering little more than caloric requirements, they serve food that lacks nutritional content.[46] They use inexpensive and unhealthy fillers or substitutes like margarine and soy to increase caloric intake, leaving people hungry, exacerbating chronic health conditions like diabetes, hypertension, and heart disease, and creating new health risks.[47] They even serve food labeled "not fit for human consumption" upon arrival[48]—its own kind of psychological warfare for those working in the kitchen.

Perhaps still worse, in efforts to avoid waste costs, these corporations ration food dangerously. They serve food that is old or contaminated or serve inadequate portions, if they do not run out altogether. In 2014, an investigation at the Gordon County Jail in Georgia, which had contracted with Trinity Services Group, revealed that incarcerated people were eating toothpaste, toilet paper, and syrup packets out of hunger.[50] Human rights violations like these committed by correctional food service providers are endless.

Michigan's experiment with private food service vendors is perhaps the most notorious. In 2014, leaked emails revealed that an Aramark employee retrieved and re-served food that had been thrown in the trash.[51] The following year, the state's correctional administrators terminated a three-year contract with Aramark early after a slew of controversies and contracted with Trinity Services Group instead.[52] But in the first 15 months of the new contract, the state fined Trinity Services Group over $2 million for various violations, including unauthorized meal substitutions, delays in serving meals, and sanitation violations.[53]

> When Aramark was the food service vendor in Florida, it often shorted meals with small portions and missing ingredients. On one occasion when I was assigned as a kitchen worker, an Aramark employee berated me for draining water off the vegetables after they were cooked. "Water is part of the serving," the employee said.
>
> – David M. Reutter, incarcerated food service worker and journalist for *Prison Legal News*[49]

After two failed experiments with private food service providers, Governor Rick Snyder announced in 2018 that the state would move back to running its own prison food service.[54]

> Their supervisor will give them a recipe to serve 900 prisoners. Our institution holds 1,100 normally, and depending on which meal it is, they will add water to all of their stuff to make their products stretch.

> On some days if they don't run out, there will be other problems with the food. Raw, undercooked, sometimes burnt, sometimes it's soupy. If they don't run out, they screw it up somehow.

> I watched a prisoner pull a rock out of his mouth. . . . Wasn't two feet over from me where I scan my IDs, and he's like, "What in the . . . ?" And he reaches into his mouth and pulls a rock out bigger than a pea . . . drops it on the table. Tink, tink, tink. I was like, "What is that?" And he says, "It's a rock."

> I've seen a bug that big in them collard greens, like I couldn't even handle it. A perfect big ol' bug right on the collard greens. . . . A well-cooked bug.

> We had spaghetti one day, and one of the officers came over and he was eating, and he pulled a mop string out.

> — Various anonymous Michigan corrections officers[55]

Michigan's decision to bring food service back in-house was a rare one. Despite the abundance of these stories and, in many cases, agreement among incarcerated people and corrections officials about the shortcomings of private food service, many prison and jail administrators continue to outsource food service to corporations that put profit over people to deprive them of something as simple as food.

In 2013, for example, Aramark was awarded a two-year $110 million contract to provide food service across Ohio's prisons.[56] Less than a year later, there were numerous reports of service failures, including 65 instances when it failed to serve food or ran out of it and five instances when it served food with maggots.[57] Though the state took the rare step of penalizing the corporation, Aramark took the $272,300 in fines in stride and won the next contract award with the state in 2015, despite a cheaper competing bid from a public union.[58]

However, perhaps the most egregious example of food-related abuse in corrections facilities occured in Alabama, where a Depression-era law allows sheriffs to personally pocket any savings from food provision in their jails. What follows is probably obvious: sheriffs skimp on food costs for the people in their custody to bolster their personal income. In Etowah County, for instance, the sheriff kept more than $750,000 of taxpayer money intended to feed people at the county's jail over a three-year period and bought himself a beach home. Altogether, the sheriff owns $1.7 million in properties on a $93,000 annual salary. Meanwhile, people incarcerated at the jail reported going hungry.[59]

SAMPLE JAIL FOOD COSTS

	El Paso County Jail, CO[60]	Hall County Jail, GA[61]	Lake County Jail, IN[62]
Provider	Aramark	Trinity Food Service	Summit Food Services (The Elior Group)
Cost Per Meal	$1.26	$0.99	$1.22
Number of Meals Served Daily	5,220	2,550	2,550

Unsurprisingly these efforts to cut food costs have had a really damaging impact on the lives of incarcerated people. Incarcerated people are over six times more likely to suffer from a food-related illness than people in the general public.[63] Between 1998 and 2014, correctional facilities reported 200 food-borne outbreaks and 20,625 illnesses, 204 hospitalizations, and five deaths resulting from food sickness.[64]

Finally, illness is not the only consequence of cost-cutting measures;

enslavement is yet another. Many prisons, some of which are on former plantations in the South, put incarcerated people to work on farms to harvest food for the facility and generate revenue for the agency. Today, the Federal Bureau of Prisons and all 50 states have incarcerated people working in agriculture.[65] In Georgia, for example, over 300 incarcerated people work, completely unpaid, to produce 42 percent of food required by the state's prisons.[66]

While prison and jail administrators weaponize food to exact nutritional punishment and enslave incarcerated people, incarcerated people have used their bodies as counter weapons in political struggles, practicing what some have termed "gastronomical resistance."[67] Throughout history, across political movements, people with no weapons have used their bodies to fight injustice and oppression.[68] Incarcerated people have time and time again effectively used hunger strikes, one form of gastronomical resistance, to protest prison conditions and labor practices. In 2013, for example, nearly 30,000 incarcerated people in California participated in a hunger strike that led to the end of indefinite solitary confinement in state prisons.[69]

COMMISSARY

In prisons and jails, commissaries can offer an expansive reprieve from the depravity of kitchen food. While egregiously priced, off-brand products can be innovatively transformed into pleasurable community meals that serve as another form of gastronomical resistance.[71] Yet commissary food comes with its own problems. Prepackaged foods are high in sugar and sodium,[72] for example, and can cause or exacerbate chronic health

conditions, leaving incarcerated people to choose between two types of
poison while private corporations collect the spoils.

Some states and municipalities
stock and operate their own commissaries, usually charging a markup on
the resale of products to cover operating costs and even turn a profit. Many
others choose to outsource their commissary operations to private corporations in exchange for a commission

> We live in an environment
> designed to deprive the
> senses. Our world is almost
> completely devoid of colors,
> pleasant scents, or tender
> physical contact. Our senses
> are starving to death. In such a
> bland artificial existence, even
> a simple sugar treat can be
> mistaken for an exotic ecstasy.
>
> – John Adams, incarcerated
>   essayist for PEN America[70]

on sales. While the latter model is more profitable for commissary corporations, they benefit from both because they manufacture and supply
many of the unique products sold in commissaries in either case. Under
both models, operators inflate product prices while offering substandard
brands to generate more profit. With a captive consumer, sales are essentially guaranteed, especially since commissary is used to meet basic food,
hygiene, and clothing needs that have not been met by prison and jail
administrators.

More specifically, besides foods, incarcerated people often purchase simple hygiene products like shampoo and deodorant in commissary. These
products are often incredibly low in quality—lotion the consistency of
water—and yet exorbitantly priced. And culture-specific hygiene products
are even harder to come by and more egregiously priced.

In most cases, it is the families supporting incarcerated loved ones who
provide funds to purchase these items given the insufficiency and subse-
quent garnishment of prison wages, if wages are paid at all. A 2018 study
of three state prison agencies found that, on average, incarcerated people
spent $947 annually on commissary products, substantially more than the
$180 to $660 typically earned annually by incarcerated people working in

these states.[73] And jails offer even fewer paid job opportunities, meaning families supporting loved ones in pretrial detention, who often cannot afford to pay bail, are also exploited by these commissary schemes.

JASMA'S STORY

I was a young woman when I went to prison. It was the most dehumanizing experience of my life. Every day, I dealt with the profound racism and misogyny of the system. Male guards constantly threatened to rape me and the other women if we didn't comply with their orders. On other days, they just maliciously denied us necessary hygiene products. They used their power to terrorize and degrade us.

Jasma Credle
New York

I spent my first menstrual cycle in solitary. I was given just two cheap sanitary napkins a day. The result was humiliating. I bled through my clothes and had no option but to sit in it for hours. Back in general population, we did not get sanitary napkins or tampons at all. We had to buy them from commissary, which we could only do once every two weeks, or suffer the humiliation of bloodied bottoms.

And purchasing menstrual hygiene products from commissary was not an easy task. I had to plan ahead, determining what I needed and, more importantly, what I could afford. Low-quality, generic brand tampons cost twice as much on the inside—more than $5 for a pack of 18—while our pay scale ranged from just $0.10 to $0.25 an hour. I would work 50 hours just to afford decency during my cycle.

Of course, sanitary napkins were not the only thing we needed from commissary. There were other things like deodorant, shampoo, shower slippers, and even food. We had to buy pre-packaged food to supplement the inedible, unhealthy, and limited diet served in the mess hall. Again, all at high costs on low wages.

The truth is that prisons provide little of what you really need to survive—from sustenance to basic hygiene. Instead, you need to rely on your family for all that. But most families supporting people behind bars don't have the money. They can't afford to give their loved ones doing time the money needed to buy even a shred of dignity inside.

CARE PACKAGES

Recognizing that commissary falls short of meeting the basic human needs of incarcerated people, many corrections agencies have historically allowed incarcerated people to receive homemade care packages from family, friends, and support groups. These care packages are subject to strict content guidelines and weight restrictions that vary from institution to institution and can change without notice.

Increasingly, however, corporations are stepping in and convincing agencies to prohibit homemade care packages and introduce sterile, privatized care package programs that give families a limited menu of egregiously priced "pre-approved" products. Prison and jail administrators receive commissions and corporations collect profits hand over fist. In its bid for the West Virginia contract, for example, Union Supply Group, which runs the care package program Union Supply Direct, projected that the state would earn about $95,000 per year thanks to a 17 percent commission rate on annual sales.[74]

Privatized care package programs are no more than external-facing commissary stores. In fact, most care package programs are run by commissary operators. They merely allow families to shop directly from a comparably terrible menu with a few more brand name items. When these programs are introduced, families are generally barred from sending fresh fruit and vegetables or filling bags with cheaper items from their local bodega, dollar store, or superstore. Instead, they must pay much more to the few corporations that control the care package program for their loved one's facility. And families that may have previously used social benefits to pay for items included in homemade care packages no longer have that option either, putting care packages even further out of reach for the economically distressed communities targeted by the criminal legal system. Moreover, ordering packages is not easy for people without internet access or computer literacy, which is not uncommon for those impacted by incarceration.

In 2018, New York piloted a privatized care package program. Of the six approved vendors the state selected, only one sold menstrual hygiene products—at four times the cost at the local chain retailer. Thankfully, advocates forced the state to cancel the pilot and prevented it from taking permanent hold.[76] But, in 2022, New York introduced a revised policy. Despite expanding the list of approved vendors beyond typical prison corporations, the new directive still bans incarcerated people from receiving food packages from family and friends outside.[77] Other states are considering or have already implemented similar policies.[78]

> My support network isn't very technologically aware. My mom doesn't even own a computer, let alone know how to place orders. I won't even mention what she can't afford. Essentially, I was one of the few major financial contributors for my family. Now DOCCS is attempting to institute another punitive restriction on our families.
>
> — John K., incarcerated person, New York[75]

Limiting the items that incarcerated people can receive and privatizing care packages is not just financially exploitive, but also emotionally depraved. Homemade packages are sent and received with love, carefully crafted to include favorite snacks and childhood reminders. Care packages built in warehouses by strangers cannot carry the same weight. Privatizing care packages removes some of the last reminders of the outside world that bring hope to an otherwise hopeless place.

VENDING MACHINES

For incarcerated people, vending machines are limited to visiting rooms. They typically offer more enjoyable ready-made items like pizzas and burgers. But the small corporations in this market take advantage of their captive audience with expensive prices. Sharing a hot meal can have a significant positive impact on a visit—food has the power to create memories—and should be encouraged, not exploited.

But depending on the length of one's visit, food can also be more of a necessity than a luxury. In 2018, family relationships were strained when Pennsylvania temporarily suspended vending machine access during prison visits.[79] "If you are elderly or diabetic or have a small child, it is impossible now for you to visit your loved one," explained Claire Shubik-Richards, head of the Pennsylvania Prison Society.[80] Families were eager to see vending machines returned to visit rooms despite the hefty cost of food items.

The exploitation of basic human needs like food is both anathema to human rights and the perfect encapsulation of how the prison industry functions. Corporations, and sometimes government agencies, profit by spending as little as possible to feed those in their care. Worse yet, failures in one service line can, in fact, drive revenue in another, creating remarkably dangerous incentives. Legal, regulatory, and procurement weaknesses allow corporations to avoid any meaningful or long-lasting consequences for their dehumanizing, reprehensible food practices. The state of prison and jail food is a crisis within a crisis.

LEARN MORE

- *Ending the Hidden Punishment of Food in Prison*, Impact Justice (2020)
- *Billions Served: Prison Food Regimes, Nutritional Punishment, and Gastronomical Resistance*, Anthony Ryan Hatch (2019)
- "Michigan's Failed Effort to Privatize Prison Kitchens and the Future of Institutional Food," *Civil Eats* (2018)
- "In Florida Prisons, Canteens Are Big Money. But Not Everyone Pays the Same Price," *Florida Times Union* (2018)
- "Prison Food and Commissary Services: A Recipe for Disaster," *Prison Legal News* (2018)
- *The Company Store: A Deeper Look at Prison Commissaries*, Prison Policy Initiative (2018)
- "Maggots with a Side of Dirt? What Privatization Does to Prison Food," *Governing* (2018)
- "Prison Food Is Making U.S. Inmates Disproportionately Sick," *The Atlantic* (2017)
- "The Big Business of Prisoner Care Packages," The Marshall Project (2017)
- "Prison Food Politics: The Economics of an Industry Feeding 2.2 Million," *The Guardian* (2017)
- *Prison Food in America*, Erika Camplin (2017)
- *Paging Anti-Trust Lawyers: Prison Commissary Giants Prepare to Merge*, Prison Policy Initiative (2016)
- "What's in a Prison Meal?" The Marshall Project (2015)

HEALTHCARE

> The company's efforts to reduce costs interfered with my ability, and with the staff's ability, to provide appropriate levels of care to inmates.
>
> — *Charles Pugh, MD, former Medical Director at Corizon*[1]

With the introduction of asylums, the 1700s marked the beginning of the inhumane warehousing of people with mental illnesses.[2] Limited relief came in the late 1800s when psychiatric hospitals were established to treat rather than torture people suffering from mental illness.[3] At the peak of their popularity in 1955, there were 560,000 people in psychiatric hospitals in the United States.[4] But the introduction of antipsychotic medications began a deinstitutionalization trend[5] that would eventually lead to a substantial increase in people with mental illness behind bars.

Description: Corrections agencies contract with healthcare corporations to provide a variety of healthcare services to incarcerated people, namely medical and behavioral healthcare, including mental health and substance abuse treatment. Correctional healthcare corporations also provide specialized healthcare services such as pharmacy services, diagnostic testing and screening, ambulatory services, and hospice care.

In 1965, Medicaid accelerated dein-stitutionalization by excluding state psychiatric hospitals and other similar state-run institutions from federal funding.[6] People with serious mental illnesses were moved to nursing homes or released to community programs that were supported by federal funding under the Community Mental Health Act passed just two years earlier. By the late 1970s, there were nearly two million people with mental illnesses in community health facilities.[7] But, in 1981, the Omnibus Budget Reconciliation Act substantially cut federal funding to community-based treatment programs.[8] Many people with mental illnesses were put out and had their treatment denied. Unsurprisingly, without support, they quickly began to fill prisons and jails unequipped to manage their needs.

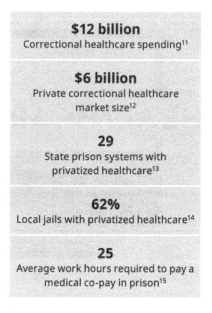

$12 billion
Correctional healthcare spending[11]

$6 billion
Private correctional healthcare market size[12]

29
State prison systems with privatized healthcare[13]

62%
Local jails with privatized healthcare[14]

25
Average work hours required to pay a medical co-pay in prison[15]

Around the same time, the targeting of Black, brown, and Indigenous communities by racist policing and criminal policies caught up with the long-term underinvestment in the health and well-being of the same communities to exacerbate medical needs inside prisons and jails. Soon, the history of racism in medicine, public health, and mental health was on full display across the correctional landscape,[9] which was offering little more than first aid at the time.[10]

But, in 1976, the Supreme Court affirmed the constitutional right to healthcare for incarcerated people when it determined that "deliberate indifference to [the] serious medical needs of prisoners" constituted a violation of the Eighth Amendment's prohibition against cruel and unusual punishment in *Estelle v. Gamble*.[16] Correctional administrators quickly turned to alternative healthcare systems for support, including university systems, nonprofit hospitals, and the private sector.[17]

In 1973, New York City became the first jurisdiction to outsource correctional healthcare when it contracted with Montefiore Hospital, a nonprofit hospital in the Bronx.[18] However, it was in 1978 when the first for-profit correctional healthcare corporation, Prison Health Services, Inc. (PHSi), which later became Corizon Health (now YesCare), came on the scene. The industry expanded significantly over the next few decades as the deinstitutionalization of people with mental illness continued, particularly in smaller to midsize counties with tighter budgets and fewer public options.[19] Today, corrections agencies provide medical and mental healthcare, along with a myriad of other health services, to those in their custody through a matrix of for-profit, nonprofit, and government options.

HOW MUCH MONEY IS AT STAKE?

The United States spends $12 billion annually on correctional healthcare, roughly 15 percent of all correctional spending.[20] State corrections agencies increased spending on healthcare by 41 percent in the ten-year period between 2001 and 2011, and the federal prison system increased spending on healthcare by 24 percent between just 2010 and 2014.[21] This rapid growth over the past few decades has made the market incredibly attractive to the private sector.

In 2005, an estimated 40 percent of correctional spending was flowing to correctional healthcare corporations.[22] By 2018, 56 percent of state prisons systems and 62 percent of jails had privatized healthcare in full or in part.[23] Today, these corporations make claim to over $5 billion of correctional spending, contracted to provide correctional healthcare services in 29 states.[24]

MAP OF PRIVATIZATION DELIVERY SYSTEMS

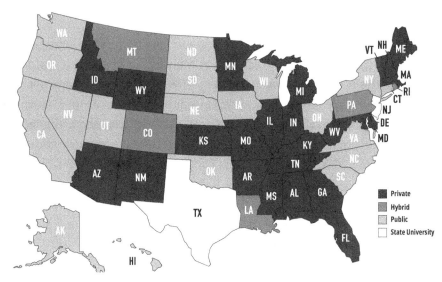

Source: Worth Rises.

Beyond the sheer numbers, the serious healthcare needs of those in correctional environments draw in providers eager to capitalize on the idea that incarcerated people need increased services, whether or not they are indeed provided. Disproportionately Black, brown, and Indigenous and often economically distressed, the nearly 2 million people in prisons and jails are more likely to suffer from medical and mental health ailments even before their incarceration due to the lack of investment in the health and well-being of these communities.[25] Pre-existing health conditions are then compounded by unhealthy and traumatic correctional environments to make incarcerated people more likely to suffer from chronic illness, infectious diseases, substance abuse, and mental health ailments than people in the general population.[26]

More than 50 percent of all those in prison or jail have some mental health need.[27] Approximately 15 percent of the national prison population and 20 percent of the national jail population, or more than 350,000 people, have a serious mental illness—ten times as many people as there are psychiatric beds in hospitals.[28] And an estimated 65 percent of people in prison suffer from alcohol or drug dependency,[29] making corrections an attractive market for pharmaceutical corporations that produce antipsychotic and addiction drugs.

All these healthcare concerns are more acute and costly for elderly people in prisons, a population that has been rapidly growing due to punitive sentencing laws. Between 2000 and 2010, the number of people behind bars who were 55 years old or older grew by 181 percent while the total prison population grew by 17 percent over the same period. It costs roughly three times as much to incarcerate an older person than a younger person due in large part to their healthcare needs,[30] money that flows largely to correctional healthcare corporations.

Finally, incarcerated women and transgender people also encounter unique and costly healthcare needs that are attractive to providers.

WHAT CORPORATIONS ARE INVOLVED?

Founded in 1978, PHSi was the first for-profit correctional healthcare corporation.[31] Correctional Medical Services, which would later merge with PHSi, was founded in 1979.[32] MHM Services followed in 1981,[33] California Forensic Medical Group in 1983,[34] and PrimeCare Medical in 1986.[35] NaphCare came on the scene in 1989.[36] In 1994, Wexford Health Sources emerged.[37] Correct Care Solutions and Armor Correctional Health Services were founded in 2003[38] and 2004,[39] respectively.

Mergers and acquisitions have begun to consolidate the correctional healthcare market. In 2011, the two oldest correctional healthcare corporations, PHSi and Correctional Medical Services, merged to form Corizon Health,[40] the largest player in the market at the time,[41] which later rebranded as YesCare. A couple of years later, in 2013, MHM Services, which historically focused its services on behavioral healthcare, entered into a joint venture with publicly traded Centene Corporation to create Centurion Health.[42] Centene then acquired its partner, MHM Services, in 2018.[43] Centene quietly offloaded Centurion without disclosing the buyer or sale price in 2023.

Also in 2018, H.I.G. Capital executed the largest deal in the market when it purchased Correct Care Solutions and merged it with Correctional Medical Group Companies[45] to create Wellpath, now the largest correctional healthcare corporation with an estimated $2.7 billion in annual revenues.[46] Its dominance in the field gives the corporation considerable bargaining power with corrections agencies that have committed to outsourcing healthcare, a decision that is not always easy to reverse. On occasion, Wellpath or one of its competitors may be the only provider bidding on a contract, creating an imbalance of power, which deeply impacts quality of care.

> If you're the only dance in town, you can pretty much call your own shots.
>
> – Bobby F. Kimbrough Jr., sheriff of Forsyth County, NC, on Wellpath[44]

TOP MARKET PLAYERS

	Wellpath[47]	YesCare[48]	Centurion Health[49]	Naphcare[50]	Wexford Health[51]
Estimated Annual Revenues	$2,650 Mn	$855 Mn	$752 Mn	$550 Mn	$425 Mn
States	37	17	15	37	13
Facilities	550	52	250	N/A	120
Employees	15,000	4,000	8,000	2,400	2,700
Incarcerated Patients	300,000	50,000	275,000	150,000	97,000

MEDICAL CARE

While the U.S. Supreme Court established a constitutional right to healthcare for incarcerated people in 1976, there have been no consistent or enforced quality-of-care standards. In fact, only six state prison systems formally require and integrate quality monitoring systems in their oversight of healthcare.[52] And quality is rarely a factor when determining the cost of care, which, in 2015, varied from $2,173 in Louisiana to $19,796 in California on average per person per year.[53]

Introducing profit motives into opaque correctional environments, which are already rife with abuse, critically exacerbates the harm incarcerated people suffer as correctional healthcare providers measure the cost of a person's health and well-being against the cost to their bottom line. Often paid a flat fee, these corporations are incentivized to cut costs as much as possible to pocket what they do not spend. They routinely under-staff facilities, hire unqualified practitioners, avoid preventative care, refuse pain relief, and even deny life-saving treatments and hospitalizations. Even well-intentioned medical professionals working for these corporations have reported pressure to provide the cheapest possible care even if inadequate to meet a patient's medical needs.[56]

> Corizon is just hiring bodies, trying to get their numbers up. . . . There's RNs there that don't even know how to start an IV. There are nurses that can't operate an oxygen tank. A lot of them have no type of training.
>
> – Jose Vallejo, former Corizon nurse[54]

Predictably, these cost-cutting tactics result in substandard care with dire consequences. For instance, between 2011 and 2012, Corizon cut the cost of hospitalizations from its predecessor by 53 percent, increasing its profit margin from 15 percent to 24 percent by 2013. Over the next few years, Corizon faced repeated wrongful death suits across the country with a common fact pattern: healthcare professionals determine a suffering patient needs to go to the hospital, the corporation denies hospitalization to save on costs, and the patient dies shortly after. Whether it was a tight chest, a hip pain, or insufferable detox, in each case, the treatable condition was relayed to a Corizon medical practitioner and ignored, resulting in death.[57]

Corizon, now YesCare, is far from the only correctional healthcare provider with such a tragic résumé. A survey of the nation's 523 largest jails revealed that those that outsourced health-care to the private sector had mortality rates that were 18 to 58 percent higher than those that used a publicly managed medical service, depending on the corporation.[58] NaphCare and Armor had the highest rates, followed by Corizon, or YesCare, and Well-path.[59] And two-thirds of those who died were awaiting trial.[60]

> While it's true that there's this rubric of using private vendors, it is designed to absolve the sheriffs of responsibility and involvement. It does not, however, improve quality.
>
> – Homer Venters, former Chief Medical Officer for Correctional Health Services in New York City[55]

Over the past few decades, correctional healthcare providers have also turned to telemedicine to mitigate the need for onsite staffing. By 2011, 30 states used telemedicine for at least one medical subspecialty or diagnostic service.[61] While offering some small benefits to incarcerated people, such as faster access to specialty doctors, the major benefit is realized by the providers and correctional administrators in cost savings related to having practitioners on-site.[62] Telemedicine has birthed new market players like KaZee, which equips corrections facilities with telemedicine capabilities and saved the Texas Department of Criminal Justice nearly a billion dollars over a decade.[63]

Desperate for care, incarcerated people have brought tens of thousands of medical malpractice lawsuits over the years against correctional health-care providers. Between 2009 and 2014, Corizon, the nation's largest prison healthcare corporation at the time, was sued 1,364 times, or more than once every other day, for providing inadequate care.[64] While correctional healthcare providers claim these lawsuits are often frivolous or unsubstan-tiated, their 7 percent success rate is only slightly lower than that of medical malpractice lawsuits in the general public,[65] even with the significant disadvantage facing incarcerated plaintiffs in court. In one case, a court rejected the malpractice claim of an incarcerated patient who received a late diagnosis of lymphoma after months of reported pain because he could not present expert testimony as to whether the care he received "departed from accepted medical practice."[66]

In fact, the veracity of these cases presents such a threat to correctional healthcare providers that some are going to great lengths to get out from under them. For example, in 2022, to evade hundreds of mounting medical malpractice lawsuits, Corizon leveraged a controversial bankruptcy tactic known as the "Texas Two-Step." Executives divided Corizon into two new entities: YesCare, which was given all its assets, largely existing contracts, and Tehum Care Services, which received all the liabilities and then filed for bankruptcy. The liabilities amounted to more than a billion dollars in lawsuits, which Tehum then tried to settle for pennies on the dollar in a fast-tracked bankruptcy proceeding, spurring efforts to quash the bankruptcy altogether. As of 2024, bankruptcy proceedings were still ongoing, while YesCare continued to operate as one of the industry's largest players. Notably, the proceedings were initiated by an opaque group of investors with a history of running nursing homes that recently acquired the corporation with the intention of creating a prison-to-nursing-home pipeline.[67]

These corporate cost-cutting strategies shift real costs onto taxpayers in the short and long term. In the short term, avoiding preventative healthcare exacerbates both acute and chronic illnesses, often leading to hospitalizations that carry higher costs. Over 45,000 incarcerated people are transported out of facilities each month for healthcare services, and $90 million is spent annually just transporting incarcerated people to hospitals.[68] In the long term, releasing people with compromised health into communities creates a cost burden for public healthcare and social service agencies. Yet the biggest cost of this profiteering is measured in human lives: the mortality rate of formerly incarcerated people is 3.5 times higher than others in the general population.[69]

SHERON'S STORY

Five years ago, when I was in federal prison, I got a bacterial infection and suffered nerve poisoning. I spent three months on life support. When I regained consciousness, I was paralyzed with severe respiratory issues. I was moved to a facility in Atlanta, Georgia, to complete my recovery and undergo physical therapy. It took nearly a year to just walk, talk, and eat again.

Sheron Edwards
Mississippi

Just as I started to reclaim my life, I finished my federal prison sentence and was extradited to Mississippi to serve a second, 20-year sentence for the same crime in state prison. I walked into Mississippi's notorious Parchman plantation prison in the summer of 2017. I brought all my prescriptions and treatments, but once they ran out, I quickly learned I wasn't getting any more.

Centurion was the healthcare provider at the time. One of their nurses informed me that the company wouldn't provide the prescription medications, breathing treatments, or physical therapy I needed because they exceeded the prison's per-person budget allocation. Still recovering, I had to do what I could to heal on my own. I started by doing planks to strengthen my core, then moved on to push-ups and wall squats.

It was far from easy. One day, I accidentally shattered my ankle because my bones were still brittle from the paralysis. Once the swelling went down, I had to have a six-inch rod and screws inserted in my ankle. After the surgery and once my cast was removed, Centurion gave me just one physical therapy session. A few years later, Centurion was sued for malpractice, and they dropped their contract with the Mississippi Department of Corrections. But while they may no longer serve our facility, I still feel the long-term effects of their cheap healthcare, or lack thereof.

BEHAVIORAL HEALTH

Over half of incarcerated people suffer from mental illness,[70] with 14 percent of those in federal and state prisons and 26 percent of those in local jails suffering from a serious mental illness.[71] In fact, there are roughly ten times as many people in prison or jail with a serious mental

24601 (b. 1995), State Correctional Institution Muncy, PA. "Money falls freely for psychiatric medications for prisoners. It's easier and cheaper to drug than to heal."

illness as there are psychiatric beds in the United States.[72] Even so, these statistics—based on self-reported data—underestimate the prevalence and severity of mental illness among incarcerated people, especially Black, brown, and Indigenous people whose illness is less often properly diagnosed and treated.[73]

Given the high levels of untreated mental illness, it is unsurprising that substance abuse and addiction are also particularly high in the incarcerated population. More than 1.6 million people are arrested for drug possession every year.[74] And more than half of the people in federal and state prisons and two-thirds of the people in local jails meet the diagnostic criteria for drug dependency or abuse (excluding alcohol)—again based on self-reported data, meaning the true figures could be still higher.[75] Among women, the problem is even deeper, with 82 percent of women suffering from a serious substance abuse disorder.[76] A 2013 report revealed that women were twice as likely to die from drug or alcohol intoxication while incarcerated.[77]

Despite the overwhelming prevalence of mental illness and substance abuse and addiction among incarcerated people, behavioral health needs may be among those least adequately met by correctional healthcare providers. Roughly a million people arrested each year are at risk for untreated drug or alcohol withdrawal in jail.[78] This is in part because government agencies fail to allocate appropriate funding. Only 14 percent of correctional healthcare spending is spent on mental health and 5 percent on substance abuse and addiction treatment.[79] As a result, corporations often choose quick pharmaceutical options over the time-intensive work required to treat patients with these disorders effectively.

In doing so, correctional healthcare providers help pad the pockets of pharmaceutical corporations that shamelessly market to the correctional field. For example, Alkermes, the manufacturer of Aristada and Risperdal, treatments for schizophrenia, and Vivitrol, a treatment for opioid dependency, advertises its drugs in correctional brochures and at correctional conferences.[80] Worse yet, its drugs are injected to forcibly restore pretrial competency in persons deemed unfit to stand trial.[82]

Again, the outcomes are devastating. Suicide has been the leading cause of death in local jails since 2000.[83] Many have suffered dangerous, even fatal, detoxes during their incarceration.[84] And overdoses are the leading cause of death among formerly incarcerated people upon release.[85]

> Drug and alcohol withdrawal protocols were routinely not followed. We worked three days on and two days off, and many times I recall returning to duty to find a patient in full-blown detox.
>
> – Inga Jones, former Corizon nurse[81]

CO-PAYS

Despite the substandard care offered in prisons and jails, incarcerated people are often expected to pay medical co-pays for physician visits, medications, dental treatment, and other health services. At times paid to the for-profit healthcare provider and at others to the government agency, co-pays in state prisons typically run between $2 to $5 and are meant to recoup the cost of care and deter unnecessary doctor visits.[86]

However, considering what little money incarcerated people have—either earned through penny wages[87] or sent in by loved ones on the outside—and the other costs of incarceration, these co-pays put healthcare out of reach for many. An incarcerated minimum-wage worker in North Carolina would need to work 100 hours to afford the $5 co-pay required for a doctor's visit.[88] By comparison, an equivalent co-pay for a non-incarcerated minimum-wage worker in North Carolina would be $725.[89]

Thirty-eight states charge incarcerated people medical co-pays, eight of which do not pay at least some, if not all, for work.[90] For example, until recently, Texas, which does not pay any incarcerated workers, charged people incarcerated in its state prisons a $100 annual medical co-pay[91] to the tune of roughly $2 million per year in revenue for the state.[92] Advocacy moved the legislature to drop the $100 annual fee, but it replaced the fee with a $13.55 co-pay per visit, still the highest for any state prison system in the country.[93]

And the costs do not end with co-pays. Incarcerated people are some-times expected to pay for hospitalizations, rendered medical services, and even basic, over-the-counter medications, ointments, or treatments.[94] At times, corporations operating commissaries and providing healthcare com-pete to exploit people while correctional administrators referee. Some jails have removed basics like Tylenol from their commissary lists to force incar-cerated people to pay the costly co-pay for a doctor's visit to get simple pain relief—a practice that earned the medication the nickname "the $20 Tylenol" in one North Carolina jail.[95]

Regardless of how paltry the care they provide is, correctional healthcare corporations make billions of dollars every year. And each year, new cor-rections agencies consider privatizing the provision of healthcare in their facilities, ignoring the decades of lawsuits, critical independent studies, and desperate pleas of incarcerated people for quality care. Meanwhile, incar-cerated people, particularly Black, brown, and Indigenous people, whose health is already compromised due to racial disparities in medicine, public health, and mental health, are dying.

The grim state of correctional healthcare was particularly exposed dur-ing the pandemic. Incarcerated people suffered disproportionate infection rates as staff carried the virus into facilities where access to testing, hygiene products, personal protective equipment, and medical supplies was limited and social distancing virtually impossible. There was only one solution that medical professionals and advocates could agree on: jurisdictions had to release people. But not all government officials saw it the same way, and many incarcerated people died.[96]

The bottom line is that prisons and jails are not made for care; they worsen health outcomes and perpetuate trauma. Thankfully, incarcerated people and their advocates continue to bring lawsuits, running out correc-tional healthcare corporations that put profit over people and demanding more investment in the health and well-being of people in custody.[97] And, importantly, many are simultaneously demanding divestment from prisons altogether and investment in community health and healing.[98]

LEARN MORE

- "Health, Access to Care, and Financial Barriers to Care Among People Incarcerated in U.S. Prisons," *Journal of the American Medical Association* (2024)
- Custodial Mortality Project, UCLA (2023)
- "Hidden Investors Took Over Corizon Health, a Prison Healthcare Company. Then They Deployed the Texas Two-Step," *Business Insider* (2023)
- "Special Report: U.S. Jails Are Outsourcing Medical Care—and the Death Toll Is Rising," *Reuters* (2020)
- "The Private Option," *The Atlantic* (2019)
- "The Jail Health-Care Crisis," *New Yorker* (2019)
- "Corizon, the Prison Healthcare Giant, Stumbles Again," The Appeal (2019)
- *State Prisons and the Delivery of Hospital Care*, Pew Charitable Trusts (2018)
- *Providing Healthcare in the Prison Environment*, HDR (2018)
- *Prison Health Care: Costs and Quality*, Pew Charitable Trusts (2017)
- *The Current State of Public and Private Prison Healthcare*, University of Pennsylvania, Wharton Public Policy Initiative (2017)
- *The Steep Cost of Medical Co-pays in Prison Puts Health at Risk*, Prison Policy Initiative (2017)
- *Incorrect Care: A Prison Profiteer Turns Care into Confinement*, Grassroots Leadership (2016)
- *Profits vs. Prisoners: How the Largest U.S. Prison Health Care Provider Puts Lives in Danger*, Southern Poverty Law Center (2016)
- "Private Healthcare Providers Are Making Big Bucks Contracting with Prisons," *Consumerist* (2016)
- "Punished for Addiction: Women Prisoners Dying from Lack of Treatment," *ReWire News* (2015)

TRANSPORTATION

You route the prisoner like a package, but miss a single deadline, and you lose money.

— Kent Bradford, former Director of Operations at TransCor America[1]

The Extradition Clause of the U.S. Constitution requires states to honor extradition orders made by other states. However, in an 1860 ruling, the U.S. Supreme Court decided that federal courts could not enforce this requirement, giving states discretion on whether to comply with interstate extradition orders.[6] Then in 1987, in *Puerto Rico v. Branstad*, the court overturned its prior ruling, holding that federal courts could, in fact, enforce such interstate orders and that states have no discretion as it relates to honoring interstate extradition orders.[7]

Paired with the racist dog whistle

Description: Corrections agencies contract with transportation corporations to relocate incarcerated or detained people in response to transfer, extradition, and deportation orders. While most operate by land, some transportation corporations operate by air.

540,000
Annual extraditions nationwide[2]

26
States using privatized correctional transportation[3]

politics and "tough-on-crime" policies of the 1980s and 1990s, this decision is presumed to have spurred the interstate extradition business. While long distance, interstate travel has always been commonplace for the Federal

> One flat fee for both male and female inmates, including juveniles.
>
> – Inmate Services Corporation
>   promotional material[10]

Bureau of Prisons, which depends on the U.S. Marshals Service to transport people, it presented a new challenge for state and local correctional administrators with limited transportation operations.

Quickly, small specialty prison transportation businesses began to crop up. Corrections agencies, facing staffing constraints and unexpected costs, eagerly turned to them to fulfill extradition orders.[8] Some agencies even came to depend on these corporations to transport incarcerated people for court appearances, facility transfers, and hospital visits. Over the next 20 years, these small businesses ballooned into crudely run corporations with dangerous cost-cutting practices and deadly consequences.[9]

In the immigration system, the privatization of transportation is slightly more recent. At their inception in 2003, U.S. Immigration and Customs Enforcement (ICE) and Customs and Border Patrol (CBP) used the U.S. Marshals Service to transfer and deport people in their custody. But the agencies quickly privatized

> **$420 million**
> Annual ICE budget for transportation and removals[4]

> **Over 175,000**
> Annual removals and transfers by ICE Air[5]

transportation to cut costs, starting with the most expensive transportation method: flights.[11] ICE kicked off the privatization of deportations when it created the ICE Flight Operations Unit, also known as ICE Air, in 2006,[12] and immediately partnered with CSI Aviation, an aviation corporation and military contractor, to charter its flights.[13]

That same year, CBP began outsourcing ground transportation services at the border to save federal agents the task,[14] awarding its first contract to G4S.[15] In 2007, private prison giant the GEO Group formed GEO Transport to meet ground transportation needs at an ICE processing center it managed.[16] And with that, privatized transportation corporations became a regular part of the immigration detention and deportation machine.

HOW MUCH MONEY IS AT STAKE?

The U.S. Marshals Service is responsible for the transportation of people within the federal prison system, moving more than 265,000 people per year.[17] States and local corrections agencies across the country also generally have their own transportation services. Though there is no concrete data regarding the number of incarcerated people state and local correctional administrators move each year, it is likely to fall into the millions. As of 2016, 26 states used privatized transportation to move people in their custody. Paid between $0.75 and $1.50 per person per mile for hundreds of thousands of trips every year, these corporations rake in the revenue.[18]

ICE outsources most of its domestic and international transportation needs. In 2021, ICE spent $419 million on transportation and removals, which included 61 charter flights, 16.3 million miles of ground transportation, and 1.2 million hours of contracted guards directly related to transportation, among other things[19]—a 49 percent increase from $282 million in 2016.[20] Additionally, ICE transports unaccompanied children using commercial airlines, about 120,000 children in 2021, more than a 700 percent increase from just over 15,000 the prior year—a number it expects to remain high.[21]

STATES CONTRACTING WITH EXTRADITION CORPORATIONS

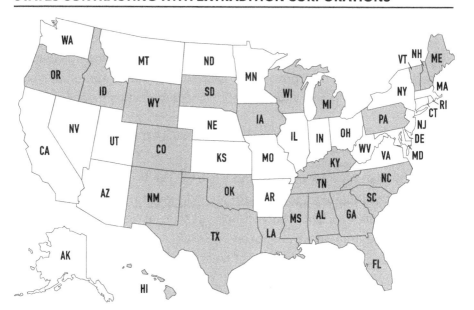

Source: The Marshall Project.

WHAT CORPORATIONS ARE INVOLVED?

Though there are many small correctional transportation corporations, just a handful control the majority of the market. There are 24 correctional transportation corporations registered with the U.S. Department of Transportation, but only seven have state extradition contracts.[22]

Prisoner Transportation Services of America (PTS) is the largest correctional transportation corporation in the country, partnering with 1,200 agencies and moving more than 30,000 people each year.[23] In the past ten years, Massachusetts alone paid PTS more than $1.3 million.[24] TransCor America, a subsidiary of private prison giant CoreCivic, contracts with over 2,000 facilities largely across the South and Southwest[25] and averages 2.2 million miles annually.[26] GEO Transport, a subsidiary of the other private prison giant, the GEO Group, maintains a fleet of 400 armed transportation officers and has transported 2.3 million people since starting up in 2007.[27] Other major players include U.S. Corrections, Inmate Services Corporation, and Security Transport Services.

In the immigration context, ICE carries out its deportations with the help of GEO Transport[28] and G4S, the world's largest security corporation,[29] on the ground and Classic Air Charter and CSI Aviation in the air.[30] Classic Air Charter was awarded the contract in 2018 when it beat out CSI Aviation, ICE's long-standing air partner since it privatized flights in 2018.[32] Classic Air Charter collected $793 million through 2023,[31] when ICE returned to its partnership with CSI Aviation. While ICE typically spends nearly $8,000 per flight hour,[33] Omni Air international, a charter responsible for higher-profile deportations, charges ICE an incredible $33,500 per flight hour.[34]

CORRECTIONS

State and local correctional administrators routinely outsource transportation services to corporations to avoid the staffing costs needed to move incarcerated people. Paid per person per mile traveled, these corporations go to great lengths, quite literally, to maximize their profits at the grave expense of their passengers and, in many cases, even their drivers.[35] This revenue model incentivizes contractors to pack as many incarcerated people as possible in vans and drive them along the most circuitous paths to their destination. Chained together, people are regularly hauled for days and, in many cases, even weeks.[36] In one instance, a passenger being extradited from Ohio to Colorado for a parole violation was subjected to a torturous 20-day journey in the back of a TransCor van, though the corporation claimed its average trip was 4 to 5 days.[37]

Worsening matters, drivers are generally paid only while on the road and expected to pay out-of-pocket for accommodations and other needs along their routes. This discourages stopping, with disastrous consequences.[38]

Source: The New York Times. *Deadly crash involving a Prisoner Transportation Services of America van and driver who fell asleep at the wheel.*

Since 2000, private transportation vans have been involved in more than 50 car accidents, many related to driver fatigue,[39] and in most cases, incarcerated passengers were shackled but not wearing seat belts.[40] In fact, many vans do not actually have working seat belts.[41] In 2009, a PTS driver fell asleep at the wheel in the wee hours of the morning, killing two guards and one incarcerated person onboard.[42]

Under these conditions, drivers ignore not only their own needs, but also the needs of their incarcerated passengers. Corporate policies allow drivers to limit food and ration water,[43] force people to urinate and defecate on themselves, and ignore medical emergencies.[44] Sweltering heat and faulty air-conditioning further exacerbate these horrific conditions.[45] In 2012, for example, a man was put on a PTS van from Florida to Ohio to answer for a warrant for failure to pay child support. The air-conditioning was not working on a particularly hot day and the extreme heat made him delusional. Rather than address his medical needs, transport guards beat him. A few hours later, the man died in the van.[46] PTS still charged the extraditing county $1,061 for his extradition.[47]

For incarcerated women and gender-nonconforming people, private transportation vans present even more concerns. Women have been forced to menstruate in McDonald's wrappers while transport guards watched.[49] Faulty safety equipment has endangered pregnant passengers and their fetuses.[50] Sexual abuse is also a constant threat. Since 2000, at least 14 women have reported being sexually assaulted, some repeatedly, by staff while caged in private transportation vans.[51] In one instance, a van driver for Extraditions International sexually assaulted a passenger under threat of death in a bathroom during a rare stop.[52] Despite alerting corporate staff at the stop, she was returned to the van with the same driver for the remainder of her four-day trip.[53] Litigation revealed that the corporation hired the guard after he was fired from his last job as a corrections officer for assaulting another incarcerated person.[54]

> My prisoners got sick and threw up on each other all the time. They passed out from heatstroke—the windows barely opened, for security reasons, and the air-conditioning was always broken. It got so hot that they would strip down to their underwear, and I would have to buy them buckets of ice and water.
>
> — Fernando Colon,
>   former employee at
>   U.S. Corrections[48]

Notwithstanding the extensive harm they cause, correctional transportation corporations have been allowed to operate with near impunity. Only one federal law regulates the correctional transportation industry: the Interstate Transportation of Dangerous Criminals Act, commonly known as Jeanna's Act.[55] Named after the original victim of a man who later escaped from a private extradition van, the bill focuses on preventing escapes.[56] The Act also requires standards be set for passenger safety but allows the

American Correctional Association and correctional transportation corporations to weigh in.[57] Investigative journalism over the past few years has sparked congressional inquiries into the industry,[58] but there has yet to be meaningful change,[59] leaving incarcerated people subject to private transportation without many protections.

JOSEPH'S STORY

In 2014, I was detained by police in New York. Though I was facing no charges or warrants in the state, a warrant came up for my arrest in Florida. So, instead of releasing me, I was booked and locked up. The Orange County Sheriff's Department in Florida was planning on extraditing me and had 21 days to do so.

Joseph Delaluz
New York

Over the coming weeks, they asked for multiple extensions. After 45 days, I was still in New York. When I was called to court again, my family and I were hopeful because we thought I would be released. We were wrong and it broke us all.

Instead, the officers who brought me to court removed my handcuffs and handed me off to two armed men in plain clothes, who put me in their own handcuffs. They gave me 15 minutes to say goodbye to my crying family and then took me to the airport. I didn't learn until later in the trip that these men were with a private transportation service.

They paraded me through the airport in shackles in front of everyone. There was a chain around my waist connected to my handcuffs. They strapped a large Taser to my right bicep that would deliver a shock if I moved more than six feet away. I had to board the plane first—in front of all the other passengers. People stared at me in shock, and parents covered their children's eyes as I passed. On the plane, my feet were also shackled. During our three-hour layover, the officers hid me in the back of a restaurant while we waited for our connection. I ate and used the bathroom in shackles too.

The whole extradition experience was humiliating. After traveling for 11 hours, we finally arrived and the transportation officers removed my shackles. They passed me off to the Orange County officers and went on with their lives. I was held for eight months before the state of Florida dropped the charges and released me. In the meantime, they lost all of my property, including the $300 I had when I was arrested, and refused to help me get back to New York. I never would have made it home if my mom hadn't bought me a Greyhound bus ticket back from Orlando.

IMMIGRATION DETENTION

Many people come to the United States to avoid war, violence, abuse, and poverty in their home countries,[60] conditions that in many cases resulted from more than a century of U.S. military–backed coups and privatized plundering.[61] Now, they are being forced back into danger and desperation with the help of large private transportation corporations.

> I thought I would take my last breath in the back of that van.
>
> — Floricel Liborio Ramos,
>   immigrant detained by ICE[62]

The immigration detention transportation industry is dominated by a handful of large conglomerates notorious for varied types of abuses across the world. Immigrants are forced onto their vans, buses, and planes, chained together in leg restraints like cattle.[63] If they refuse to board, they are Tasered, put in body bags, and thrown on.[64] Throughout their journey, they are handcuffed and often denied meals and medication and subjected to extreme conditions.[65] In the worst cases, they are beaten.[66]

In 2017, for example, according to a lawsuit filed later, four detained immigrants were transported in a windowless van operated by G4S between two immigration detention facilities. They were shackled at their wrists, waist, and ankles and denied meals and medication. Unable to withstand the sweltering heat of the van cage, they vomited and fainted. During the 24-hour trip that should have taken just five hours, their cries for help were ignored.[67]

That same year, 92 people were put on a privately chartered plane to be deported to Somalia.[68] For undisclosed reasons, the plane was grounded in Senegal for almost 23 hours, during which passengers were kept handcuffed, prevented from using the restroom, and verbally and physically assaulted.[69] The abuse was only revealed because the plane, with all its passengers, was forced to return to the United States. In most cases, accounts of abuse aboard deportation flights never make it back to the United States but instead remain abroad with deported people.

Paid per person per mile, correctional and immigration detention transportation corporations guard their bottom lines by overcrowding vans, taking extended routes, avoiding stops, and ignoring the needs of their shackled passengers. With few government protections or legal remedies available to those harmed, these corporations create some of the most inhumane conditions for incarcerated and detained people.

LEARN MORE

- "They Let a Sick Inmate Die in a Van. Now They Won't Pay His Family $650,000," *New York Times* (2019)
- "Investigation Reveals Disturbing Conditions for Prisoners Transported by For-Profit Companies," *Mother Jones* (2016)
- "Death, Abuse and Sexual Assault: The Horrific and Unregulated Private Prison Van Transport Business," Democracy Now! (2016)
- "Inside the Deadly World of Private Prisoner Transport," The Marshall Project (2016)
- "The Horrible Things I Saw Driving a Van Packed with Prisoners," The Marshall Project (2016)
- "How to Investigate Private Prisoner Transport in Your State," The Marshall Project *(2016)*

COMMUNITY CORRECTIONS

For me, you are walking money. I own your body.

— *Michelle Esquenazi, President of Empire Bail Bonds*[1]

The community corrections industry grew out of centuries of bail and pre-trial reform. Historically, families and friends served as sureties for those accused of crimes. But in the 1700s, as people became more mobile and corporal punishment, including imprisonment, began to replace fines assessed for crimes, concerns about people fleeing before trial rose. Bail became arbitrary and increasingly less affordable, creating a natural entry point for the commercial bail bond industry.[2]

Description: Government agencies contract with community corrections corporations to provide correctional supervision outside of secured facilities like prisons and jails. They include bail bond agencies, diversion programs, electronic monitoring, probation and parole supervision, residential reentry centers, and day reporting centers.

In 1898, the first commercial bail bond agency, McDonough Brothers, emerged in San Francisco, and quickly similar agencies began to pop up across the country.[4] By the 1920s, researchers were publishing studies about the inequities of the money bail system,[5] but it was not until the 1950s that the U.S. Supreme Court ruled that access to bail was fundamental to the presumption of innocence—though not an absolute right.[6] In the 1960s, disdain for commercial bail bond agencies was mounting amid reports of abuse and corruption and led to the passage of the 1966 Federal Bail Reform Act, which, among other things, introduced pretrial supervision with the intention of curbing pretrial detention.[7] By 1999, the federal system and nearly every state had created a pretrial supervised release practice.[8]

Probation evolved alongside money bail in the late 1800s as a way to divert people from prison.[9] Massachusetts was the first state to pass probation legislation in 1878, but because some considered it too lenient a sentence, it took nearly 80 years for the federal system and all states to adopt probation laws.[10] Nevertheless, by the 1970s, probation was no longer about helping people succeed in the community but about control, and a new industry emerged. Politicians seeking to be "tough-on-crime" pushed for strict new requirements for people on probation, such as mandatory reporting and drug testing.[11] Florida was the first state to outsource probation in 1975, but it was not until 1989 that legislation in Missouri and Tennessee really opened the door to for-profit probation agencies.[12] Today, Georgia, which passed legislation permitting private probation in 2000 largely due to a $75,000 industry bribe,[13] is the largest proponent of private probation, with 80 percent of its courts outsourcing probation supervision.[14]

> [I]n too many instances, the [commercial bail bond] system . . . neither guarantees security to society nor safeguards the right of the accused.
>
> — Arthur L. Beeley, *The Bail System in Chicago* (1927)[3]

In its modern-day form, parole had its start slightly later than probation in 1907 in New York, but it scaled faster.[15] As the use of parole grew, so did residential reentry centers, more commonly known as halfway houses. By 1944, the federal system and all states had adopted parole systems,[16] and halfway houses were primarily run by nonprofits and religious organizations providing substance abuse treatment, counseling, and job training.[17] By the 1980s, as racist fear-mongering and "tough-on-crime" rhetoric began discouraging early release,[18] the U.S. Congress passed sentencing reform that eliminated parole in the federal system[19] and management of halfway houses was increasingly turned over to private operators.[20] The 1994 Crime Bill then pushed states to enact "truth-in-sentencing" laws that restricted early release.[21]

As probation and parole evolved and technology advanced, so did the tools for control. Electronic monitoring was first introduced in the 1960s to monitor youths' compliance with parole conditions and reward positive behavior.[22] By the 1980s, corrections agencies were using electronic monitoring on a much wider population, claiming it allowed them to release people from overcrowded prisons while still keeping them under supervision. By charging supervision fees, corrections agencies could also use electronic monitoring to shift the cost of incarceration onto those under supervision.[23] In recent years, new technology is once again expanding the reach of community supervision as ankle monitors are slowly being replaced with smartphone apps.[24]

Since the 2008 financial crisis, government budgets have been strained and public outrage over the scope of mass incarceration has grown, leading centrist politicians and private corporations to position community corrections as the future of the criminal legal system. They refer to diversion programs, probation and parole supervision, and electronic monitoring as "alternatives to incarceration" and shift the costs of these so-called alternatives on to those subjected to them.[25] They have poured government funding into the community corrections industry through legislation like the 2018 First Step Act with enthusiastic support from the private prison industry, which has spent years preparing for this shift.[26]

HOW MUCH MONEY IS AT STAKE?

The "tough-on-crime" era did more than just cause the prison population to explode. It also grew the pretrial population and those under other forms of correctional supervision—all to the benefit of the community corrections sector. Altogether, there are now 3.7 million people, or 1 in 100 people, in the United States under correctional control through either incarceration or supervision.[27]

Overpolicing has created a steady flow of customers for the bail bond and diversion industries. About 10.7 million people are booked into jail each year.[28] Only 23 percent are released on their own recognizance.[29] Diversion programs are offered to another 8 percent by the one-third of jurisdictions offering them.[30] The overwhelming balance are held on bail. While there is no national data about how many people are bailed out by commercial bail bond agencies, in New York City alone, before bail was reformed in 2019, about 77,400 people were released on bail annually, and nearly 80 percent used a commercial bail bond agent.[31] In total, the bail bond industry issues about $15.9 billion in bonds each year, collecting $1.3 billion in premiums from people accused of crimes and their families.[32]

Between 1980 and 2018, the number of people under community supervision in the United States more than tripled from 1.3 million to a peak of 4.4 million people, before decreasing to 3.7 million by the end of 2021. Probation accounts for 2.9 million, many of whom are supervised by private probation agencies that have penetrated more than a dozen states thus far. Parole accounts for the remaining 800,000, many of whom are often subjected to the hundreds of private halfway house operators across the country.[33] The federal prison system alone has about 7,000 people at any given time in 171 such residential reentry centers, nearly all of which are run by private corporations.[34]

All those under community supervision are at risk for electronic monitoring. Between 2005 and 2022, the number of people under community supervision subjected to electronic monitoring grew over 180 percent from 53,000 to more than 150,000.[35] Electronic monitoring has also crossed over into the immigration landscape in recent years. In 2022, more than 360,000 immigrants were on electronic monitors on any given day—11 times the number of people held in detention—bringing the total number of adults under electronic monitoring in the United States to over half a million.[36] In 2022, BI, the nation's largest electronic monitoring corporation in both the criminal and immigration systems, reported that it alone had 195,000 people in its electronic monitoring program.[37] All this brings the electronic monitoring industry in North America an estimated $1.2 billion each year.[38]

WHAT CORPORATIONS ARE INVOLVED?

▪ BAIL BONDS

The bail bond industry operates in two distinct tiers: brick-and-mortar bail bond agencies and the large financial sureties that insure them, which together are estimated to rake in $1.4 to $2.4 billion every year. There are as many as 25,000 bail bond agents nationwide.[39] One of the largest is Aladdin Bail Bonds, which has over 50 locations across 8 states and collects $14 million in revenue annually.[40] The immigration bond market is dominated by Libre by Nexus.[41]

Behind bail bond agencies are more than 30 insurance corporations, but 9 insure the vast majority of the $15.9 billion in bonds posted each year.[42] Major players include Tokio Marine, Fairfax Financial Holdings, and R&Q.

▪ DIVERSION PROGRAMS

The privatized diversion industry is highly fragmented. CorrectiveSolutions is one major player that entered the private diversion market in the late 1980s and now has contracts to run programs in 100 jurisdictions across 17 states.[43] Drug treatment programs, which are largely unregulated,[44] are also offered by a patchwork of larger providers like BounceBack and regional nonprofits like Human Service Associates, a Florida-based diversion provider that was shut down in 2014 after embezzling state funds.[45] But household names like Exxon, Shell, and Walmart have also played a role in privatized diversion programs, contracting with addiction rehabilitation programs that push unpaid hard work as a treatment for addiction.[46]

■ COMMUNITY SUPERVISION

Probation and parole supervision is a fragmented and localized market with just a few major players, like Judicial Corrections Services, a subsidiary of correctional healthcare giant Wellpath,[47] and Sentinel Offender Services. Although the size of the industry is hard to determine, Sentinel was generating an estimated $5 million in revenues annually in Georgia alone—just a fraction of its business—before pulling out of the state in 2016 due to waning profitability.[48] Notably, in 2018, private prison giant CoreCivic bought in to this market with the $15.9 million acquisition of Recovery Monitoring Solutions, which manages more than 6,500 people under correctional supervision in addition to thousands in its various monitoring programs.[49]

■ ELECTRONIC MONITORING

The electronic monitoring industry is dominated by a few players. The largest, BI, has 195,000 people on its electronic and alcohol monitors across 50 states and is a subsidiary of private prison giant the GEO Group, making up 21 percent of its revenues.[50] Like its parent company, BI also plays a major role in the immigration system, with an exclusive contract with ICE to monitor undocumented immigrants.[51] Between 2021 and 2022 alone, the GEO Group's electronic monitoring business increased its annual revenue by $217 million, or 78 percent, due to an increase in the number of people on its electronic monitors in both the criminal and immigration systems.[52] The immigration bail bond agency Libre by Nexus also forces its customers to wear ankle monitors as a condition of their bail.[53] Other major electronic monitoring corporations include Attenti, SuperCom, SCRAM Systems, and Satellite Tracking of People (STOP), a subsidiary of prison telecom provider Securus.[54]

▪ RESIDENTIAL REENTRY AND DAY REPORTING CENTERS

The residential reentry (or halfway house) and day reporting market is comprised of a mix of private prison operators, nonprofits, and mom-and-pop house managers. Since 2005, the two largest private prison operators, the GEO Group and CoreCivic, have rapidly expanded into community corrections through the acquisition of halfway house operators and similar businesses in an effort to diversify their revenue streams with their private prison business under attack.[55] The GEO Group has been particularly aggressive, making over a billion dollars in acquisitions to establish its position as the nation's largest residential reentry and day reporting center operator.[56] The largest of these was the 2017 purchase of Community Education Centers for $360 million.[57] As of 2022, the GEO Group managed 42 residential reentry centers with over 10,000 beds and 87 day reporting centers, and had nearly half a million people under community supervision.[58] CoreCivic has taken similar steps, acquiring Avalon Correctional Services in 2015 for $158 million as well as other smaller regional providers.[59] As of 2022, CoreCivic managed 23 residential reentry centers with more than 5,000 beds.[60]

BAIL BONDS

After someone is arrested and charged with a crime, a judge decides whether they can await trial in the community or must do so in a jail cell. In most cases, whether someone is detained pretrial is dependent on their ability to post a bond—a refundable payment to the court meant to ensure that they will return for trial.[61] Often, judges have complete discretion in deciding whether someone is set bail and how much. The national median bail for a felony is $10,000.[62]

It is estimated that as many as 500,000 people held in local jails are there solely because of their inability to pay bail.[64] Many spend time in jail because they owe as little as $250.[65] The vast majority are Black, brown, and

Indigenous people.[66] Confinement, worsened by inhumane conditions in jails, leads many to plead guilty simply to get out on time served or avoid a trial penalty.[67] In the end, rather than offering people a path to freedom, money bail drives the growth of pre-trial detention while the number of convicted people in jail has remained roughly the same since 2000.[68] Money bail has created a two-tiered system of justice in the United States.[69] Wealthy people charged with crimes post bail and go home, but people without financial means in the same position are forced to depend on exploitative commercial bail bond agencies or remain in jail until their cases are resolved, which can take months or even years.

Faced with the prospect of spending months in jail before trial or pleading guilty, many people turn to bail bond

2
Countries that allow commercial bail bonds[70]

$15.9 billion
Bail value posted every year[71]

What has been made clear . . . is that our present attitudes toward bail are not only cruel, but really completely illogical. . . . Usually only one factor determines whether a defendant stays in jail before he comes to trial. That factor is not guilt or innocence. It is not the nature of the crime. It is not the character of the defendant. That factor is, simply, money. How much money does the defendant have?

– U.S. Attorney General Robert Kennedy (1965)[63]

agents to post their bonds in exchange for a nonrefundable premium, typically 10 percent of the bond amount. Bail bond agents also tack on hidden fees and collateral requirements and intimidate families to pay up. Families that struggle are often trapped in cycles of debt while contending with the looming threat of their loved one's incarceration if they fall behind on their payments.[72]

There has been local, state, and federal-level movement to curtail the influence of the commercial bail bond industry.[74] In recent years, advocates have organized bail funds and done crowdfunding to bail people out of jail.[75] The results of these bail outs undermine the central argument that undergirds the bail bond industry: that money bail is necessary to ensure people return to face trial.[76] One study by a charitable bail fund found that 95 percent of people bailed out returned to court though they had no personal financial obligation to.[77]

Some states have even had success in curtailing or even eliminating cash bail. For example, in 2019, New York passed legislation banning money bail for most cases involving misdemeanors and lower-level felonies and requiring the "least restrictive" conditions to ensure a person's return to court, though opponents managed to repeal the latter.[78] In 2023, advocates in Illinois passed legislation ending money bail entirely, and included strict limitations on the pretrial imposition of electronic monitoring. The industry and other opponents challenged the constitutionality of the bill all the way up to the Illinois supreme court but lost.[79]

> This [industry] is completely dominated by retired state probation people and wardens of state prisons. They created this industry for themselves.
>
> – Sheriff Howard Sills of Putnam County, Georgia[73]

In the immigration system, the situation is often worse. Detained immigrants can often post bail to be freed while awaiting their deportation proceedings, which typically last more than two years. But the median immigration bond is $7,500, far beyond what many can afford on undocumented wages. Immigration bail bond agencies, like Libre by Nexus, post immigration bonds in exchange for a 20 percent nonrefundable premium. But often, before paying the bond, Libre forces people to agree to wear an electronic monitor.[80] These monitors come with outrageous fees that can rival the cost of the bond itself: $460 activation fee, $50 device delivery fee, and $420 in monthly device lease charges. Many are unaware of these charges—hidden in contracts written in a foreign language—until they receive the bill. If people are unable to pay, Libre threatens them and their families with deportation.[81]

DIVERSION PROGRAMS

Diversion programs are another example of a so-called "alternative to incarceration" used to extort low-income people. In counties across the country, agencies have outsourced these diversion programs to private corporations that use the threat of incarceration to force people facing charges into costly and ineffective programs. Consequently, wealthy people can pay their way out of a jail sentence while people in poverty must choose between incarceration and debt.

In practice, privatized diversion is more like extortion than rehabilitation. Many diversion corporations partner with prosecutor offices, who often receive a percentage of the fees paid by participants, giving them an incentive to push them into diversion programs and inflate fees. Yet, in some jurisdictions, these corporations have entirely replaced prosecutors, going so far as to target and contact people suspected of petty crimes before they have even been charged, threatening them with prosecution unless they pay hundreds of dollars to enter their diversion program.[82]

For example, in Illinois, dozens of counties contract with two diversion corporations, CorrectiveSolutions and BounceBack. People who accept one of CorrectiveSolutions' diversion plans can end up with hundreds of dollars in fees—up to $175 for classes, $35 for administrative fees, and countless other charges for rescheduling classes or late payments. In one county, the corporation sent notices to over 3,000 people demanding they enter its program or face charges—1,342 people completed it. However, the state's attorney's office ended up charging only 11 of the hundreds of people who

··· WARNING OF CRIMINAL CHARGES ···

The State's Attorney's Office has received a complaint against you for issuing a worthless check(s) . (See list below.) Issuing a worthless check with knowledge of insufficient funds and with the intent to defraud is a criminal offense punishable with jail time and/or fines. It appears that you have ignored the demand by the recipient of the listed check(s) to make restitution. Under Illinois Statutes, this can constitute criminal intent and a Warrant for your arrest can be issued.

It is still possible to avoid a CRIMINAL CONVICTION

The Kankakee County State's Attorney's Check Enforcement Program allows check writers facing possible criminal action an opportunity to avoid that action. But you must comply with the conditions of this diversion program.

Source: ProPublica: CorrectiveSolutions letter threatening criminal charges.

never entered the program, suggesting that many people paid for diversion for charges that would never have been brought.[83]

Hundreds of private sober homes across the country also serve as diversion programs and trap people in cycles of debt and addiction.[84] In many cases, these homes offer no treatment and are nothing more than insurance scams. In Florida, for example, treatment provider Whole Recovery ordered their residents to undergo unnecessary drug tests and confiscated their keys and phones to prevent them from leaving, all the while charging thousands of dollars in fraudulent claims to their insurance firms.[85] And one Philadelphia-based rehabilitation corporation, Humble Beginnings, sent countless patients to recovery centers in Florida like Whole Recovery in exchange for kickbacks.[86] This scheme has become so commonplace that it is widely known as the "Florida Shuffle."[87]

Still, perhaps the worst diversion abuse is seen in drug rehabilitation programs that push unpaid hard work as a treatment for addiction. Investigative journalism in 2020 revealed at least 300 drug and alcohol rehabilitation facilities in 44 states that required unpaid work. In some cases, this work was contracted out to corporations; participants worked in oil refineries for

Exxon and Shell, other stocked warehouses for Walmart, and still others slaughtered chickens for Simmons Foods. These corporations paid program operators, often nonprofits, which used the funds to pay their executives' generous salaries.[90]

COMMUNITY SUPERVISION

Currently, almost 70 percent of adults under the control of the criminal legal system are not incarcerated, but under community supervision.[91] While not confined to a carceral cell, people under community supervision often have their travel rights restricted and remain under the ever-present threat of incarceration and scrutiny of the government.

Pretrial supervision, probation, and parole function similarly but as different systems. Pretrial supervision is imposed on people facing charges based on their "suitability" to

3.7 million
Adults on probation or parole[88]

25%
Prison admissions for technical violations of probation or parole[89]

remain free before trial.[92] Probation is a sentence that allows people who are convicted of a crime to avoid incarceration if they agree to a series of conditions, fines, and fees.[93] The average person on probation has 15 conditions placed on their freedom.[94] Parole offers release from prison or jail after a person has served a minimum sentence at the cost of similarly onerous conditions.[95]

The conditions imposed by these various community supervision regimes are invasive and nearly impossible to meet, setting people up for rearrest for technical violations, not new crimes. This is particularly true in Black, brown, and Indigenous communities that are subjected to overpolicing and for people with low incomes whose lack of resources make certain requirements particularly hard to meet.[96]

As a result, community supervision has created a revolving door to our prisons and jails, sending people behind bars for trivial technical violations like showing up late to an appointment. There are nearly 150,000 prison admissions each year for technical violations—a staggering 25 percent of admissions nationwide. In some states, the number is even higher. For instance, in Kentucky, technical violations account for 63 percent of prison admissions and 45 percent of the prison population on any given day.[98]

> It is my sense that the imposition and enforcement of probation conditions has become more punitive in nature, and I think much of that may be attributed to the types of persons we are attracting to the probation profession.
>
> – Dan Beto, former Texas probation director[97]

In many states, probation and parole are increasingly outsourced to private corporations that boldly advertise shifting government costs onto supervisees to win contracts. Under this model, courts pay nothing, and individuals are required to pay out of pocket for all costs associated with their probation or parole. For example, Providence Community Corrections (PCC) charges people supervision fees that range from $35 to $44 per month.[99] It adds fees for services such as drug testing or mandatory classes that are compelled as conditions of probation or parole. In one case, PCC charged a woman surviving on disability payments $20 per randomized drug test though her original offense was not drug related.[100] For those with low incomes who are disproportionately targeted by the criminal legal system, even seemingly low costs are extremely burdensome and can snowball exponentially over time. People who cannot afford to pay these fees are often incarcerated.[101]

ELECTRONIC MONITORING

Electronic monitoring is used to incarcerate people in their own homes or restrict their movement to a particular geographic area, making life in the community nearly as restrictive as life in a prison. And like privatized supervision, electronic monitoring is increasingly funded by the people subjected to it.

Electronic monitoring is often deceptively portrayed as a tool to free people from incarceration. However, in reality, electronic monitoring has merely expanded the number of people under correctional control, transformed private spaces into carceral structures, and shifted correctional costs from the government onto individuals, disproportionately Black, brown, and Indigenous people.[103] These costs include hefty setup fees of up to $200 and daily monitoring fees that can reach $40, meaning that the cost of electronic monitoring can easily exceed the monthly cost of rent for many. And if a device is damaged, those on supervision can be charged as much as $1,200 to replace it. When people fall behind on their payments, they can be punished with home confinement, if not already subjected to it, until they can come up with the money—a nearly impossible task if they cannot leave their houses.[104]

Although people under supervision are often required to work, the very presence of an electronic monitor can make it difficult to find or keep a job. These devices carry a stigma for the

> They really don't care what you do, as long as you hand over your money. It's like paying protection to the Mafia.
>
> — Anonymous 20-year-old student under supervision by Judicial Correctional Services[102]

> No one wants to give you a job . . . because employers see the monitor and they don't like it. They don't like it at all.
>
> — Undocumented woman required to wear an ankle monitor by ICE[105]

people who wear them, often leading co-workers and supervisors to pass judgment. One study revealed that 22 percent of people forced to wear an ankle monitor had been terminated from a job because of it.[106] They also make it difficult for people working physical labor jobs like construction to wear necessary protective gear.[107]

But electronic monitors jeopardize more than one's ability to work; they also threaten the health and well-being of those wearing them and that of their families. Monitors prevent people from accessing necessary care and can even present new health hazards. For example, an electronic monitor can jeopardize one's participation in an anonymous substance abuse treatment program, prevent a person from appropriately caring for themselves or family in emergencies, or subject a person to discrimination by healthcare providers. These devices also exact a psychological toll. For instance, many have gone through the humiliating experience of charging a monitor in public given their limited battery life.[108]

Newer devices are even more invasive. Agencies around the country increasingly require people convicted of driving under the influence to wear devices that measure the blood alcohol level in their perspiration. These alcohol monitors alert law enforcement if they detect that someone has consumed alcohol, but they are prone to false positives that are triggered by everyday products like lotion or cologne.[109] The spread of smartphones has created yet another frontier for electronic monitoring. Invasive applications like Guardian by Telmate and Touchpoint by SCRAM allow law enforcement to live-monitor people through their cellphones, putting the freedom of many at risk.[110] Other smartphone applications like Promise claim to be change agents that offer people reminders about court dates, databases of service referrals, and online courses, all on the government's dime,[111] but are still paid per person, giving it little incentive to help people leave the system.[112] Far from being tools for decarceration, as their developers claim, these applications are just 21st-century shackles.[113]

SARAH'S STORY

The day my baby was born was supposed to be the happiest day of my life. Instead, I spent the day defending my right to motherhood and right to care. That's when I came to understand that the stigma associated with wearing an ankle monitor can kill you. It can also steal your child.

Sarah Faye Hanna
Texas

When I returned home from the hospital after giving birth, I got a call from Child Protective Services informing me that a case manager was coming to do a home inspection to make sure my baby was safe. Apparently, a nurse had called the agency after she saw my ankle monitor. I was shocked and hurt because I straightened out my life for my baby.

My ankle monitor is a probation requirement I've had since I was released from jail, then rehab. I can only leave my house between 7 a.m. and 7 p.m., and when I'm home, I have to be tethered to the wall for two hours every day to charge my monitor. Imagine tending to a crying baby attached to a wall or worrying about being arrested for taking your baby to the emergency room?

For all this trouble, my husband and I have to pay $300 per month on top of the $250 per month to simply be on probation. When I'm late on a payment, the monitoring company calls and threatens to have me jailed again. They provide no other support. They didn't even tell me when my ankle monitor was going to be removed—but it was finally taken off just a few weeks ago.

Electronic monitoring has caused me physical, psychological, and financial hurdles since the day I came home, not a pathway to recovery and reentry. People claim it's an alternative to incarceration, but I served my sentence. I'm on probation—I still have to report and test for drugs. It's not replacing anything.

RESIDENTIAL REENTRY AND DAY REPORTING CENTERS

Residential reentry centers, or halfway houses, are intended to transition people successfully from correctional settings to free society by providing a supportive structure. However, they often require people to navigate confusing and often contradictory requirements while living in conditions that can resemble the worst prisons and jails.[114]

In most cases, halfway house residents are required to find employment if not enrolled in a program, but they do not often get to keep what they earn. In the federal system, for instance, halfway houses can take up to 25 percent of residents' wages, preventing them from becoming financially independent.[116] Unsurprisingly, these houses generate huge profits for their operators but few benefits for the people in them. In Pennsylvania, for example, the state spends $110 million annually on private halfway houses, but in 2013, a study revealed that these halfway houses had worse recidivism rates among their residents than people who are released directly from state prisons onto the street.[117]

> The living conditions were worse than prison. When it rained, the halfway house staff would break out a dozen five-gallon buckets. . . . We had two bathrooms for over 70 guys.
>
> — Shon Hopwood, Georgetown Law professor and former private halfway house resident[115]

In New Jersey, private halfway houses cut costs with disastrous consequences. After officials decided to move thousands of people incarcerated in state prisons to private halfway houses in the late 1990s,[118] the state signed a contract with Community Education Centers (CEC) worth $71 million per year. Although CEC executives paid themselves millions in salaries and bonuses, the conditions in their facilities were abysmal. Residents reported widespread sexual assault, rampant drug use, and unqualified staff,[119] leading many to run away.[120] A series of investigations revealed that then–New Jersey governor Chris Christie had close ties with top executives of the corporation, and many were also paid as state advisers.[121] Despite all these troubles, the GEO Group, which acquired CEC in 2017 for $360 million, continues to proclaim that its facilities in New Jersey are a national model.[122]

Private day reporting centers also suffer from many of the same issues, though they do not have a residential component. Corporations in the space typically sign contracts with state agencies that pay per diem rates for each person in their programs. Unsurprisingly, this model creates a strong incentive to create abusive program requirements that keep people enrolled perpetually. In California, for example, the GEO Group's programs—often focused on behavioral thinking rather than education or vocational training—require people to take courses at the center for 12 hours a day, 7 days a week.[123]

Support has grown across the political spectrum for community-based restorative justice and substance abuse treatment. But with the criminal legal system still in control, the increasing involvement of private corporations has simply given rise to a treatment industry incentivized to keep people in the system.[124] These corporations have lobbied to increase the use of residential reentry and day reporting centers.[125] In 2018, they successfully secured increased funding for these community corrections solutions in the federal First Step Act.[126]

Bail bond agencies reinforce a system that allows wealthy people to pay their way out of jail and working-class people—disproportionately Black, brown, and Indigenous—to suffer behind bars. While they claim to perform a public service, their history of abuse and lobbying for punitive laws reveals their mere parasitic dependency on racist and classist policing and policies. Fortunately, communities around the country are standing up to this powerful industry. The end of the money bail system is on the horizon, but corporate lobbyists are vehemently fighting back.

The community supervision industry has corporate lobbyists at work too. Private prison operators drafted the blueprint for mass incarceration and lobbied for its implementation. Now, as they watch their business model come under attack by culture change, they profess support for reforms that would decrease the carceral population and likely their bottom line. However, in the background, they have spent millions lobbying to make community corrections the solution of the future and preparing for the shift. But the people who created our carceral crisis cannot be trusted to solve it.

For that same reason, the rise of surveillance technology should be viewed with serious suspicion, not welcomed with open arms. Despite the industry's attempt to portray dystopian technology like electronic monitoring as an "alternative to incarceration," community surveillance will, at best, replace physical shackles with digital ones fueled by the same racist systems of financial exploitation and, at worst, widen and deepen the net cast by the criminal legal system. And these innovations will not save taxpayer money; they will merely impose a hidden regressive tax on overpoliced Black, brown, and Indigenous communities and those in poverty. We must reevaluate these so-called solutions and dream of new ones if we are to truly free people.

LEARN MORE

- *People on Electronic Monitoring*, Vera Institute of Justice (2024)
- *Understanding E-Carceration*, James Kilgore (2022)
- Challenging E-Carceration Project, Media Justice and Urbana-Champaign Independent Media Center
- "Street-Level Surveillance," Electronic Frontier Foundation
- *Prison by Any Other Name: The Harmful Consequences of Popular Reforms*, Maya Schenwar and Victoria Law (2020)
- "Many of Miami's Immigrants Wear Ankle Monitors. Will Technology Betray Them?" *Miami Herald* (2019)
- "Digital Jail: How Electronic Monitoring Drives Defendants into Debt," *New York Times* (2019)

- "How a Criminal Justice Reform Became an Enrichment Scheme," *Politico* (2019)

- "In Oklahoma, Private Companies Run Pretrial Services, Driving People into Debt," The Appeal (2019)

- *Confined and Costly: How Supervision Violations Are Filling Prisons and Burdening Budgets*, Council of State Governments Justice Center (2019)

- *Fact Sheet: Electronic Monitoring Devices as Alternatives to Detention*, National Immigration Forum (2019)

- *No More Shackles*, Media Justice (2018, 2019)

- "Electronic Monitors: How Companies Dream of Locking Us in Our Homes," *In These Times* (2018)

- *Set Up to Fail: The Impact of Offender-Funded Private Probation on the Poor*, Human Rights Watch (2018)

- "From Cages to the Community: Prison Profiteers and the Treatment Industrial Complex," *Prison Legal News* (2018)

- *Community Cages: Profitizing Community Corrections and Alternatives to Incarceration*, American Friends Service Committee (2016)

CONCLUSION

That was a lot. And sadly, it still is far from everything that could be said about the prison industry. As impacted communities know too well, there are millions of examples of every harm that was enumerated and there are still countless others that went unmentioned. There are also many more actors who inflict this harm in using the carceral system to build their wealth and livelihood—and not just in the private sector, but also in government, unions, and nonprofit organizations.

In fact, even unknowingly, many of us are implicated. Our tax dollars are funding the prison industry and the harm it causes. Our personal savings sit with banks that provide billions in financing to it. The financial aid that helps us make tuition payments is, at times, supplied by the prison industry. Our pension funds and retirement accounts are invested in it—in the corporations covered here and a myriad of others. Even our favorite sports teams and cultural institutions are owned and supported by executives that build their wealth off of the people suffering in our carceral system.

The prison industry is ubiquitous in our lives. For many, this is entirely news. For those in impacted communities, it is not—it is just a new articulation of painfully familiar experiences. But whether you picked up new information or just a new perspective, we encourage you to reflect on what you learned, share it with your networks, and find time for meaningful discussion.

Understanding our oppressive system is just the first step in moving toward the abolition of our carceral system. The work is still ahead of us. We hope you will channel what rage or frustration this book conjured up toward creating change in your community, however big or small. A seem-ingly impossible task, we must do our best to carry forward the torch of our brave and brilliant elders and ancestors. With their enduring guidance, we can dismantle the prison industry—root out its racist, classist, and patriar-chal core—and build in its place a truly liberated world.

NOTES

Architecture + Construction

1. "San Mateo County Maple Street Correctional Center," HOK, n.d., www.hok.com/projects.

2. Zach Chouteau, "U.S. Census Bureau Report Shows Dip in Government Correctional Construction," *Correctional News*, July 18, 2018, correctionalnews.com.

3. Wendy Sawyer and Peter Wagner, "Mass Incarceration: The Whole Pie 2023," Prison Policy Initiative, March 2023, www.prisonpolicy.org. This number includes state prisons, federal prisons, juvenile correctional facilities, local jails, immigration detention facilities, and Indian Country jails.

4. Chris Mai, Mikelina Belaineh, Ram Subramanian, and Jacob Kang-Brown, "Broken Ground: Why America Keeps Building More Jails and What It Can Do Instead," Vera Institute of Justice, November 2019, www.vera.org/downloads/publications.

5. Zhen Zeng, "Jail Inmates in 2021," Bureau of Justice Statistics, Office of Justice Programs, U.S. Dept. of Justice, December 2022, https://bjs.ojp.gov/sites.

6. German Lopez, "Nixon Official: Real Reason for the Drug War Was to Criminalize Black People and Hippies," *Vox*, March 23, 2016, www.vox.com.

7. Emily Posner, "Public Comment on Behalf of Abolitionist Law Center," Abolitionist Law Center, October 28, 2017, fighttoxicprisons.files.wordpress.com/2017/11/alc-comments.

8. Hillary Shelton and Inimani Chettiar, "Want to Shrink Prisons? Stop Subsidizing Them," *Washington Post*, November 11, 2016, www.washingtonpost.com/news/in-theory.

9. Keely Herring, "Was a Prison Built Every 10 Days to House a Fast-Growing Population of Nonviolent Inmates?" *PolitiFact*, July 31, 2015, www.politifact.com/factchecks.

10. John Eason, "Why Prison Building Will Continue Booming in Rural America," *The Conversation*, March 12, 2017, theconversation.com; Jon Schuppe, "Does America Need Another Prison?" *NBC News*, March 22, 2018, www.nbcnews.com/specials/kentucky-prison-coal-countr/.

11. Chouteau, "U.S. Census Bureau Report Shows Dip in Government Correctional Construction."

12. "Prison and Jail Construction Report Gives Snapshot of Industry," *Correctional News*, January 3, 2013, correctionalnews.com.

13. Ibid.

14. Mai, et al., "Broken Ground: Why America Keeps Building More Jails and What It Can Do Instead."

15. "Top 10 Major Upcoming Courthouse and Jail and Prison Construction Projects, U.S.—May 2019," ConstructConnect, May 16, 2019, canada.constructconnect.com/joc/news/economic.

16. Matthew Haag, "4 Jails in 5 Boroughs: The $8.7 Billion Puzzle Over How to Close Rikers," *New York Times*, September 4, 2019; Mark Buckshon, "NYC Selects Six Design-Build Teams for $8.2 Billion Borough-based Jails to Replace Rikers Island," *New York Construction Report*, January 6, 2022, www.newyorkconstructionreport.com.

17. "Justice: Innovating Justice Architecture," HDR Inc., n.d., www.hdrinc.com/markets/justice.

18. "Justice," HOK, n.d., www.hok.com/projects/market/justice.

19. IBISWorld, report unavailable.

20. "The Construction Companies: Hochtief-Vinci," Corporate Watch, February 11, 2013, corporatewatch.org; Robert Gellately, *The Oxford Illustrated History of the Third Reich* (Oxford: Oxford University Press, 2018).

21. James Kilgore, "Monitors to Phones to Meals: These 5 Corporations Are Quietly Making Billions off Incarceration," *Occupy*, February 13, 2015, www.occupy.com.

22. "Correctional Facilities," Gilbane Building Company, n.d., www.gilbaneco.com/markets/overview-2/criminal-justice/correctional-facilities.

23. "Government + Justice," Hensel Phelps, n.d., www.henselphelps.com/industry/government-justice.

24. "Correctional & Judicial," Clark Construction, n.d., www.clarkconstruction.com/our-work/sector/correctional-judicial.

25. Lauren Gill, "LA County Supervisors to Vote on Canceling Jail Contract," The Appeal, August 8, 2019, theappeal.org.

26. Ruth Delaney, Ram Subramanian, Alison Shames, and Nicholas Turner, "Reimagining Prison Web Report," Vera Institute of Justice, October 2018, www.vera.org.

27. Ibid.

28. Stephanie Wykstra, "The Case Against Solitary Confinement," *Vox*, April 17, 2019.

29. "Calculating Torture," Solitary Watch and Unlock the Box Campaign, May 2023, solitary-watch.org/calculating-torture.

30. Jean Casella and Sal Rodriguez, "What Is Solitary Confinement?." *The Guardian*, April 27, 2016, www.theguardian.com/world; Joshua Manson, "How Many People Are in Solitary Confinement Today?" Solitary Watch, January 4, 2019, solitarywatch.org; "Calculating Torture," Solitary Watch and Unlock the Box Campaign.

31. For example, Shauneen Miranda, "The Angola 3's Albert Woodfox, Who Survived Decades of Solitary Confinement, Dies," NPR, August 5, 2022, www.npr.org.

32. "United States: Prolonged Solitary Confinement Amounts to Psychological Torture, Says UN expert," United Nations Human Rights Office of the High Commissioner, February 28, 2020, www.ohchr.org; Wykstra, "The Case Against Solitary Confinement"; Michael Sorkin, "Drawing the Line: Architects and Prisons," *The Nation*, August 27, 2013, www.thenation.com.

33. "United States: Prolonged Solitary Confinement Amounts to Psychological Torture, says UN expert," United Nations Humans Rights Office of the High Commissioner.

34. Rachael Slade, "Is There Such a Thing as 'Good' Prison Design?" *Architectural Digest*, April 30, 2018, www.architecturaldigest.com.

35. David N. Pellow, Jasmine Vazin, Harrison Ashby, Michaela A. Austin, Sage Kime, Shannon Mcalpine, and Yue (Rachel) Shen, "Environmental Injustice Behind Bars: Toxic Imprisonment in America," September 2018, gejp.es.ucsb.edu.

36. Daniel Moattar, "U.S. Scraps Prison Plan for Abandoned Coal Mine," *DW*, June 19, 2019, www.dw.com.

37. Michael Waters, "How Prisons Are Poisoning Their Inmates," *The Outline*, July 23, 2018, theoutline.com/post/5410/toxic-prisons-fayette-tacoma-contaminated.

38. Pellow, et al., "Environmental Injustice Behind Bars: Toxic Imprisonment in America."

39. Panagioti Tsolkas, "Florida County Votes Against New Jail on Former EPA Superfund Site, Opts to Stay in Flood Zone," *Prison Legal News*, February 8, 2017, www.prisonlegalnews.org.

40. Eli Hager, "Hal Rogers Wants a Prison in Letcher County. The Trump Administration Has Doubts," *Lexington Herald Leader*, November 8, 2017, www.kentucky.com.

41. Sam Adams, "Feds, Anti-Prison Forces Reach Pact to Dismiss Lawsuit," *Mountain Eagle*, August 21, 2019, www.themountaineagle.com.

42. Candice Bernd, Zoe Loftus-Farren, and Maureen Nandini Mitra, "America's Toxic Prisons: The Environmental Injustices of Mass Incarceration," *Earth Island Journal*, earthisland.org/journal.

43. Ibid.

44. Lauren McGaughy, "Texas' Prison Heat Bill a 'Cop Out' Because It No Longer Forces Units to Lower Temps, Advocates Say," *Dallas Morning News*, August 23, 2019, www.dallasnews.com/news/politics.

45. Wes Venteicher, "Bacteria That Killed California Inmate Found to Be Widespread in Stockton Prison," *Sacramento Bee*, April 17, 2019, www.sacbee.com/news/politics-government/the-state-worker/article.

46. Francisco Aviles Pino, "Los Angeles County Votes to Stop Construction of New Jail-Like Facility, Adding Momentum to National Abolition Movement," *The Intercept*, August 22, 2019, theintercept.com.

47. Mai, et al., "Broken Ground: Why America Keeps Building More Jails and What It Can Do Instead."

48. "New Utah State Correctional Facility," Layton Construction, n.d., www.laytonconstruction.com/portfolio/justice.

49. Nate Carlisle, "New Utah prison Is Running About 20% Over Budget, 18 months Behind Schedule, and Will Hold Fewer Inmates than Planned," *Salt Lake Tribune*, Wednesday, August 16, 2017, www.sltrib.com/news/politics. Photo by Scott Sommerdorf.

50. Mathew Burciaga, "'Professional Negligence' Led to Delays on Northern Branch Jail Project, County Lawsuit Claims," *Lompoc Record*, August 6, 2019, lompocrecord.com/news/local/crime-and-courtsl.

51. "Juvenile Hall Replacement Project," Humboldt County, n.d., humboldtgov.org; Shomik Mukherjee, "Juvenile Hall Construction Stalled as Humboldt County Talks New Terms," *Times-Standard*, October 5, 2019, www.times-standard.com.

52. Raphael Sperry, "Is 'Justice Architecture' Just?" *Aggregate*, March 6, 2015, www.we-aggregate.org.

Operations + Management

1. Erik Larson, "Captive Company," *Inc.*, June 1, 1988, www.inc.com.

2. Kelsey Oliver, "Incarceration Nation: Prison Overcrowding and Government Attitudes Will Benefit the Industry," *IBISWorld*, December 2018.

3. E. Ann Carson, "Prisoners in 2021," Bureau of Justice Statistics, Office of Justice Programs, U.S. Dept. of Justice, December 2022, bjs.ojp.gov.

4. Eunice Cho, "Unchecked Growth: Private Prison Corporations and Immigration Detention, Three Years into the Biden Administration," ACLU, August 7, 2023, www.aclu.org/news.

5. Cody Mason, "Too Good to Be True: Private Prisons in America," The Sentencing Project, 2012, sentencingproject.org.

6. "2018 ESG Report," CoreCivic, 2018, www.corecivic.com; Shane Bauer, *American Prison: A Reporter's Undercover Journey into the Business of Punishment* (New York: Penguin Books, 2019), p. 21.

7. Shane Bauer, "Today It Locks up Immigrants. But CoreCivic's Roots Lie in the Brutal Past of America's Prisons," *Mother Jones*, October 1, 2018, www.motherjones.com.

8. Ibid.

9. Michael Rigby, "Wackenhut Changes Name to Geo Group, Politics Remain the Same," *Prison Legal News*, June 15, 2004, www.prisonlegalnews.org/news; "GEO Group History Timeline," The GEO Group, n.d., www.geogroup.com.

10. Brigette Sarabi and Edwin Bender, "The Prison Payoff: The Role of Politics and Private Prisons in the Incarceration Boom," Western Prison Project, November 2000, www.prisonpolicy.org.

11. Rebecca Cooper, et al., "Hidden Corporate Profits in the U.S. Prison System: The Unorthodox Policy-Making of the American Legislative Exchange Council," *Contemporary Justice Review* 19, no. 3 (June 18, 2016), p. 380–400, https://doi.org/10.1080/10282580.2016.1185949.

12. Mike Elk and Bob Sloan, "The Hidden History of ALEC and Prison Labor," *The Nation*, August 1, 2011, www.thenation.com; "Ending the School-to-Prison Pipeline: Hearing Before

the Subcommittee on Constitution, Civil Rights and Human Rights of the Committee on the Judiciary," United States Senate, One Hundred Twelfth Congress, Second Session, 2012, www .govinfo.gov.

13. Lauren-Brooke Eisen, *Inside Private Prisons: An American Dilemma in the Age of Mass Incarceration* (New York: Columbia University Press, 2019), p. 24.

14. Elk and Sloan, "The Hidden History of ALEC and Prison Labor."

15. "Profiting from Public Dollars: How ALEC and Its Members Promote Privatization of Government Services and Assets," *In the Public Interest*, 2012, www.inthepublicinterest.org.

16. Elk and Sloan, "The Hidden History of ALEC and Prison Labor."

17. Eisen, *Inside Private Prisons*, p. 25.

18. Philip Mattera, Mafruza Khan, and Stephen Nathan, "Corrections Corporation of America: A Critical Look at Its First Twenty Years," Prison Policy Initiative, May 2003, www.prisonpolicy .org/scans/grassrootsleadership; Dan Pens, "Prison Realty/CCA Verges on Bankruptcy," *Prison Legal News*, July 15, 2000, www.prisonlegalnews.org.

19. "Prison Realty Announces Restructuring Led by Fortress and Blackstone Investor Group," CoreCivic, December 27, 1999, ir.corecivic.com.

20. "Fatal Mismanagement at Ohio CCA Prison," *Prison Legal News*, June 15, 1998, www .prisonlegalnews.org.

21. Mattera, et al., "Corrections Corporation"; Pens, "Prison Realty/CCA."

22. Eisen, *Inside Private Prisons*, p. 147.

23. Mattera, et al., "Corrections Corporation"; Pens, "Prison Realty/CCA."

24. Eisen, *Inside Private Prisons*, p. 148.

25. Ibid.

26. Ibid.

27. Eileen Sullivan, "Obama Administration to End Use of Private Prisons," *PBS NewsHour*, August 18, 2016, www.pbs.org/newshour/nation.

28. "Statement by Secretary Jeh C. Johnson on Establishing a Review of Privatized Immigration Detention," Department of Homeland Security, August 29, 2016, www.dhs.gov/news.

29. Hanna Kozlowska, "The American Private Prison Industry Has Scored Another Big Win with the U.S. Government," *Quartz*, December 1, 2016, qz.com.

30. Jeff Sommer, "Trump's Win Gives Stocks in Private Prison Companies a Reprieve," *New York Times*, December 3, 2016, www.nytimes.com.

31. "Private Prison Company The GEO Group's Pay to Play," Campaign Legal Center, December 8, 2017, campaignlegal.org/cases-actions.

32. Sharita Gruberg, "Trump's Executive Order Rewards Private Prison Campaign Donors," Center for American Progress, June 28, 2018, www.americanprogress.org/issues/immigration /news.

33. Amy Brittain and Drew Harwell, "Private-Prison Giant, Resurgent in Trump Era, Gathers at President's Resort," *Washington Post*, October 25, 2017, www.washingtonpost.com/politics.

34. Charles P. Pierce, "It Sounds Like Jeff Sessions Is Planning on Locking a Lot of People Up," *Esquire*, January 30, 2018, www.esquire.com/news-politics.

35. "Private Prison Company the GEO Group's Pay to Play."

36. Liliana Segura, "The First Step Act Could Be a Big Gift to CoreCivic and the Private Prison Industry," *The Intercept*, December 22, 2018, theintercept.com.

37. Lauren-Brooke Eisen, "Breaking Down Biden's Order to Eliminate DOJ's Private Prisons Contracts," Brennan Center for Justice, August 27, 2021, www.brennancenter.org/our-work/research-reports.

38. Cho, "Unchecked Growth."

39. "CoreCivic 2022 Annual Report," CoreCivic, February 2023, ir.corecivic.com; "The GEO Group 2022 Annual Report," the GEO Group, February 2023, investors.geogroup.com.

40. Carson, "Prisoners in 2021."

41. "Immigration Detention: An American Business," Worth Rises, June 2018, worthrises.org/immigration.

42. Oliver, "Incarceration Nation," p. 3.

43. Eric Schlosser, "The Prison-Industrial Complex (Part Two)," *The Atlantic*, September 1997, www.theatlantic.com.

44. "CoreCivic Supplemental Financial Information for the Quarter Ended December 31, 2022," CoreCivic, February 8, 2023, ir.corecivic.com; "The GEO Group 2022 Annual Report."

45. Christopher Zoukis, "From Cages to the Community: Prison Profiteers and the Treatment Industrial Complex," *Prison Legal News*, March 6, 2018, www.prisonlegalnews.org/news.

46. Oliver, "Incarceration Nation," p. 27.

47. Kara Gotsch and Vinay Basti, "Capitalizing on Mass Incarceration U.S. Growth in Private Prisons," The Sentencing Project, July 2018, www.sentencingproject.org.

48. "CoreCivic 2022 Annual Report."

49. Ibid.

50. "The Banks That Finance Private Prison Companies," *In the Public Interest*, November 2016, www.inthepublicinterest.org.

51. Alvarado, et al., "These People Are Profitable."

52. "The GEO Group 2019 Annual Report."

53. Dealbook, "GEO to Buy Cornell Companies for $685 Million," *New York Times*, April 19, 2010, archive.nytimes.com/dealbook.nytimes.com.

54. "The Banks That Finance Private Prison Companies."

55. Oliver, "Incarceration Nation," p. 27.

56. "Newsroom," MTC, n.d., www.mtctrains.com/about-us/newsroom.

57. "The GEO Group 2022 Annual Report"; "Our Location," The GEO Group, n.d., www .geogroup.com/Locations.

58. "CoreCivic 2022 Annual Report."

59. Oliver, "Incarceration Nation."

60. "LaSalle Southwest Corrections," LaSalle Southwest Corrections, n.d.,www .lasallecorrections.com.

61. "DHS Awards AGS Contract to Support Krome Detention Center," Akima Global Services, May 13, 2014, www.akimaglobalservices.com.

62. Helen Warrell, "Future of Problem Prisons in Question as G4S Contract Is Stripped," *Financial Times*, April 3, 2019, www.ft.com.

63. "Sodexo," American Friends Service Committee, 2018, investigate.afsc.org.

64. Ibid.

65. "Buying Influence: How Private Prison Companies Expand Their Control of America's Criminal Justice System," *In the Public Interest*, October 2016, www.inthepublicinterest.org.

66. "Board of Directors," The GEO Group, n.d., www.geogroup.com/board_of_directors.

67. Bauer, *American Prison*, p. 48.

68. Ibid., p. 67.

69. Ibid., p. 68.

70. Ibid., p. 48.

71. Oliver, "Incarceration Nation," p. 20; Mason, "Too Good to Be True."

72. Benjamin Hart, "Shane Bauer Talks Working Undercover at a Private Prison," *New York Magazine*, September 21, 2018, /nymag.com/intelligencer.

73. David Reutter, "CoreCivic Prison in Tennessee Plagued with Problems," *Prison Legal News*, January 31, 2018, www.prisonlegalnews.org/news.

74. Bauer, *American Prison*, p. 150.

75. Nicole Flatow, "Private Prison Firm to Pay Idaho $1 Million for False Records That Left Key Security Posts Vacant," *Think Progress*, February 6, 2014, thinkprogress.org.

76. "Review of the Federal Bureau of Prisons' Monitoring of Contract Prisons," Office of the Inspector General, U.S. Department of Justice, August 2016, oig.justice.gov/reports; Ray Downs, "DOJ Audit Says GEO Group Misspent $3 Million in Troubled Prison," *New Times Broward-Palm Beach*, April 27, 2015, www.browardpalmbeach.com/news.

77. Kendall Downing, "Low Pay Contributes to Staffing Problems at Mississippi Prisons," WLOX, August 22, 2019, www.wlox.com.

78. Joseph Neff and Alysia Santo, "Mississippi Prison Killings: Five Factors Behind the Deadly Violence," The Marshall Project, January 8, 2020, www.themarshallproject.org.

79. Ibid.

80. Joseph Neff and Alyssia Santo, "What Happened When This Prison Couldn't Hire Enough Guards? It Put Gangs in Charge," *USA Today*, June 25, 2019, www.usatoday.com.

81. Arielle Dreher, "Private Prison Trial Starts Today Over Alleged Squalor, Rats, Deaths," *Jackson Free Press*, March 5, 2018, www.jacksonfreepress.com.

82. Robert Kahn, "Refugees Say Private Prison Guards Savaged Them," *Courthouse News*, May 30, 2018, www.courthousenews.com.

83. Madison Pauly, "In 3 Months, 3 Immigrants Have Died at This Private Detention Center," *Mother Jones*, June 23, 2017, www.motherjones.com; Adry Torres, "Moment female guard and her colleague attack and pepper-spray eight ICE detainees who were on a 72-HOUR hunger strike protesting 'appalling' conditions at California detention center," *Daily Mail*, February 6, 2020, www.dailymail.co.uk.

84. Rebecca Plevin, "How a Private Prison Giant Has Continued to Thrive in a State That Wants It Out," *Desert Sun*, January 25, 2020, www.desertsun.com.

85. Lora Adams, "State and Local Governments Opt Out of Immigrant Detention," Center for American Progress, July 25, 2019, www.americanprogress.org; David Rubenstein and Prathpeepan Gulasekaram, "Privatized Detention and Immigration Federalism," *Stanford Law Review*, March 11, 2019, www.stanfordlawreview.org.

86. "TRAC Immigration Data," Syracuse University, 2016, trac.syr.edu/immigration/reports.

87. Sarah Macaraeg, "Inside a Private Prison's $150M Deal to Detain Immigrants in New Mexico," *New Mexico in Depth*, October 26, 2017, nmindepth.com.

88. Loren Collingwood, Jason L. Morin, and Stephen Omar El-Khatib, "Expanding Carceral Markets: Detention Facilities, ICE Contracts, and the Financial Interests of Punitive Immigration Policy," *Race and Social Problems* 10, no. 4 (July 2, 2018), p. 275–92, doi.org.

89. "CCA Board of Directors Authorizes REIT Conversion," CoreCivic, February 7, 2013, ir .corecivic.com/news-releases; "The GEO Group Completes Company Restructuring and Health Care Divestiture; Began Operating in Compliance with REIT Rules Effective January 1, 2013," *BusinessWire*, January 2, 2013, www.businesswire.com/news.

90. "An Examination of Private Financing for Correctional and Immigration Detention Facilities," *In the Public Interest*, June 2018, www.inthepublicinterest.org.

91. Ibid.

92. "The Banks Still Financing Private Prisons," Center for Popular Democracy, May 3, 2019, populardemocracy.org/blog.

93. "Fitch Downgrades CoreCivic's IDR to 'BB-'; Negative Outlook," Fitch Ratings, April 21, 2020, www.fitchratings.com/research/non-bank-financial-institutions.

94. Catherine Kim, "A Growing Number of States Are Banning Private Prisons," *Vox*, December 2019, www.vox.com.

95. Sue Sturgis, "Private Prisons Form Alliance, Hire Flack from pro-Trump Attack Group," *Facing South*, November 8, 2019, www.facingsouth.org.

96. "Three Private Prison Firms Form Advocacy Group," *Crime Report*, October 28, 2019, thecrimereport.org/.

97. Aziza Kasumov, "Private Prison Companies Move to Cut Debt as Activists Hit Home," *Financial Times*, August 20, 2020, www.ft.com; Dan Weil, "GEO Shares Fall as It Drops REIT Structure and Turns C Corp," *The Street*, December 2, 2021, www.thestreet.com.

98. Christopher Zoukis, "From Cages to the Community: Prison Profiteers and the Treatment Industrial Complex," *Prison Legal News*, March 6, 2018, www.prisonlegalnews.org.

99. Maya Schenwar and Victoria Law, *Prison by Any Other Name* (New York: The New Press, 2020).

Personnel

1. Brett Murphy, Nick Penzenstadler, and Gina Barton, "A Security Empire Deployed Guards with Violent Pasts Across the U.S. Some Went on to Rape, Assault or Kill," *USA Today*, March 26, 2020, www.usatoday.com.

2. "1892 Homestead Strike," AFL-CIO, n.d., aflcio.org/about/history/labor-history-events.

3. Jennifer Bayot, "George Wackenhut, 85, Dies; Founded Elite Security Firm," *New York Times*, January 8, 2005, www.nytimes.com; Beryl Lipton, "From FBI Reject to Private Warlord: The Rise of George Wackenhut," *MuckRock*, January 10, 2017, www.muckrock.com.

4. Brett Murphy, Nick Penzenstadler, and Gina Barton, "Five Takeaways from Our Investigation into the World's Largest Private Security Company," *USA Today*, December 15, 2019, www.usatoday.com.

5. "Securitas and Pinkerton to Form World Leader in Security," Securitas, February 22, 1999, www.securitas.com/media/pressreleases.

6. *City of Canton, Ohio v. Harris,* 489 U.S. 378 (1989).

7. "A Jailhouse Lawyer's Manual: Your Right to Be Free from Assault by Prison Guards and Other Prisoners," *Columbia Human Rights Law Review*, May 2017, jlm.law.columbia.edu.

8. Ingrid Eagly and Joanna Schwartz, "The Privatization of Police Policymaking," *Texas Law Review* 96, no. 5, n.d., texaslawreview.org.

9. Shannon Heffernan and Weihua Li, "New Data Shows How Dire the Prison Staffing Shortage Really Is," The Marshall Project, January 10, 2024, www.themarshallproject.org.

10. Chelsea Donovan, "North Carolina Prison Staffing Shortage: 39% of NC's Correctional Officer Positions Are Vacant," WRAL News, January 30, 2024, www.wral.com.

11. Matt McKillop and Alex Boucher, "Aging Prison Populations Drive Up Costs," Pew Charitable Trusts, February 20, 2018, www.pewtrusts.org/en/research-and-analysis/articles.

12. "Review of the Federal Bureau of Prisons' Medical Staffing Challenges," Department of Justice Office of the Inspector General, March 2016, oig.justice.gov/reports; Deborah Shelton, Bill Barta, and Louise Reagan, "Correctional Nurse Competency and Quality Care Outcomes," *Journal for Evidence-Based Practice in Correctional Health* 2, no. 1 (November 2018), opencommons.uconn.edu.

13. Shelton, et al., "Correctional Nurse Competency."

14. Anna Amir, "Stand Guard: Electronic Security Systems Will Pose a Threat to Industry Revenue Growth," *IBISWorld*, November 2018.

15. Murphy, "A Security Empire."

16. "USA Spending," n.d., www.usaspending.gov/search.

17. "U.S. Immigration and Customs Enforcement Fiscal Year 2019 Enforcement and Removal Operations Report," U.S. Immigration and Customs Enforcement, 2019, www.ice.gov.

18. Ibid.

19. Heather Rohrlich and Justin Timmons, "The U.S. Border Patrol Is Fast-Tracking a $50 Million Job Due to the Shutdown," *Quartz*, January 24, 2019, qz.com.

20. "U.S. Immigration and Customs Enforcement: Fiscal Year 2023 ICE Annual Report," U.S. Immigration and Customs Enforcement, December 29, 2023, www.ice.gov.

21. "Corrections Officers and Jailers," U.S. Bureau of Labor Statistics, September 6, 2023, www.bls.gov/oes; "Corrections Officers and Bailiffs," U.S. Bureau of Labor Statistics, May 2022, www.bls.gov.

22. Donovan, "North Carolina Prison Staffing Shortage: 39% of NC's Correctional Officer Positions Are Vacant."

23. William Langewiesche, "The Chaos Company," *Vanity Fair*, March 18, 2014, www.vanityfair .com.

24. "USA Spending," 2022, www.usaspending.gov.

25. "Correctional Facilities Security," Securitas Technology, n.d., www.securitastechnology .com.

26. Timothy Landhuis, "Largest Healthcare Staffing Firms in the United States," *Staffing Industry Analysts*, August 31, 2018, www2.staffingindustry.com/Research/Research-Reports.

27. "Online Corrections Training," CorrectionsOne Academy, 2020, www.corrections oneacademy.com.

28. "Training for Corrections Professionals," National Institute of Corrections, March 7, 2017, nicic.gov/training.

29. "Mock Prison Riot 2020," Mock Prison Riot, n.d., www.mockprisonriot.org.

30. Scott Morris, "Police Policy for Sale." The Appeal, February 2, 2019, theappeal.org/lexipol -police-policy-company.

31. "Kronos Incorporated," PrivCo, n.d., system.privco.com/company/kronos-incorporated.

32. "Optimize Staffing Using Kronos TeleStaff," Kronos, n.d., www.kronos.com/customers /california-department-corrections-and-rehabilitation.

33. "Corrections | Operational Workforce Management Software," Orion Communications, n.d., www.orioncom.com/corrections.

34. "Best-in-Class Jail Scheduling and Workforce Management," InTime, n.d., intime.com /industries/corrections.

35. David Reutter, "Georgia Medical Prison Rife with Dysfunction, Abuse and Dilapidated Conditions," *Prison Legal News*, September 3, 2018, www.prisonlegalnews.org.

36. Ibid.

37. Danny Robbins, "State Official Failed to Delve into Prison Doctor's Troubled Past," *Atlanta Journal Constitution*, July 13, 2018, www.ajc.com.

38. Ibid.

39. "Online Corrections Training," CorrectionsOne Academy, n.d., www.corrections oneacademy.com.

40. Eagly and Schwartz, "The Privatization of Police Policymaking."

41. "Online Corrections Training."

42. "The NIC Learning Center," National Institute of Corrections, n.d, nicic.gov/how-can-nic -help/training-and-ecourses.

43. Morris, "Police Policy for Sale."

44. Evan Hill, "The Mock Prison Riot: Where Guards Play Jail," *Al Jazeera America*, May 20, 2014, america.aljazeera.com/multimedia; Dave Gilson, "My So-Called Riot," *Mother Jones*, December 2009, www.motherjones.com.

45. Gilson, "My So-Called Riot."

46. "Kronos: Police & Corrections," Kronos, 2019, www.ukg.com/industry-solutions; Wendy Sawyer, "How Much Do Incarcerated People Earn in Each State?" Prison Policy Initiative, 2017, www.prisonpolicy.org.

Labor + Programs

1. Julia O'Donoghue, "Sheriff: Louisiana's Early Release of Prisoners Means Loss of 'The Ones You Can Work,'" *Times-Picayune*, October 13, 2017, www.nola.com.

2. "Black Codes and Pig Laws," PBS, 2017, www.pbs.org.

3. Angela Davis, *Are Prisons Obsolete?* (New York: Seven Stories Press, 2003), collectivelibera tion.org.

4. Matthew J. Mancini, "Race, Economics, and the Abandonment of Convict Leasing," *Journal of Negro History* 63, no. 4 (October 1978), p. 339–52, doi.org.

5. "Convict Lease System," University of Houston, 2019, www.digitalhistory.uh.edu.

6. Blake Randol, "Auburn System," *Encyclopedia of Criminology and Criminal Justice*, January 22, 2014, doi.org.

7. "Convict Leasing," PBS, 2017, www.pbs.org.

8. "Prison Industries Enhancement Certification Program," American Legal History, n.d., moglen.law.columbia.edu.

9. "PIECP Final Guideline," National Correctional Industries Association, n.d., www .nationalcia.org.

10. "Factories with Fences: 75 Years of Changing Lives," UNICOR, n.d., www.unicor.gov/publications/corporate.

11. Michael J. Berens and Mike Baker, "Broken Prison Labor Program Fails to Keep Promises, Costs Millions," *Seattle Times*, December 13, 2014, projects.seattletimes.com.

12. Wendy Sawyer, "How Much Do Incarcerated People Earn in Each State?" Prison Policy Initiative, April 10, 2017, www.prisonpolicy.org/.

13. Ibid.

14. *Captive Labor: Exploitation of Incarcerated Workers*, American Civil Liberties Union (ACLU), 2022, www.aclu.org/publications.

15. Sawyer, "How Much Do Incarcerated People Earn in Each State?"

16. *Captive Labor: Exploitation of Incarcerated Workers*, ACLU.

17. Worth Rises estimate based on data from Steve Bronars and Coleman Bazelon, *A Cost-Benefit Analysis: The Impact of Ending Slavery and Involuntary Servitude as Criminal Punishment and Paying Incarcerated Workers Fair Wages*, Edgeworth Economics, January 31, 2024, endthe exception.com.

18. Gerard Robinson and Elizabeth English, "The Second Chance Pell Pilot Program: A Historical Overview," American Enterprise Institute, September 2017, www.aei.org.

19. Mike Elk and Bob Sloan, "The Hidden History of ALEC and Prison Labor," *The Nation*, August 1, 2011, www.thenation.com.

20. "Prison Industry Enhancement Certification Program," U.S. Department of Justice, March 2004, www.ncjrs.gov.

21. Jerome G. Miller, "The Debate on Rehabilitating Criminals: Is It True That Nothing Works?" Prison Policy Initiative, March 1989, www.prisonpolicy.org.

22. Travis C. Pratt, Jacinta M. Gau, and Travis W. Franklin, *Key Ideas in Criminology and Criminal Justice* (Thousand Oaks, CA: Sage Publications, 2011), p. 71–85, us.sagepub.com.

23. Ashley A. Smith, "Momentum for Prison Education," *Inside Higher Ed*, November 6, 2018, www.insidehighered.com.

24. "Federal Bureau of Prisons Education Program Assessment Final Report," Department of Justice—Federal Bureau of Prisons, November 29, 2016, www.justice.gov.

25. Richard P. Seiter and Karen R. Kadela, "Prisoner Reentry: What Works, What Does Not, and What Is Promising," *Crime & Delinquency* 49, no. 3 (July 2003), p. 360–88, doi.org..

26. Matthew Clarke, "Prison Education Programs Threatened," *Prison Legal News*, May 19, 2014, www.prisonlegalnews.org.

27. Nicholas Turner, "Unlocking Potential for Incarcerated People Through Pell Grant Reinstatement," *Boston Globe*, July 13, 2023, www.bostonglobe.com.

28. Mack Finkel and Wanda Bertram, "More States Are Signing Harmful 'Free Prison Tablet' Contracts," Prison Policy Initiative, March 7, 2019, www.prisonpolicy.org.

29. P.R. Lockhart, "Colorado Passes Amendment A, Voting to Officially Abolish Prison Slavery," *Vox*, November 7, 2018, www.vox.com/policy-and-politics.

30. Kiara Alfonseca, "U.S. Constitution's Exception for Slavery Faces Renewed Battle Ahead of Juneteenth," ABC News, June 15, 2023, abcnews.go.com.

31. "Abolition Amendment," #EndTheException, n.d., endtheexception.com.

32. Moe Clark, "Forced Labor Continues in Colorado, Years After Vote to End Prison Slavery." *BOLTS Magazine*, September 19, 2023, boltsmag.org/colorado-prison-slavery; Michael Levenson, "Prisoners Sue Alabama, Calling Prison Labor System 'A Form of Slavery,'" *New York Times*, December 12, 2023, www.nytimes.com.

33. Wendy Sawyer and Peter Wagner, "Mass Incarceration: The Whole Pie 2023," Prison Policy Initiative, March 14, 2023, www.prisonpolicy.org.

34. Whitney Benns, "American Slavery, Reinvented," *The Atlantic*, September 21, 2015, www.theatlantic.com.

35. Kevin Rashid Johnson, "Prison Labor Is Modern Slavery. I've Been Sent to Solitary for Speaking Out," *The Guardian*, August 23, 2018, www.theguardian.com.

36. *Captive Labor: Exploitation of Incarcerated Workers*, ACLU.

37. Ibid.

38. Bronars and Bazelon, *A Cost-Benefit Analysis: The Impact of Ending Slavery and Involuntary Servitude as Criminal Punishment and Paying Incarcerated Workers Fair Wages*.

39. "2006 Awards—Life Skills for State and Local Prisoners Program," U.S. Department of Education, August 1, 2006, web.archive.org; www2.ed.gov/programs/lifeskills/2006awards; "Corrections & Reentry," CrimeSolutions, National Institute of Justice, n.d., www.crimesolutions.gov/TopicDetails.

40. Lois M. Davis, et al., "Evaluating the Effectiveness of Correctional Education," Rand Corporation, 2013, p. 33, www.rand.org.

41. Christopher Zoukis, "The Second Step: Invest in Prison Education Programs, Reinstate Pell Grants," *Prison Legal News*, July 2019, www.prisonlegalnews.org.

42. "Prison Education: Guide to College Degrees for Inmates and Ex-Offenders," The Best Schools, July 9, 2019, thebestschools.org/magazine/prison-inmate-education-guide.

43. "Prison Labor and the Private Sector: The Corporate Exploitation of Prison Labor Reaches Deep into the Supply Chain," Worth Rises, December 9, 2021, worthrises.org/blog.

44. Joseph Zimmer, "This Constitution Week Let's Stop Using Brands That Support Prison Slavery," *Common Dreams*, September 23, 2022, www.commondreams.org.

45. Mike Baker and Michael J. Berens, "Why License Plates Have Cost Us So Much," *Seattle Times*, December 15, 2014, projects.seattletimes.com.

46. "License Plate Manufacturing Solutions for Correctional Facilities," 3M, n.d., www.3m.com.sg/3M/en_SG/road-safety-sg/applications/vehicle-registration/correctional-facility-solutions.

47. Steve Rendle, "Modern Slavery Statement," VF Corporation, October 2019, www.vfc.com.

48. "NCIA Corporate Members," NCIA, n.d., web.archive.org.

49. Robin McDowell and Margie Mason, "Prisoners in the U.S. Are Part of a Hidden Workforce Linked to Hundreds of Popular Food Brands," Associated Press, January 29, 2024, apnews.com.

50. "Cargill's Human Rights Policy," Cargill, January 2024, www.cargill.com.

51. "Except for Me: Britt," #EndTheException, n.d., endtheexception.com/exceptforme.

52. John Washington, "Mike Bloomberg Exploited Prison Labor to Make 2020 Presidential Campaign Phone Calls," *The Intercept*, December 24, 2019, theintercept.com.

53. "About," Televerde, n.d., televerde.com/about.

54. Anthony Evans, Taylor Gilmor, and Saager Buch, "The Economic, Social and Fiscal Impact of Televerde's Prison Workforce Program," Arizona State University Seidman Research Institute, December 9, 2019, televerde.com/wp-content.

55. Gary Mohr and Gayle Bickle, "An Intermediate Outcome Evaluation of the Thinking for a Change Program," Ohio Department of Rehabilitation and Correction, 2013, www.drc.ohio .gov.

56. "Prison Reform: Reducing Recidivism by Strengthening the Federal Bureau of Prisons," U.S. Department of Justice, March 6, 2017, www.justice.gov/archives/prison-reform; "Federal Bureau of Prisons Education Program Assessment Final Report," U.S. Department of Justice, Federal Bureau of Prisons, November 29, 2016, www.justice.gov.

57. "Moral Reconation Therapy—MRT Facilitator Training, Cost Proposal," Correctional Counseling, Inc., 2018, www.ccimrt.com.

58. Brian Belardi, "McGraw-Hill Education Expands Accessibility for Adult Ed Test Preparation Tools with New Offline and Spanish Offerings," McGraw Hill Education, April 23, 2015, investors .mheducation.com/investor-news/press-release.

59. "Paxen Publishing Completes the Purchase of Houghton Mifflin Harcourt's Adult Education Assets," Paxen Publishing, April 9, 2018, web.archive.org/web/20190705173646/https:// www.paxenpublishing.com.

60. Partnerships Between Community Colleges and Prisons Providing Workforce Education and Training to Reduce Recidivism," U.S. Department of Education, March 2009, www2.ed.gov /about/offices/list/ovae/pi/AdultEd/prison-cc-partnerships.

61. "About Orijin," Orijin, n.d., orijin.works/about.

62. Megan Rose Dickey, "Edovo Raises $9 Million to Provide Incarcerated People with Tablet-Based Education," *TechCrunch*, April 8, 2018, techcrunch.com.

63. "Inmate Services—Education," JPay, Inc., n.d., www.jpay.com/Education; "GTL Unveils Education Management Offering for Corrections Professionals and Inmates," Global Tel*Link (GTL), July 27, 2016, www.gtl.net..

64. Michelle Phelps, "The Return of Rehabilitation? Educational Programs for Prisoners Remain Inadequate," Society Pages, 2017, thesocietypages.org.

65. Hanna Kozlowska, "U.S. Prisoners Are Going on Strike to Protest a Massive Forced Labor System," *Quartz*, September 9, 2016, qz.com/777415/an-unprecedented-prison-strike-hopes-to-change-the-fate-of-the-900000-americans-trapped-in-an-exploitative-labor-system.

66. Alexia Fernández Campbell, "Prison Strike 2018: Federal Prisoners Work Factory Jobs for Much Less Than the Minimum Wage," *Vox*, August 24, 2018, www.vox.com.

67. Matthew Makarios, "Program Profile: Thinking for a Change," National Institute of Justice Crime Solutions, May 4, 2012, crimesolutions.ojp.gov.

68. Julie Goodridge, et al., "Prison Labor in the United States: An Investor Perspective," Northstar Asset Management, April 2018, missioninvestors.org.

69. Alexia Fernández Campbell, "The Federal Government Markets Prison Labor to Businesses as the 'Best-Kept Secret,'" *Vox*, August 24, 2018, www.vox.com.

70. Goodridge, et al., "Prison Labor in the United States: An Investor Perspective."

71. "Prison Industry Enhancement Certification Program," n.d., 4c99dc08-46a7-4bd9-b990-48103d668bb3.filesusr.com/ugd/74ff44_663948d99c9949fe8e8a5afaf8d87ae9.pdf.

72. "About Us," CleanCore Solutions, n.d., www.cleancoresol.com. PIECP workers in Nebraska get paid $305,323 per quarter in gross wages, so $3,355 per day, or $53 per person per day.

73. "Prison Industry Enhancement Certification Program (PIECP)," Cornhusker State Industries, n.d., csi.nebraska.gov/piecp.

74. Ibid.

75. "Our History," Haystack Mountain Inc., n.d., haystackmountaincheese.com/our-story.

76. Goodridge, et al., "Prison Labor in the United States: An Investor Perspective."

77. *Captive Labor: Exploitation of Incarcerated Workers*, ACLU.

78. Robin McDowell and Margie Mason, "Prisoners in the U.S. Are Part of a Hidden Workforce Linked to Hundreds of Popular Food Brands."

79. "Except for Me: Britt," #EndTheException.

80. Stian Rice, "Farmers Turn to Prisons to Fill Labor Needs," *High Country News*, June 12, 2019, web.archive.org.

81. McDowell and Mason, "Prisoners in the U.S. Are Part of a Hidden Workforce."

82. "Angola State Prison: A Short History," Voices Behind Bars: National Public Radio and Angola State Prison, n.d., ccnmtl.columbia.edu.

83. "End Plantation Prisons," Promise of Justice, n.d., promiseofjustice.org.

84. Jolie McCullough, "Inmates Are Dying in Stifling Texas Prisons, but the State Seldom Acknowledges Heat as a Cause of Death," *Texas Tribune*, June 28, 2023, www.texastribune.org.

85. Elizabeth Whitman, "How a Giant Egg Farm Made Money off Women Prisoners in Dangerous Conditions," *Cosmopolitan*, February 15, 2023, www.cosmopolitan.com/lifestyle/a42710907/women-prisoners-at-hickmans-farms.

86. *Captive Labor: Exploitation of Incarcerated Workers*, ACLU.

87. "Correctional Industries: How Governments Exploit Prison Labor to Subsidize Their Budgets," Worth Rises, January 8, 2024, worthrises.org/blog.

88. Lilah Burke, "Public Universities, Prison-Made Furniture," *Inside Higher Ed*, February 14, 2020, www.insidehighered.com/news/2020/02/14/public-universities-several-states-are-required-buy-prison-industries.

89. Christopher Robbins, "NY's New License Plates Will Still Be Made by Prisoners Earning 65 Cents an Hour," *Gothamist*, August 23, 2019, gothamist.com.

90. "State and Federal Prison Wage Policies and Sourcing Information," Prison Policy Initiative, April 10, 2017, www.prisonpolicy.org.

91. "Top Ten Benefits of Correctional Industries," National Correctional Industries Association, n.d., 4c99dc08-46a7-4bd9-b990-48103d668bb3.filesusr.com/ugd/df1d6e_27767 a82614c46da984735a047dd00b2.pdf.

92. Mike Baker and Michael J. Berens, "Why License Plates Cost Us So Much," *Seattle Times*, December 15, 2014, projects.seattletimes.com.

93. Ibid.

94. Nicole Goodkind, "Prisoners Are Fighting California's Wildfires on the Front Lines, but Getting Little in Return," *Fortune*, November 2019, fortune.com.

95. "Prisoners Are Getting Paid $1.45 a Day to Fight the California Wildfires," American Civil Liberties Union, n.d., www.aclu.org.

96. Goodkind, "Prisoners Are Fighting California's Wildfires."

97. Lakshmi Singh, "Serving Time and Fighting California Wildfires," NPR, November 18, 2018, www.npr.org.

98. Adesuwa Agbonile, "Inmates Help Battle California's Wildfires. But When Freed, Many Can't Get Firefighting Jobs," *Sacramento Bee*, September 6, 2018, www.sacbee.com; Michael James, "California Governor Signs Bill Giving Prisoners Battling Wildfires a Shot at Becoming Pro Firefighters," *USA Today*, September 11, 2020, www.usatoday.com.

99. Twitter post, Worth Rises, March 31, 2020, twitter.com/WorthRises.

100. Christina Carrega, "Nearly 100 Prison Inmates in NY to Produce 100K Gallons of Hand Sanitizer Weekly," ABC News, March 10, 2020, abcnews.go.com/Health.

101. Melissa Klein, "NYC's Potter's Field Has Buried Nearly 900 People During Coronavirus Outbreak," *New York Post*, June 27, 2020, nypost.com.

102. Julie Goodridge, et al., "Prison Labor in the United States: An Investor Perspective."

103. Beth Schwartzapfel, "Taking Freedom: Modern-Day Slavery in America's Prison Workforce," *Pacific Standard*, May 7, 2018, psmag.com/social-justice.

104. German Lopez, "America's Prisoners Are Going on Strike in at Least 17 States," *Vox*, August 22, 2018, www.vox.com.

105. Sawyer, "How Much Do Incarcerated People Earn in Each State?"

106. *Captive Labor: Exploitation of Incarcerated Workers*, ACLU.

107. "State and Federal Prison Wage Policies."

108. Bronars and Bazelon, *A Cost-Benefit Analysis: The Impact of Ending Slavery and Involuntary Servitude as Criminal Punishment and Paying Incarcerated Workers Fair Wages*.

109. Private communication to Worth Rises.

110. Bronars and Bazelon, *A Cost-Benefit Analysis: The Impact of Ending Slavery and Involuntary Servitude as Criminal Punishment and Paying Incarcerated Workers Fair Wages*; Peter Wagner and Bernadette Rabuy, "Following the Money of Mass Incarceration," Prison Policy Initiative, January 25, 2017, www.prisonpolicy.org.

111. Bronars and Bazelon, *A Cost-Benefit Analysis: The Impact of Ending Slavery and Involuntary Servitude as Criminal Punishment and Paying Incarcerated Workers Fair Wages*.

112. Grant Duwe, "The Use and Impact of Correctional Programming for Inmates on Pre- and Post-Release Outcomes," National Institute of Justice, June 2017, www.ncjrs.gov.

113. "Corrections & Reentry Programs," National Institute of Justice Crime Solutions, n.d., www.crimesolutions.gov/TopicDetails.

114. Duwe, "The Use and Impact of Correctional Programming."

115. Chris Hansen, "Cognitive-Behavioral Interventions: Where They Come From and What They Do," *Federal Probation* 72 no. 2, n.d., www.uscourts.gov; "Rules Are Made to Be Followed Workbook," Correctional Counseling, Inc., 2020, www.ccimrt.com.

116. Makarios, "Program Profile"

117. Hansen, "Cognitive-Behavioral Interventions"; Duwe, "The Use and Impact of Correctional Programming."

118. Hansen, "Cognitive-Behavioral Interventions."

119. Ibid.

120. Ibid.

121. Finkel and Bertram, "More States Are Signing Harmful 'Free Prison Tablet' Contracts."

122. Staff, "W. Va. Prisons Offer Inmate Tablets," *Register-Herald*, October 25, 2019, www.register-herald.com; C.J. Ciaramella, "West Virginia Inmates Will Be Charged by the Minute to Read E-Books on Tablets," *Reason*, November 22, 2019, reason.com.

123. Whitney Kimball, "Bloodsucking Prison Telecom Is Scamming Inmates with 'Free' Tablets," *Gizmodo*, November 26, 2019, gizmodo.com.

124. Eli Hager, "How Trump Made a Tiny Christian College the Nation's Biggest Prison Educator," The Marshall Project, December 17, 2020, www.themarshallproject.org/2020/12/17/this-tiny-christian-college-has-made-millions-on-prisoners-under-trump.

125. Finkel and Bertram, "More States Are Signing Harmful 'Free Prison Tablet' Contracts."

126. Madison Pauly, "A Notorious Tech Giant Is Poised to Cash In on Pell Grants for Incarcerated People," *Mother Jones*, February 8, 2022, www.motherjones.com/criminal-justice/2022/02/aventiv-securus-lantern-college-pell-grants-prisoners.

127. "GTL Becomes ViaPath Technologies, Launches Expanded Reintegration Services," ViaPath Technologies, January 4, 2022, www.viapath.com.

Equipment

1. Rupert Neate, "Welcome to Jail Inc: How Private Companies Make Money off U.S. Prisons," *The Guardian*, June 16, 2016, www.theguardian.com.

2. David Segal, "Prison Vendors See Continued Signs of a Captive Market," *New York Times*, August 29, 2015, www.nytimes.com; Adam Bluestein, "Tapping the Prison Market," *Inc.*, January 24, 2012, www.inc.com/magazine.

3. "The Prison Industry Corporate Database," Worth Rises, n.d., data.worthrises.org.

4. USAspending.gov, 2014–2023, www.usaspending.gov.

5. Peter Eisler, Jason Szep, and Charles Levinson, "Shock Tactics: Inmate Deaths Reveal 'Torturous' Use of Tasers," Reuters, December 6, 2017, www.reuters.com.

6. Stephen J. Beard and Gary Craig, "A Flashpoint in Prison Reform: A Visual Look at How the Attica Prison Riot Unfolded," *USA Today*, September 8, 2021, www.usatoday.com.

7. Jessica Mitford, *Kind & Usual Punishment: The Prison Business* (New York: Knopf, 1973).

8. Kathleen Frenette, "The Bureau of Prisons Purchases of Goods and Services Report," New Hampshire Procurement Technical Assistance Program, 2008, www.berlinnh.gov; "FY 2015 Appropriations Report—State Department of Corrections," Arizona Department of Corrections, n.d., www.azjlbc.gov.

9. The Freedonia Group, "Law Enforcement & Guarding Equipment—Industry Market Research, Market Share, Market Size, Sales, Demand Forecast, Market Leaders, Company Profiles, Industry Trends," August 2016, www.freedoniagroup.com.

10. Ibid.

11. Jeff McDonald, "Money Meant for Inmate Welfare Spent on Education, Staff, and Sheriff's Department Expenses," *San Diego Union-Tribune*, April 22, 2019, www.sandiegouniontribune.com/news/watchdog/story.

12. "California Code, Penal Code—PEN § 4025," Findlaw, n.d., codes.findlaw.com.

13. "Inmate Welfare Fund Audit (AD No. 14-058)," Los Angeles Police Department Audit Division, June 2015, lapdonlinestrgeacc.blob.core.usgovcloudapi.net/lapdonlinemedia..

14. "The Prison Industry Corporate Database," Worth Rises, n.d., data.worthrises.org.

15. Robert Hoshowsky, "Industry Pioneers: Cornerstone," *Construction in Focus*, November 2022, constructioninfocus.com.

16. David Segal, "Prison Vendors."

17. "History," Bob Barker, n.d., www.bobbarker.com/history.

18. Mark J. Perry, "The General Public Thinks the Average Company Makes a 36% Profit Margin, Which Is About 5X Too High, Part II," American Enterprise Institute, January 15, 2018, www.aei.org/carpe-diem; "Financing a Jail Supplies and Equipment Company," Commercial Capital, March 5, 2013, www.comcapfactoring.com/blog.

19. "Cornerstone Detention Products," PrivCo, n.d., system.privco.com/company; "2017 Detention Equipment Contractors Report," *Correctional News*, 2017, correctionalnews.com..

20. "Annual Reports & Year in Review," Stanley Black & Decker, n.d., ir.stanleyblackanddecker .com/financial-information; "Correctional Facility Security Solutions," Stanley Convergent Security Solutions, n.d., www.stanleysecuritysolutions.com.

21. "Bob Barker Company, Inc.," PrivCo, n.d., system.privco.com/company/bob-barker_private _stock_annual_report_financials.

22. "Southern Folger," PrivCo, n.d., system.privco.com/company/southern-folger_private _stock_annual_report_financials.

23. "Kane Innovations," Kane Innovations, 2017, www.kaneinnovations.com; "The Prison Industry Corporate Database," Worth Rises; "Kane Innovations," PrivCo, n.d., system.privco .com/company/kane-innovations_private_stock_annual_report_financials/financials.

24. Jack Dolan, "Objections Raised to Caging Inmates During Therapy," *Los Angeles Times*, December 28, 2010, www.latimes.com.

25. "Security Cuff Benches," Derby Industries, n.d., www.derbyindustries.com/ecommerce /products.

26. "Portable Bunk Beds," Norix Furniture, n.d., www.norix.com/products/detention -accessories/stack-a-bunk.

27. "Underbed Storage Box, 6.3 Gal. Capacity," Bob Barker, n.d., www.bobbarker.com /products/security/personal-effects-storage/storage-boxes/box-underbed-storage.

28. "Detention Food Pass Through Door," Kryptomax, n.d., www.kryptomax.com/detention -access.

29. Stephie Grob Plante, "How a Lack of Personal Care Products Contributes to Harrowing Conditions for Detained Migrants," *Vox*, July 3, 2019, www.vox.com.

30. "All-in-One Shampoo—Safety Data Sheet," Bob Barker, 2023, www.bobbarker.com.

31. "All-in-One, Maximum Security, 1 Gal.," Bob Barker, 2023, www.bobbarker.com.

32. "Pert Plus Shampoo & Conditioner, 13.5 Oz.," Bob Barker, 2023, www.bobbarker.com.

33. Eisler, et al., "Shock Tactics."

34. "Humane Restraint," Humane Restraint, 2020, www.humanerestraint.com.

35. Julie Punches, "Behavioral Restraint Use for Violent/Self Destructive Behaviors," *PolicyS-tat*, August 2016, www.coursehero.com.

36. Christie Thompson and Joseph Shapiro, "28 Days in Chains." The Marshall Project, October 26, 2016, www.themarshallproject.org.

37. Joseph Shapiro, "Federal Report Criticizes Harsh Treatment of Lewisburg Prisoners," NPR, July 13, 2017, www.npr.org/sections/thetwo-way.

38. Eli Hager, "Alternatives to Bullets," The Marshall Project, September 23, 2015, www .themarshallproject.org.

39. "Baton Trauma Zone Chart," Defense Technology, n.d., www.defense-technology.com /product.

40. Tim Reid, et al., "Shock Tactics: As Taser Warns of Risks, Cities Bear a Burden in Court," Reuters, August 23, 2017, https://www.reuters.com/investigates/special-report/usa-taser -legal.

41. "TASER® X3™, X26™, and M26™ ECD Warnings, Instructions, and Information: Law Enforcement," TASER International, 2010, fingfx.thomsonreuters.com.

42. "Tasers Credited with Reduction in Mich. CO Attacks," Corrections1 by LEXIPOL, August 26, 2013, www.correctionsone.com/products/less-lethal/taser/articles.

43. Eisler, et al., "Shock Tactics."

44. "Correctional Facilities Security," Securitas Technology, n.d., www.securitastechnology .com/industries/correctional-facilities.

45. David Grossman, "Prisons Are Building Giant Biometric Databases of Prisoners' Voices," *Popular Mechanics*, February 1, 2019, www.popularmechanics.com/technology/security.

46. Joseph Menn, "Microsoft Turned Down Facial-Recognition Sales on Human Rights Concerns," Reuters, April 16, 2019, www.reuters.com/article.

47. Tom Simonite, "The Best Algorithms Still Struggle to Recognize Black Faces," *Wired*, July 22, 2019, www.wired.com.

48. Dave Lee, "San Francisco Is First U.S. City to Ban Facial Recognition," BBC News, May 14, 2019, www.bbc.com/news/technology.

49. "Correctional Facility Face Recognition," FaceFirst, 2020, web.archive.org/web /20220315173613/https://www.facefirst.com/industry/correctional-facility-face-recognition.

50. Tim Requarth and George Joseph, "Leaked Documents Say Roughly 2,000 NY Prisoners Affected by Erroneous Drug Tests," *Gothamist*, November 21, 2019, gothamist.com/news.

51. George Joseph, "NY State Prisons Abruptly Suspend Drug Tests for Contraband," *Gothamist*, August 26, 2020, gothamist.com/news.

52. "Conferences," American Correctional Association, n.d., www.aca.org.

53. "American Correctional Association," Prison Policy Initiative, n.d., www.prisonpolicy.org.

54. "Orlando Program Book," American Correctional Association, 2018, register.aca.org.

Data + Information

1. Ronald Bailey, "Facial Recognition and the Danger of Automated Authoritarianism," *Reason*, January 21, 2020, reason.com; "Clearview AI," Kirenaga Partners, n.d., kirenaga.com /portfolio/clearview-ai.

2. Khalil Gibran Muhammad, *The Condemnation of Blackness: Race, Crime, and the Making of Modern Urban America* (Cambridge, MA: Harvard University Press, 2010).

3. "Prison Management Systems Market," Persistence Market Research, n.d., www .persistencemarketresearch.com.

4. Ibid.

5. Gail Elias, "How to Collect and Analyze Data: A Manual for Sheriffs and Jail Administrators," PREA Resource Center, July 2007, www.prearesourcecenter.org.

6. Tim Brennan, David Wells, and Jack Alexander, "Enhancing Prison Classification Systems: The Emerging Role of Management Information Systems," NICIC, July 2004, info.nicic.gov.

7. Anna Maria Barry-Jester, Ben Casselman, and Dana Goldstein, "The New Science of Sentencing," The Marshall Project, August 4, 2015, www.themarshallproject.org.

8. "Report on Algorithmic Risk Assessment Tools in the U.S. Criminal Justice System—The Partnership on AI," The Partnership on AI, April 23, 2019, www.partnershiponai.org.

9. Matt Henry, "Risk Assessment: Explained," The Appeal, March 25, 2019, theappeal.org.

10. Ethan Corey, "New Data Suggests Risk Assessment Tools Have Little Impact on Pretrial Incarceration," The Appeal, February 7, 2020, theappeal.org .

11. Henry, "Risk Assessment: Explained": Danielle Kehl, Priscilla Guo, and Samuel Kessler, "Algorithms in the Criminal Justice System: Assessing the Use of Risk Assessments in Sentencing," July 2017, dash.harvard.edu/bitstream; Nathan James, "Risk and Needs Assessment in the Criminal Justice System," Congressional Research Service, July 24, 2015, www.everycrsreport .com.

12. Henry, "Risk Assessment: Explained"; Kehl, et al., "Algorithms in the Criminal Justice System."

13. Barry-Jester et al., "The New Science of Sentencing."

14. Clare Garvie, Alvaro Bedoya, and Jonathan Frankle, "The Perpetual Line-Up," Perpetual Line Up, October 18, 2016, www.perpetuallineup.org.

15. George Joseph and Debbie Nathan, "Prisons Across the U.S. Are Quietly Building Databases of Incarcerated People's Voice Prints," The Intercept, January 30, 2019, theintercept.com.

16. "Biometric Identity System: DHS Needs to Address Significant Shortcomings in Program Management and Privacy," U.S. Government Accountability Office (GAO), September 12, 2023, www.gao.gov/products.

17. Stephen Mayhew, "History of Biometrics," Biometric Update, July 20, 2018, www .biometricupdate.com.

18. "Biometrics: Definition, Trends, Use Cases, Laws and Latest News," Thales Group, September 10, 2020, www.thalesgroup.com/en/markets/digital-identity-and-security/government /inspired/biometrics.

19. Shaun Raviv, "The Secret History of Facial Recognition," Wired, January 21, 2020, /www .wired.com; Mayhew, "History of Biometrics."

20. Doug Wyllie, "How Biometric Technologies Will Help Correctional Facilities," Corrections1 by Lexipol, May 16, 2017, www.corrections1.com/products/police-technology/investigation /biometrics-identification/articles.

21. Mayhew, "History of Biometrics."

22. Joseph, et al., "Prisons Across the U.S. Are Quietly Building Databases of Incarcerated People's Voice Prints."

23. "EXHIBIT 5 Comments Re Second Further Notice of Proposed Rulemaking: Single Call Programs," Prison Policy Initiative, January 12, 2015, static.prisonpolicy.org.

24. Mayhew, "History of Biometrics"; "Biometrics," Thales Group.

25. Natalie Prescott, "The Anatomy of Biometric Laws: What U.S. Companies Need to Know in 2020," *National Law Review*, January 15, 2020, www.natlawreview.com.

26. "Prison Management Systems Market Is Projected to Grow Significantly to Reach US$ 2,809.8 Mn by 2026—Persistence Market Research," *PRNewswire*, January 10, 2019, www .prnewswire.com/news-releases.

27. Ibid.

28. Ibid.

29. Henry, "Risk Assessment: Explained."

30. Ibid.

31. "How Many Jurisdictions Use Each Tool?" Mapping Pretrial Injustice, Movement Alliance Project & MediaJustice, n.d., pretrialrisk.com/national-landscape.

32. Ben Green, "The False Promise of Risk Assessments: Epistemic Reform and the Limits of Fairness," n.d., doi.org.

33. "Biometric System Market Size, Share & Covid-19 Impact Analysis—By Contact Type, Technology, Mobility, End-User, and Region, 2022–2029," Fortune Business Insight, n.d., www .fortunebusinessinsights.com.

34. "Biometrics," Thales Group.

35. "$65.3 Billion Biometric System," GlobeNewswire News Room.

36. "Biometrics Scan Software Industry in the U.S.—Market Research Report," *IBIS World*, October 28, 2019, www.ibisworld.com.

37. "Biometrics in 2020," Thales Group.

38. "The Syscon Story," Syscon, n.d., syscon.net/about.

39. "Corrections Tech," Syscon, n.d., syscon.net.

40. "2019 Annual Report," DXC Technology, 2019, s27.q4cdn.com/120381974/files /doc_financials.

41. Henry, "Risk Assessment: Explained."

42. "Northpointe Suite Custody Management," Equivant, n.d., www.equivant.com.

43. Karen Hao, "Amazon Is the Invisible Backbone of ICE's Immigration Crackdown," *MIT Technology Review*, October 22, 2018, www.technologyreview.com; "DXC Offender360™ Jail Management," DXC Technology, n.d., query.prod.cms.rt.microsoft.com/cms/api/am/binary /RWO7l1.

44. "Algorithms in the Criminal Justice System: Pre-Trial Risk Assessment Tools," Electronic Privacy Information Center, n.d., epic.org/algorithmic-transparency/crim-justice/.

45. Kehl, et al., "Algorithms in the Criminal Justice System"; "Level of Service Inventory—Revised (LSI-R) Profile and Associated Costs," Pennsylvania Commission on Crime and Delinquency, n.d., www.pccd.pa.gov/Funding/Documents.

46. Kehl, et al., "Algorithms in the Criminal Justice System."

47. "Northpointe Suite Custody Management," Equivant.

48. Shaila Dewan, "Judges Replacing Conjecture with Formula for Bail," *New York Times*, June 26, 2015, www.nytimes.com; "Advancing Pretrial Justice," Advancing Pretrial Policy & Research, n.d., www.psapretrial.org/about/background.

49. "Common Pretrial Risk Assessments," Mapping Pretrial Injustice, Movement Alliance Project & MediaJustice, n.d., pretrialrisk.com/the-basics/common-prai.

50. Ibid.

51. Ibid.

52. Ames Grawert and Patricia Richman, "The First Step Act's Prison Reforms," Brennan Center for Justice, September 23, 2022, www.brennancenter.org/our-work/research-reports; Marissa Gerchick, et al., "Don't Let Math Distract You: Together, We Can Fight Algorithmic Injustice," American Civil Liberties Union (ACLU), August 8, 2023, www.aclu.org/news/criminal-law-reform.

53. "Criminal ID Solutions," *Biometric Update*, n.d., www.biometricupdate.com/service-directory/criminal-id.

54. "Biometrics," Thales Group.

55. "About Us," Dataworks Plus, n.d., www.dataworksplus.com.

56. "About Idemia," Idemia, n.d., www.idemia.com/leader-identity-technologies.

57. Joseph, et al., "Prisons Across the U.S. Are Quietly Building Databases of Incarcerated People's Voice Prints."

58. "Custom Corrections and Jail Management Systems," Chetu, n.d., www.chetu.com.

59. David Pyrooz, "Using Restrictive Housing to Manage Gangs in U.S. Prisons," National Institute of Justice, June 30, 2018, nij.ojp.gov.

60. Alan Judd, "From Los Angeles, a Cautionary Tale for Georgia's New Gang Database," *Atlanta Journal-Constitution*, March 11, 2020, www.ajc.com/news.

61. Melissa del Bosque, "Immigration Officials Use Secretive Gang Databases to Deny Migrant Asylum Claims." *ProPublica*, July 8, 2019, www.propublica.org.

62. "About Us," Guardian RFID, n.d., guardianrfid.com/about.

63. Leischen Stelter, "Technology Makes Agencies Efficient, Keeps Officers and Inmates Safer," *In Public Safety*, April 1, 2016, inpublicsafety.com.

64. Camille Knighton, "Inmate Identification: Wristbands vs. ID Cards," Guardian RFID, August 10, 2018, guardianrfid.com/blog.

65. Steve Baker, "Correctional Security Trends to Watch in 2020," Stanley Convergent Security Solutions, February 11, 2020, www.stanleysecuritysolutions.com.

66. "Cloud-Based Biometrics Will Change the Face of Law Enforcement," M2SYS, March 24, 2015, www.m2sys.com/blog/public-safety.

67. "No Tech for ICE," Mijente, n.d., notechforice.com.

68. Spencer Woodman, "Palantir Provides the Engine for Donald Trump's Deportation Machine," *The Intercept*, March 2, 2017, theintercept.com; Peter Hall, "ICE Criticized for Arrest at Scranton Hospital," *Morning Call*, March 16, 2020, www.mcall.com/news/pennsylvania/mc-nws -pa.

69. "How Many Jurisdictions Use Each Tool?" Mapping Pretrial Injustice.

70. Corey, "New Data Suggests Risk Assessment Tools."

71. "An Organizer's Guide to Confronting Pretrial Risk Assessment Tools in Decarceration Campaigns," Community Justice Exchange, December 2019, www.communityjusticeexchange .org.

72. "Our Results," Brooklyn Community Bail Fund, n.d., web.archive.org.

73. "An Organizer's Guide."

74. Chelsea Barabas, Karthik Dinakar, and Colin Doyle, "The Problems with Risk Assessment Tools," *New York Times*, July 17, 2019, www.nytimes.com.

75. Julia Angwin, et al., "Machine Bias," *ProPublica*, May 23, 2016, www.propublica.org.

76. Morris L. Thigpen, Virginia A. Hutchinson, and Jim T. Barbee, "Objective Jail Classification Systems: A Guide for Jail Administrators," National Institute of Corrections, U.S. Department of Justice, February 1998, s3.amazonaws.com/static.nicic.gov/Library.

77. Adam Harris, "How We Decided to Test Racial Bias in Algorithms," *ProPublica*, May 31, 2016, www.propublica.org.

78. Julia Angwin, et al., "Machine Bias."

79. "Artificial Intelligence Research and Development to Support Community Supervision," National Institute of Justice, 2019, nij.ojp.gov.

80. Sigal Samuel, "Facial Recognition Tech Draws Controversy for Apple, Amazon, Microsoft," *Vox*, April 27, 2019, www.vox.com/future-perfect; D.J. Pangburn, "Due to Weak Oversight, We Don't Really Know How Tech Companies Are Using Facial Recognition Data," *Fast Company*, July 5, 2019, https://www.fastcompany.com; Rosalie Chan, "What to Know about Palantir, the Big Data Company That Works with ICE," *Business Insider*, July 19, 2019, www.businessinsider .com.

81. George Joseph and Debbie Nathan, "Why Is a Prison Company Storing the Voice Prints of Even Innocent People?" *Fast Company*, February 14, 2019, www.fastcompany.com.

82. "State of New York Contract Agreement—Securus Technologies," Prison Policy Initiative, New York State Department of Corrections, 2017, www.prisonphonejustice.org.

83. Joseph, et al., "Prisons Across the U.S. Are Quietly Building Databases of Incarcerated People's Voice Prints."

84. Garvie, et al., "The Perpetual Line-Up."

85. Joseph and Nathan, "Why Is a Prison Company Storing the Voice Prints of Even Innocent People?"

86. Steve Lohr, "Facial Recognition Is Accurate, If You're a White Guy," *New York Times*, February 9, 2018, www.nytimes.com.

87. Ibid.

88. Jennifer Lynch, "Face Off: Law Enforcement Use of Facial Recognition Technology," Electronic Frontier Foundation, May 2019, docs.house.gov/meetings.

89. Aaron Mak, "What's Going On with the Teenager Suing Apple Over Facial Recognition Technology?" *Slate*, April 23, 2019, slate.com/technology.

90. Bill Chappell, "ICE Uses Facial Recognition to Sift State Driver's License Records, Researchers Say," NPR, July 8, 2019, www.npr.org.

91. Vivek Kundra, "Federal Cloud Computing Strategy," The White House, February 8, 2011, obamawhitehouse.archives.gov.

92. Ibid.

93. "Biometric Identity System," GAO..

94. Justin Rohrlich, "Homeland Security Will Soon Have Biometric Data on Nearly 260 Million People," *Quartz*, November 7, 2019, qz.com.

Telecom

1. Eleanor Bell Fox and Daniel Wagner, "Time Is Money: Who's Making a Buck off Prisoners' Families?" Center for Public Integrity, September 30, 2014, publicintegrity.org/inequality-poverty-opportunity.

2. Worth Rises, unpublished data model. Includes communications revenue only.

3. Peter Wagner and Wanda Bertram, "State of Phone Justice—2022," Prison Policy Initiative, December 2022, www.prisonpolicy.org.

4. Saneta deVuono-Powell, et al., "Who Pays? The True Cost of Incarceration on Families," Ella Baker Center, Forward Together, Research Action Design, September 2015, ellabakercenter.org.

5. Steven J. Jackson, "Mapping the Prison Telephone Industry," in *Prison Profiteers: Who Makes Money from Mass Incarceration*, edited by Tara Herival and Paul Wright (New York: The New Press, 2009): pp. 236–39; Bianca Tylek and Maya Ragsdale, "Comment on *Third Report and Order* and *Order on Reconsideration* and *Fifth Notice of Proposed Rulemaking*," Worth Rises, WC Docket No. 12-375—Federal Communications Commission, September 27, 2021, www.fcc.gov.

6. "Exhibit 20: History of Securus, Securus Webpage," Prison Policy Initiative, April 22, 2013, www.prisonpolicy.org.

7. "Gores Technology Group to Acquire Global Tel*Link Corporation from Schlumberger Technologies, Inc.," The Gores Group, July 21, 2004, www.gores.com.

8. "The Gores Group and Global Tel*Link Announce Acquisition of Verizon Business' Department of Corrections Division," The Gores Group, November 13, 2006, www.gores.com.

9. Bianca Tylek and Connor McCloskey, "This Call May Be Monopolized and Recorded," The Marshall Project, July 11, 2018.

10. "GTL," American Securities, n.d., web.archive.org/web/20190913235345/https://www.american-securities.com/en/companies/GTL.

11. "Aventiv," Platinum Equity, February 2020, www.platinumequity.com/our-portfolio..

12. Kevin Dowd, "Billionaires, Buyouts and Basketball: The Gores Brothers Take on Private Equity," *PitchBook*, June 19, 2018, pitchbook.com/news.

13. Steven J. Jackson, "Ex-Communication: Competition and Collusion in the U.S. Prison Telephone Industry," *Critical Studies in Media Communication* 22, no. 4 (October 2005), pp. 263–80, doi.org.

14. Ulandis Forte, "My Grandmother's 20-Year Fight for Prison Phone Justice," *Truthout*, June 21, 2019, truthout.org.

15. "Ensuring Just and Reasonable Rates and Charges for Inmate Calling Services Report and Order on Remand and Fourth Further Notice of Proposed Rulemaking—WC Docket No. 12-375," Federal Communications Commission, July 16, 2020, docs.fcc.gov/public/attachments/DOC.

16. Jon Brodkin, "Ajit Pai Accused of Conflict for Helping Former Client, a Prison Phone Company," *Ars Technica*, August 10, 2017, arstechnica.com.

17. "Ensuring Just and Reasonable Rates and Charges for Inmate Calling Services Report and Order on Remand and Fourth Further Notice of Proposed Rulemaking—WC Docket No. 12-375."

18. *Global Tel*Link v. FCC*, No. 15-1461 (D.C. Cir. 2017).

19. "Securus Technologies Realigns Business Units, Diversifies Product Offerings Under New Corporate Parent: Aventiv Technologies," Aventiv, October 10, 2019, www.aventiv.com.

20. "GTL Becomes ViaPath Technologies, Launches Expanded Reentry Services," GTL, January 4, 2022, www.gtl.net/about-us.

21. Juliana Kim, "Biden Signs a Bill to Fight Expensive Prison Phone Call Costs," NPR, January 6, 2023, www.npr.org/2023/01/01/1146370950/prison-phone-call-cost-martha-wright-biden.

22. "Our Campaigns," Connecting Families, n.d., connectfamiliesnow.com/ourcampaigns.

23. Worth Rises, unpublished data model.

24. "Ensuring Just and Reasonable Rates and Charges for Inmate Calling Services Report and Order on Remand and Fourth Further Notice of Proposed Rulemaking—WC Docket No. 12-375."

25. Wagner and Bertram, "State of Phone Justice—2022."

26. "Comment Letter on Report and Order on Remand and Fourth Further Notice of Proposed Rulemaking—WC Docket No. 12-375," Worth Rises, November 23, 2020, docs.fcc.gov/public/attachments.

27. "Data," Connecting Families, n.d., connectfamiliesnow.com/data.

28. Sottile, "Making Phone Calls from Prison Is Now Free in Massachusetts"; Katie Honan, "New York City Jail Inmates Can Now Make Free Phone Calls," *Wall Street Journal*, May 1, 2019, www.wsj.com; "All Campaigns," Connect Families Now, n.d., connectfamiliesnow.com/ourcampaigns.

29. "Request for Proposals for Incarcerated Person Communication Services RFP # SHF | 2019-11/ Sourcing Event No. 0000003286," City and County of San Francisco, December 20, 2019.

30. "Contract Number 21PSX0109: Inmate Communications Services—State of Connecticut and Securus Technologies, LLC.," CT Source, August 8, 2023, webprocure.proactiscloud.com/maincontractboard.

31. Wagner and Bertram, "State of Phone Justice."

32. Bernadette Rabuy and Peter Wagner, "Screening Out Family Time: The For-Profit Video Visitation Industry in Prisons and Jails," Prison Policy Initiative, January 2015, static.prisonpolicy.org.

33. Jack Smith IV, "'Video Visitation' Is Ending in-Person Prison Visits—and Prisons Are Going to Make a Ton of Money," *Business Insider*, May 5, 2016, www.businessinsider.com.

34. Timothy B. Lee, "Jails Are Replacing Visits with Video Calls—Inmates and Families Hate It," *Ars Technica*, May 14, 2018, arstechnica.com/tech-policy.

35. "Tablets," Pennsylvania Department of Corrections, n.d., www.cor.pa.gov/Inmates/Pages/Tablets.aspx.

36. Matt Clarke and Ed Lyon, "Tablets and E-Messaging Services Expand in Prisons and Jails, as Do Fees," *Prison Legal News*, April 2, 2018, www.prisonlegalnews.org.

37. Ibid.; Tonya Riley, "'Free' Tablets Are Costing Prison Inmates a Fortune," *Mother Jones*, October 5, 2018, www.motherjones.com.

38. Olivia Carville, "Ex-Cons Create 'Instagram for Prisons,' and Wardens Are Fine with That," Bloomberg, February 6, 2019, www.bloomberg.com.

39. Mike Wessler, "SMH: The Rapid and Unregulated Growth of E-Messaging in Prisons," Prison Policy Initiative, March 2023, www.prisonpolicy.org.

40. "Securus Technologies: Public Lender Presentation," *Huffington Post*, April 15, 2015, big.assets.huffingtonpost.com.

41. Worth Rises, unpublished data model.

42. Ibid.

43. Ibid.

44. "Order Accepting Settlement with Modification, Granting Certificate of Authority, and Closing Dockets P-0524/CT-94-386 and P-5024/NA-94-387," Minnesota Public Utilities Commission, July 17, 1996, www.edockets.state.mn.us.

45. Bianca Tylek, "Testimony Regarding Hearing: America for Sale? An Examination of the Practices of Private Funds, Before Committee on Financial Services, U.S. House of Representa-

tives," Worth Rises, November 18, 2019, ourfinancialsecurity.org/wp-content/uploads/2019/12/Worth-Rises-Testimony-HFSC-Hearing-11.19.19.pdf.

46. Josh Kosman, "Prison Phone Profit," *New York Post*, August 19, 2011, nypost.com.

47. "American Securities Completes Acquisition of Global Tel*Link," American Securities, December 15, 2011, www.american-securities.com..

48. Tashenma Lawrence, "RE: Alabama PSC Annual Financial Statements," Unpublished data, January 10, 2024.

49. Worth Rises, unpublished data model.

50. Laurence Darmiento, "Troubled Companies Made Him Billions. but This One Made Him Enemies," *Los Angeles Times*, September 5, 2019, www.latimes.com..

51. Wagner and Bertram, "State of Phone Justice."

52. Ibid.

53. "Securus Technologies Sold to Abry Partners," meshDETECT, March 28, 2013, prisoncellphones.com.

54. Tylek, "Testimony Regarding Hearing: America for Sale? An Examination of the Practices of Private Funds."

55. "Platinum Equity's Prison Telecom Company Securus Sees Debt Trade at Up to 50 Percent Discount," Private Equity Stakeholder Project, February 6, 2020, pestakeholder.org.

56. Kevin Bliss, "Securus Technologies Rebrands as Aventiv," *Prison Legal News*, January 9, 2020, www.prisonlegalnews.org.

57. "Affordability, Accountability, Innovation and Reform," Platinum Equity, n.d., www.platinumequity.com/securus-transformation.

58. Paula Seligson, "Platinum's Prison Phone Firm Cut to CCC by S&P on Default Risk," *Bloomberg Law*, October 31, 2023, news.bloomberglaw.com/bankruptcy-law.

59. Connor McCleskey, "Will the FCC Finally Stop a Prison Telecom Merger?" Worth Rises, July 18, 2018, worthrises.org/blog.

60. Eric Markowitz, "Amid Death Threats, an Embattled Prison Phone Company CEO Speaks Out," *International Business Times*, January 26, 2016, www.ibtimes.com.

61. "Securus Technologies, Inc. Completes Transaction to Acquire JPay Inc," Securus Technologies, July 31, 2015, www.prnewswire.com/news-releases.

62. "GTL Acquires Telmate, a Leading Provider of Secure Corrections Solutions and Community Corrections and Probation, Parole Applications," PR Newswire, August 1, 2017, www.telmate.com.

63. Bianca Tylek, "How the Fight for 'Prison Phone Justice' Scored a Major Victory," *Crime Report*, April 23, 2019, web.archive.org/web/20210422104603/https://thecrimereport.org/2019/04/23/how-the-fight-for-prison-phone-justice-scored-a-major-victory.

64. McCleskey, "Will the FCC Finally Stop a Prison Telecom Merger?"

65. "Securus' Bilateral Patent License Agreements Allow Facilities to Share Technology Developed and Bring More Products to Corrections/Law Enforcement Quicker," Securus Technologies, September 29, 2016, www.prnewswire.com/news-releases.

66. Wagner and Jones, "State of Phone Justice"; McCleskey, "Will the FCC Finally Stop a Prison Telecom Merger?"; "Workshop on Further Reform of Inmate Calling Services," Federal Communications Commission, 2014, docs.fcc.gov/public/attachments.

67. Worth Rises, unpublished data model.

68. "About Unisys," Unisys, n.d., www.unisys.com/about-unisys.

69. Tashenma Lawrence, "RE: Alabama PSC Annual Financial Statements," unpublished data, January 10, 2024; "Workshop on Further Reform of Inmate Calling Services," Federal Communications Commission.

70. Davide Scigliuzzo, "HIG Plans Spinoff of Prison Phone Operator After Failed Merger." Bloomberg, January 24, 2020, www.bloomberg.com/news.

71. Jessica Miller, "With Captive Customers, Utah Jails Charge Vastly Different Rates for Phone Calls from Loved Ones. They Can Be More Than $10 for 15 Minutes," *Salt Lake Tribune*, April 29, 2019, www.sltrib.com/news.

72. "Our Companies," TKC Holdings, n.d., www.tkcholdings.com; Stephen Raher, "Paging Anti-Trust Lawyers: Prison Commissary Giants Prepare to Merge," Prison Policy Initiative, July 5, 2016, www.prisonpolicy.org.

73. Scigliuzzo, "HIG Plans Spinoff of Prison Phone Operator After Failed Merger."

74. "Public Notice: Applications Filed for the Transfer of Control of Centurylink Public Communications, Inc. to Inmate Calling Solutions, LLC D/B/A ICSolutions Non-Streamlined Pleading Cycle Established WC Docket No. 20-150," Federal Communications Commission, June 25, 2020, docs.fcc.gov/public/attachments.

75. Wagner and Bertram, "State of Phone Justice."

76. Tashenma Lawrence, "RE: Alabama PSC Annual Financial Statements." Unpublished data, January 10, 2024.

77. Ibid.

78. Ibid.; All non-revenue data from "Data," Connecting Families, connectfamiliesnow.com/data.

79. Joan Petersilia, *When Prisoners Come Home: Parole and Prisoner Reentry* (New York: Oxford University Press, 2009), p. 246. "*Every* known study that has been able to directly examine the relationship between a prisoner's legitimate community ties and recidivism has found that feelings of being welcome at home and the strength of interpersonal ties outside prison help predict postprison adjustment" (emphasis in original).

80. "Connecting Families Compelling Messaging for Prison Phone Justice Campaigns," Worth Rise, March 2020, worthrises.org/resources.

81. "Prison Phone Fact Sheet," Campaign for Prison Phone Justice, n.d., web.archive.org/web/20210125184851/https://ecfsapi.fcc.gov/file/60001328413.pdf.

82. "Rates and Kickbacks," Prison Phone Justice, n.d., www.prisonphonejustice.org.

83. Drew Kukorowski, Peter Wagner, and Leah Sakala, "Please Deposit All of Your Money: Kickbacks, Rates, and Hidden Fees in the Jail Phone Industry," Prison Policy Initiative, May 8, 2013, www.prisonpolicy.org.

84. "Ensuring Just and Reasonable Rates and Charges for Inmate Calling Services Report and Order on Remand and Fourth Further Notice of Proposed Rulemaking—WC Docket No. 12-375."

85. Karina Wilkinson, "Massachusetts Prison and Jail Phone Rates Reform Background Sheet," Prison Policy Initiative, July 2020, www.prisonpolicy.org..

86. "Data," Connecting Families.

87. Worth Rises, unpublished analysis.

88. "Data," Connecting Families.

89. "About Us," ICSolutions, n.d., www.icsolutions.com/FacilitiesHome/AboutUs.

90. Breanna Edwards, "Dawn Freeman's Mission to Help Returning Citizens Restart Their Lives," *Essence*, January 17, 2020, www.essence.com/feature/dawn-freeman-securus -foundation-criminal-justice-reform..

91. "Rate Quote," Securus Technologies, available at securustech.online/#/rate-quote.

92. "Information Processing Systems Agreement (#10ITZ0119MA), between the State of Connecticut acting by Its Department of Administrative Services and Securus Technologies, Inc.," Connecticut Department of Administrative Services, March 1, 2012.

93. "Rate Quote," Securus Technologies, available at securustech.online/#/rate-quote.

94. Wagner and Bertram, "State of Phone Justice."

95. Anthony Accurso, "Prison Telecom Giant GTL Agrees to $67 Million Settlement in Class-Action Over Inactive Account Seizure Policy," *Prison Legal News*, April 1, 2022, www .prisonlegalnews.org.

96. "TX Prison Issues: Phones," TX Prisoners Network Support, n.d., brokenchains.us.

97. DeVuono-Powell, et al., "Who Pays? The True Cost of Incarceration on Families."

98. Ibid.

99. Victoria Law, "Imagine Pleading Guilty Because You Can't Afford to Call Your Lawyer," *Truthout*, February 17, 2019, truthout.org.

100. Ibid.

101. Jimmie E. Gates, "State Supreme Court Upholds 12-Year Sentence for Man Who Brought Cellphone into Jail," *Clarion-Ledger*, January 16, 2020, www.clarionledger.com; Stevie Borrello, Daniel Fetherston, and Katherine Tutrone, "Prisoners Are Going Viral on TikTok," *Vice News*, November 12, 2020, www.vice.com.

102. Lee, "Jails Are Replacing Visits with Video Calls."

103. Rabuy and Wagner, "Screening Out Family Time."

104. Smith IV, "'Video Visitation' Is Ending In-Person Prison Visits."

105. Rabuy and Wagner, "Screening Out Family Time."

106. Lee, "Jails Are Replacing Visits with Video Calls."

107. Jorge Antonio Renaud, "Video Visitation: How Private Companies Push for Visits by Video and Families Pay the Price," Grassroots Leadership and Texas Criminal Justice Coalition, October 2014, grassrootsleadership.org.

108. Hanna Kozlowska, "Prison Communications Company Securus Will No Longer Require Jails to Ban In-Person Visits," *Quartz*, May 5, 2015, qz.com.

109. Lee, "Jails Are Replacing Visits with Video Calls."

110. Danielle Wiley, "Telmate Tablets Create Positive Environment for Inmates," *Idaho Press*, January 23, 2016, web.archive.org/web/20200406080912/https://www.idahopress.com/news/crime_courts/jail/telmate-tablets-create-positive-environment-for-inmates.

111. Ibid.

112. "TN Man Faces Charges After Drugs Spotted on Video Call," WKRN News 2, February 9, 2024, www.youtube.com.

113. Stephen Raher, "You've Got Mail: The Promise of Cyber Communication in Prisons and the Need for Regulation," Prison Policy Initiative, January 21, 2021, www.prisonpolicy.org.

114. "NYS DOCCS Inmate Services," JPay, n.d., www.jpay.com.

115. Victoria Law, "How Companies Make Millions Charging Prisoners to Send an Email," *Wired*, August 3, 2018, www.wired.com.

116. Riley, "'Free' Tablets Are Costing Prison Inmates a Fortune."

117. Ibid.

118. Karen L. Murtagh, "Commentary: Why Is New York Giving Tablets to All State Prisoners?" *Fortune*, February 2, 2018, fortune.com/2018/02/02/jpay-tablets-prisoners-rape-new-york-state.

119. Riley, "'Free' Tablets Are Costing Prison Inmates a Fortune."

120. Michael Waters, "Free Tablets for the Incarcerated Come with a Price," *The Outline*, December 3, 2019, theoutline.com.

121. "Apple Music," Apple, n.d., www.apple.com. Apple Music is $15 for a family of six, or $2.50 per person.

122. Riley; Ben Conarck, "Florida Inmates Spent $11.3 Million on MP3s. Now Prisons Are Taking the Players," *Florida Times-Union*, August 8, 2018, www.jacksonville.com.

123. Mack Finkel and Wanda Bertram, "More States Are Signing Harmful 'Free Prison Tablet' Contracts," Prison Policy Initiative, March 7, 2019, www.prisonpolicy.org.

124. "The Cost of 'Free' Prison Tablets," Appalachian Prison Book Project, November 20, 2019, appalachianprisonbookproject.org.

125. Ibid.

126. Samantha Michaels, "People in Prison Are Way More Likely to Have Dyslexia. The Justice System Sets Them Up to Fail," *Mother Jones*, April 30, 2019, www.motherjones.com/crime-justice.

127. Jordan Smith, "Securus Settles Lawsuit Alleging Improper Recording of Privileged Inmate Calls," *The Intercept*, March 15, 2016, theintercept.com.

128. Ella Fassler, "Prison Phone Companies Are Recording Attorney-Client Calls Across the U.S.," *Vice*, December 13, 2021, www.vice.com.

129. George Joseph and Debbie Nathan, "Prisons Across the U.S. Are Quietly Building Databases of Incarcerated People's Voice Prints," *The Intercept*, January 30, 2019, theintercept.com.

130. Ibid.

131. George Joseph and Debbie Nathan, "Why Is a Prison Company Storing the Voice Prints of Even Innocent People?" *Fast Company*, February 14, 2019, www.fastcompany.com.

132. "U.S. Prisons and Jails Using AI to Mass-Monitor Millions of Inmate Calls," LEO Technologies, October 24, 2019, leotechnologies.com.

133. Joseph, et al., "Prisons Across the U.S. Are Quietly Building Databases of Incarcerated People's Voice Prints."

134. "Intelligence Bundles—Global Tel Link Request for Proposals," Shelby County, TN, 2016, www.documentcloud.org/documents.

135. "U.S. Prisons and Jails Using AI," LEO Technologies.

136. Jordan Smith and Micah Lee, "Massive Hack of 70 Million Prisoner Phone Calls Indicates Violations of Attorney-Client Privilege," *The Intercept*, November 11, 2015, theintercept.com /2015/11/11/securus-hack-prison-phone-company-exposes-thousands-of-calls-lawyers-and -clients.

137. Ibid.

138. Kieren McCarthy, "Remember When Securus Was Sued for Recording 14,000 Calls Between Prison Inmates and Lawyers? It Just Settled," *The Register*, May 21, 2020, www .theregister.com.

139. "FTC Takes Action Against Global Tel*Link Corp. for Failing to Adequately Secure Data, Notify Consumers After Their Personal Data Was Breached," Federal Trade Commission, November 16, 2023, www.ftc.gov/news-events/news/press-releases.

Financial Services

1. Arun Gupta, "The Financial Firm That Cornered the Market on Jails," *The Nation*, August 1, 2016, www.thenation.com.

2. Daniel Wagner, "Megabanks Have Prison Financial Services Market Locked Up," Center for Public Integrity, October 2, 2014, publicintegrity.org/inequality-poverty-opportunity.

3. Mia Francis-Poulin, "Electronic Payments: A Brief History," Forte Blog, February 2, 2018, blog.forte.net.

4. Ariel Schwartz, "Here's the Real Story Behind the Apple of Prison Tech," *Business Insider*, July 2015, www.businessinsider.com.

5. Matthew Desmond, "American Capitalism Is Brutal. You Can Trace That to the Plantation," *New York Times*, August 14, 2019, www.nytimes.com.

6. Wagner, "Megabanks Have Prison Financial Services."

7. Daniel Wagner, "Prison Bankers Cash in on Captive Customers," Center for Public Integrity, September 30, 2014, publicintegrity.org/inequality-poverty-opportunity.

8. Ibid.

9. Stephen Raher, "The Multi-Million Dollar Market of Sending Money to an Incarcerated Loved One," Prison Policy Initiative, January 18, 2017, www.prisonpolicy.org.

10. "Securus Technologies: Public Lender Presentation," *Huffington Post*, April 15, 2015, big .assets.huffingtonpost.com.

11. Ibid.; Laura Maruschak and Todd Minton, "Correctional Populations in the United States, 2017–2018," Bureau of Justice Statistics, Office of Justice Programs, U.S. Dept. of Justice, August 2020, www.bjs.gov. Estimate based on 2.123 million people (2018) making 12 transactions a year that generate an average of $6 per transaction.

12. "Securus Technologies: Public Lender Presentation."

13. Wendy Sawyer, "Since You Asked: How Many People Are Released from Each State's Prisons and Jails Every Year?" Prison Policy Initiative, August 25, 2022, www.prisonpolicy.org.

14. "Use of Debit Card for Inmate Release Funds," Correctional Leaders Association, n.d., www.webcitation.org.

15. "Securus Technologies: Public Lender Presentation."

16. Ibid.; Maruschak and Minton, "Correctional Populations in the United States, 2017–2018." Estimate based on 4.399 million people (2018) making 12 transactions a year that generate an average of $5 per transaction.

17. Maruschak and Minton, "Correctional Populations in the United States, 2017–2018."

18. "JPay, the Apple of the U.S. Prison System," *Bloomberg Business*, September 13, 2012, www .bloomberg.com; Tim Ryan, "A Brief History of Western Union Money Transfer Services," Street-directory.com, 2018, www.streetdirectory.com/travel_guide; "TouchPay Holdings Company Profile: Acquisition & Investors," Pitchbook, n.d., pitchbook.com/profiles; "Access Corrections," Keefe Group, n.d., www.keefegroup.com; "Stored Value Cards Inc.," All Biz, n.d., www.allbiz .com; "Rapid Financial Solutions," Worth Rises—The Prison Industry Corporate Database, n.d., data.worthrises.org.

19. "The Prison Industry: Mapping Private Sector Players," Worth Rises, n.d., worthrises.org.

20. Catherine Akenhead, "How States Can Take a Stand Against Prison Banking Profiteers." *George Washington Law Review* 85, no. 4 (, July 2017), www.gwlr.org.

21. "Securus Technologies: Public Lender Presentation."

22. Wagner, "Prison Bankers Cash in on Captive Customers."

23. "Securus Technologies: Public Lender Presentation."

24. "Securus Preliminary Consolidated Balance Sheet," Prison Policy Initiative, 2018, www .prisonpolicy.org/phones/financials; "About JPay," JPay, n.d.,www.jpay.com/AboutUs.

25. Wagner, "Megabanks Have Prison Financial Services."

26. Andrew Stewart, "Debit Card Issuers Still Prey on People Released from Prisons and Jails: HRDC Lawsuits Challenge Companies in Court," *Prison Legal News*, December 1, 2020, www .prisonlegalnews.org.

27. Stephen Raher, "The Multi-Million Dollar Market of Sending Money to an Incarcerated Loved One."

28. Akenhead, "How States Can Take a Stand."

29. Amirah Al Idrus, "Debit Cards Slam Released Prisoners with Sky-High Fees, Few Protec-tions," Center for Public Integrity, September 30, 2014, publicintegrity.org; Stephanie Clifford and Jessica Silver-Greenberg, "In Prisons, Sky-High Phone Rates and Money Transfer Fees," *New York Times*, June 26, 2014, www.nytimes.com.

30. Akenhead, "How States Can Take a Stand"; Wagner, "Prison Bankers Cash in on Cap-tive Customers."

31. Akenhead, "How States Can Take a Stand."

32. "Money Order/Check Deposit Form," JPay, n.d., static1.squarespace.com.

33. Ibid.

34. Emails received by Worth Rises.

35. "Money Order/Check Deposit Form."

36. Wagner, "Prison Bankers Cash in on Captive Customers."

37. Ibid.

38. "NYS DOCCS Has Renegotiated Its Contract with JPay to Lower Rates," Worth Rises, n.d., worthrises.org.

39. Aleks Kajstura, "Consumer Financial Protection Bureau Should Regulate Release Cards," Prison Policy Initiative, March 18, 2015, www.prisonpolicy.org.

40. Ibid.

41. "'Release Cards' Turn Inmates and Their Families into Profit Stream," Malta Justice Initia-tive, n.d., maltajusticeinitiative.org.

42. Mia Armstrong and Nicole Lewis, "What Gate Money Can (and Cannot) Buy for People Leaving Prison," The Marshall Project, September 10, 2019, www.themarshallproject.org.

43. Paul Tassin, "Numi Financial Skims Unauthorized Fees from Inmates' Accounts, Class Action Says," Top Class Actions, March 31, 2017, topclassactions.com/lawsuit-settlements /lawsuit-news.

44. Kajstura, "Consumer Financial Protection Bureau."

45. Ibid.

46. Wagner, "Prison Bankers Cash in on Captive Customers."

47. David Brancaccio, "JPMorgan Chase Settles Debit Card Lawsuit with Former Inmates," *Marketplace*, August 5, 2016, www.marketplace.org.

48. "HRDC Files Joint Comment with CFPB Re Release Debit Cards," Human Rights Defense Center, March 24, 2015, www.humanrightsdefensecenter.org; Herb Weisbaum, "Inmates Charged Fee After Leaving Jail," NBC News, March 24, 2015, www.nbcnews.com..

49. Daniel Wagner, "Feds Probe Prison Banker as NYC Leaders Try to Cap Its High Fee,." *BuzzFeed News*, December 2, 2016, www.buzzfeednews.com.

50. "'Release Cards' Turn Inmates and Their Families into Profit Stream."

51. Consumer Financial Protection Bureau, "CFPB Penalizes JPay for Siphoning Taxpayer-Funded Benefits Intended to Help People Re-enter Society After Incarceration," CFPB Newsroom, October 19, 2021, www.consumerfinance.gov/about-us/newsroom.

52. "Securus Technologies: Public Lender Presentation"; Maruschak and Minton, "Correctional Populations in the United States, 2017–2018." Estimate based on 4.4 million people (2018) making 12 transactions a year that generate an average of $5 per transaction.

53. "Securus Technologies: Public Lender Presentation."

54. Arthur Pepin, "2015–2016 Policy Paper, The End of Debtors' Prisons: Effective Court Policies for Successful Compliance with Legal Financial Obligations," Conference of State Court Administrators, 2016, cosca.ncsc.org.

55. Ethan Bronner, "Poor Land in Jail as Companies Add Huge Fees for Probation," *New York Times*, July 2, 2012, www.nytimes.com.

56. Ibid.

57. "Directive No. 9250: Supervision Fees (Community Supervision)," New York Department of Corrections and Community Supervision, March 19, 2019, perma.cc/VCW2-LRCA; "JPay Payments," Department of Corrections and Community Supervision, n.d., web.archive.org/web/20200218185333/https://doccs.ny.gov/jpay-payments.

58. Tammy Gamerman, "Fees, Fines and Fairness: How Monetary Charges Drive Inequity in New York City's Criminal Justice System," New York City Office of the Comptroller, September 10, 2019, comptroller.nyc.gov/reports.

59. Ibid.; Estimate based on 16,000 people on parole paying $1.99 monthly as a payment fee to JPay.

Food + Commissary

1. Tom Perkins, "Michigan's Failed Effort to Privatize Prison Kitchens and the Future of Institutional Food," *Civil Eats*, August 20, 2018, civileats.com.

2. "Prison Food in America 2016."

3. *Hutto v. Finney*, 437 U.S. 678 (1978).

4. "United States Catering & Food Services for Correctional Facilities Market 2020," HTF Market Intelligence, October 2020.

5. "Prison Food in America 2016," edoc.bike, n.d., edoc.bike.

6. Madison Pauly, "The Surprising Benefits of Serving Prisoners Better Food," *Mother Jones*, March 2019, www.motherjones.com/crime-justice/2019/03/prison-food-health-commissary-strike-public-health-chronic-disease-pelican-bay.

7. "Prison Food in America 2016."

8. Tim Michling, "What's in This Macaroni? Privatization Is a Tool, Not a Panacea," Citizens Research Council of Michigan, March 9, 2018, crcmich.org.

9. Daniel Wagner, "Megabanks Have Prison Financial Services Market Locked Up," Center for Public Integrity, October 2, 2014, publicintegrity.org/inequality-poverty-opportunity/megabanks-have-prison-financial-services-market-locked-up.

10. Stephen Raher, "Paging Anti-Trust Lawyers: Prison Commissary Giants Prepare to Merge," Prison Policy Initiative, July 5, 2016, www.prisonpolicy.org.

11. "Keefe Commissary Network," Keefe Group, n.d., www.keefegroup.com.

12. Stephen Raher, "The Company Store," Prison Policy Initiative, 2018, www.prisonpolicy.org/reports/commissary.

13. David Reutter, "Prison Food and Commissary Services: A Recipe for Disaster," *Prison Legal News*, August 4, 2018, www.prisonlegalnews.org.

14. "United States Catering & Food Services for Correctional Facilities Market 2020," HTF Market Intelligence, October 2020.

15. "12 Need-to-Know Statistics," North American Association of Food Equipment Manufacturers, 2018, www.thenafemshow.org/wp-content/uploads/Corrections; Avery Davis, "The Disgusting Truth Behind Prison Food in America," *Spoon University*, July 19, 2016, spoonuniversity.com.

16. "Food Services—Correctional Facility," Aramark, n.d., web.archive.org/web/20201112025806/https://www.aramark.com/industries/business-government/correctional-facilities/food-services.

17. Leslie Soble, Kathryn Stroud, and Marika Weinstein, "Eating Behind Bars: Ending the Hidden Punishment of Food in Prison," Impact Justice, 2020, impactjustice.org.

18. Raher, "Paging Anti-Trust Lawyers: Prison Commissary Giants Prepare to Merge"; Raher, "The Company Store."

19. Ibid.

20. "Fact Sheet: Private Equity-Owned Firms Dominate Prison and Detention Services," Private Equity Stakeholder Project, September 17, 2018, pestakeholder.org; "Keefe Commissary Network."

21. Raher, "Paging Anti-Trust Lawyers."

22. Ben Conarck, "Florida Prisons Roll Out More For-Profit Services While Weighing Visitation Cuts," *Florida Times-Union*, June 1, 2018, www.jacksonville.com.

23. Anthony Ryan Hatch, *Captivating Technology: Race, Technoscience, and the Carceral Imagination* (Durham, NC: Duke University Press, 2019), pp. 67–84.

24. Mecca Bos, "Don't Go to Jail for the Dining Experience," *Food Service News*, February 2018, www.foodservicenews.net.

25. "Correctional Facilities," Aramark, n.d., www.aramark.com/industries/business -government/correctional-facilities.

26. "United States Catering & Food Services for Correctional Facilities Market 2020," HTF Market Intelligence, October 2020.

27. Ibid.

28. "About Us," Trinity Services Group, n.d., www.trinityservicesgroup.com; "Prison Food in America 2016"; "United States Catering & Food Services for Correctional Facilities Market 2020," HTF Market Intelligence, October 2020.

29. "About Us," Trinity Services Group; "Trinity Services Group, Inc.," PrivCo, n.d., system .privco.com/company/trinity-services-group-inc.

30. "Prison Food in America 2016."

31. "The Prison Industry Corporate Database," Worth Rises, n.d., data.worthrises.org.

32. "Companies," Keefe Group, 2019, www.keefegroup.com/companies-101.

33. "Swanson Services Corporation Is Now Part of Trinity Services Group," Trinity Services Group, 2016, web.archive.org.

34. "Union Supply Group," Union Supply Group, 2020, unionsupply.com.

35. Stephanie Simon, "Jailbirds Order Up Hot Wings," *Wall Street Journal*, April 27, 2010, www .wsj.com/articles.

36. "Keefe Commissary Network," Keefe Group, 2019, www.keefegroup.com.

37. Tim Barker, "Prison Services Are Profitable Niche for Bridgeton Company," *St. Louis Post-Dispatch*, February 15, 2015, www.stltoday.com.

38. Taylor Elizabeth Eldridge, "The Big Business of Prisoner Care Packages," The Marshall Project, December 21, 2017, www.themarshallproject.org.

39. "Fact Sheet: Private Equity-Owned Firms Dominate Prison and Detention Services," Private Equity Stakeholders Project.

40. "Keefe Commissary Network," Keefe Group, 2019, www.keefegroup.com.

41. "TKC Holdings, Inc.," PrivCo, n.d., system.privco.com/company/tkc_private_stock_annual _report_financials.

42. Julio Ojeda-Zapata, "Jails Offer Micro Markets Instead of Vending Machines," *Corrections1*, March 30, 2015, www.corrections1.com; "Jail Vending," MicroTronicus, 2020, www .microtronicus.com.

43. "Sheriff Runs Female Chain Gang," CNN, October 29, 2003, www.cnn.com.

44. H. Claire Brown and Joe Fassler, "Prison Food Is Making U.S. Inmates Disproportionately Sick," *The Counter*, January 3, 2018, newfoodeconomy.org.

45. "Prison Food in America 2016."

46. Chris Hedges, "Food Behind Bars Isn't Fit for Your Dog," *Truthdig*, December 23, 2013, www.truthdig.com.

47. Michael Owen Jones, "Eating Behind Bars: On Punishment, Resistance, Policy, and Applied Folkloristics," *Journal of American Folklore* 130, no. 515 (2017), p. 72, doi.org; Monica Eng, "Prisoners Sue over Soy Diet," *Chicago Tribune*, December 21, 2009, www.chicagotribune.com.

48. Connor Sheets, "Jail Kitchen Workers Say Donated, Spoiled Food Keeps Costs Low for 'Beach House Sheriff,'" AL.com, April 23, 2018, www.al.com/news/birmingham.

49. David M. Reutter, "Prison Food and Commissary Services: A Recipe for Disaster," *Prison Legal News*, August 4, 2018, www.prisonlegalnews.org.

50. Sarah Geraghty, "Failure to Provide Adequate Nutrition to People in the Gordon County Jail," Southern Center for Human Rights, October 28, 2014, www.schr.org.

51. Carimah Townes, "Corporation Literally Served Inmates Trash," *ThinkProgress*, March 30, 2015, archive.thinkprogress.org.

52. Kyle Feldscher, "Michigan Cancels Aramark Contract to Provide Food Service at State Prisons," *MLive*, July 13, 2015, www.mlive.com.

53. Paul Egan, "Prison Food Contractor Hit with $2M in Penalties," *Detroit Free Press*, January 20, 2017, www.freep.com.

54. Michael Gerstein and Jonathan Oosting, "State Set to End Private Prison Food Service," *Detroit News*, February 7, 2018, www.detroitnews.com.

55. Roland Zullo, "Food Service Privatization in Michigan's Prisons: Observations of Corrections Officers," March 2016, www.mco-seiu.org.

56. "Ohio Prisoners Complain of Maggots in Food," *Huffington Post*, July 15, 2014, www.huffingtonpost.com.

57. Ibid.

58. Hatch, *Captivating Technology: Race, Technoscience, and the Carceral Imagination*; Christopher Zoukis, "Ohio Experiences Continued Problems with Aramark," *Prison Legal News*, March 18, 2018, www.prisonlegalnews.org.

59. Connor Sheets, "Jail Kitchen Workers Say Donated, Spoiled Food Keeps Costs Low for 'Beach House Sheriff'"; Camila Domonoske, "Alabama Sheriff Legally Took $750,000 Meant to Feed Inmates, Bought Beach House," NPR, March 14, 2018, www.npr.org.

60. Rachel Riley, "Attempted Riot over Food at El Paso County Jail Preceded by Rise in Complaints, Warnings from Deputies," *The Gazette*, March 7, 2017, gazette.com; "Security Division," El Paso County Sheriff, n.d., www.epcsheriffsoffice.com; "Sheriff's Office Releases Monthly Statistics on Sheriff Elder's Top Priorities," El Paso County Sheriff, March 7, 2019, www.epcsheriffsoffice.com.

61. "RFP #40-004 Inmate Food Services Annual Contract," Hall County Jail, n.d., www
.hallcounty.org; "Inmate Food Services, Addendum #1," Government Contracts & Bids, June 19,
2019, www.hallcounty.org; "Hall County, GA, Official Website," Hall County Jail, n.d., www
.hallcounty.org.

62. Craig Lyons, "County Eyes Nearly $1 Million Savings with Jail Food Service Contract," *Chicago Tribune*, November 7, 2018, www.chicagotribune.com.

63. Joe Fassler and Claire Brown, "Prison Food Is Making U.S. Inmates Disproportionately
Sick," *The Atlantic*, December 27, 2017, www.theatlantic.com.

64. Mariel Marlow, et al., "Foodborne Disease Outbreaks in Correctional Institutions—
United States, 1998–2014," *American Journal of Public Health* 107, no. 7 (2017), pp. 1150–56, ajph
.aphapublications.org.

65. Carrie Chennault and Joshua Sbicca, "Prison Agriculture in the United States," Inter-
University Consortium for Political and Social Research, June 20, 2023, www.openicpsr.org..

66. "Food & Farm Services," Georgia Department of Corrections, January 2022, gdc.georgia
.gov.

67. Hatch, *Captivating Technology: Race, Technoscience, and the Carceral Imagination.*

68. Banu Bargu, *Starve and Immolate—The Politics of Human Weapons* (New York: Columbia
University Press, 2015).

69. Natasha Lennard, "Prison Strike Organizer Warns: Brutal Prison Conditions Risk 'Another
Attica,'" *The Intercept*, August 21, 2018, theintercept.com.

70. "Commissary Day," PEN America, November 19, 2012, pen.org.

71. Hatch, *Captivating Technology: Race, Technoscience, and the Carceral Imagination.*

72. Taylor Elizabeth Eldridge, "The Big Business of Prisoner Care Packages: Inside the Booming Market for Food in Pouches," *Prison Legal News*, October 8, 2018, www.prisonlegalnews
.org.

73. Raher, "The Company Store."

74. Eldridge, "The Big Business of Prisoner Care Packages: Inside the Booming Market for
Food in Pouches."

75. "Stop Package Restrictions in New York State Prisons! Take Action Now!" Critical Resistance, December 20, 2017, criticalresistance.org.

76. "Packaging Love," Worth Rises, n.d., worthrises.org/packaginglove.

77. Molly Hagan, "New York's Prison Package Ban Places New Burdens on the Incarcerated,"
The Appeal, June 2, 2022, theappeal.org.

78. Ibid.

79. Samantha Melamed, "Sharing Meals Brings Families Together, Even in Prison. Doing
Without Has Strained Ties," *Philadelphia Inquirer*, January 3, 2019, www.philly.com.

80. Ibid.

Healthcare

1. Deanna Pan, "TIMELINE: Deinstitutionalization and Its Consequences," *Mother Jones*, April 29, 2013, www.motherjones.com.

2. Renee Fabian, "The History of Inhumane Mental Health Treatments," *Talkspace*, July 31, 2017, www.talkspace.com.

3. Pan, "TIMELINE: Deinstitutionalization and Its Consequences."

4. E. Fuller Torrey, et al., "More Mentally Ill Persons Are in Jails and Prisons Than Hospitals: A Survey of the States," Treatment Advocacy Center and National Sheriffs' Association, May 2010, static.prisonpolicy.org.

5. DJ Jaffe, "Medicaid Discrimination Against People with Severe Mental Illnesses," Mental Illness Policy Org, n.d., mentalillnesspolicy.org.

6. Ibid.; Pan, "TIMELINE: Deinstitutionalization and Its Consequences."

7. Pan, "TIMELINE: Deinstitutionalization and Its Consequences."

8. Ibid.

9. Derek H. Suite, et al., "Beyond Misdiagnosis, Misunderstanding and Mistrust: Relevance of the Historical Perspective in the Medical and Mental Health Treatment of People of Color," *Journal of the National Medical Association* 99, no. 8 (August 2007), www.ncbi.nlm.nih.gov.

10. Jason Szep, et al., "Special Report: U.S. Jails Are Outsourcing Medical Care—and the Death Toll Is Rising," Reuters, October 26, 2020, kfgo.com.

11. Peter Wagner and Bernadette Rabuy, "Following the Money of Mass Incarceration," Prison Policy Initiative, January 25, 2017, www.prisonpolicy.org.

12. Worth Rises, unpublished data.

13. Worth Rises, unpublished data.

14. Szep, et al., "Special Report: U.S. Jails Are Outsourcing Medical Care—and the Death Toll Is Rising."

15. Wendy Sawyer, "The Steep Cost of Medical Co-Pays in Prison Puts Health at Risk," Prison Policy Initiative, April 17, 2017, www.prisonpolicy.org.

16. *Estelle v. Gamble*, 429 U.S. 97 (1976).

17. David Redemske, "Providing Healthcare in the Prison Environment," HDR, 2018, www.hdrinc.com.

18. Kenneth L. Appelbaum, Thomas D. Manning, and John D. Noonan, "A University-State-Corporation Partnership for Providing Correctional Mental Health Services," *Psychiatric Services* 53, no. 2 (February 1, 2002), pp. 185–89, doi.org; Noga Shalev, "From Public to Private Care: The Historical Trajectory of Medical Services in a New York City Jail," *American Journal of Public Health* 99, no. 6 (June 1, 2009), pp. 988–95, doi.org.

19. Szep, et al., "Special Report: U.S. Jails Are Outsourcing Medical Care—and the Death Toll Is Rising."

20. Wagner and Bernadette Rabuy, "Following the Money of Mass Incarceration."

21. Ana Singh, "Convicts Without Care: How the Privatization of Healthcare in the U.S. Prison System Fails to Protect Inmates' Health," *Berkeley Political Review*, January 28, 2017, bpr.berkeley .edu; "Managing Prison Health Care Spending," Pew Charitable Trusts, 2013, www.pewtrusts .org; "State Prison Health Care Spending: An Examination," Pew Charitable Trusts and the John D. and Catherine T. MacArthur Foundation, July 2014, www.pewtrusts.org.

22. Redemske, "Providing Healthcare in the Prison Environment."

23. "Prison Health Care: Costs and Quality—How and Why States Strive for High-Performing Systems," Pew Charitable Trusts, October 2017, www.pewtrusts.org; Szep, et al., "Special Report: U.S. Jails Are Outsourcing Medical Care—and the Death Toll Is Rising."

24. Worth Rises, unpublished data.

25. Nicholas Freudenberg, "Jails, Prisons, and the Health of Urban Populations: A Review of the Impact of the Correctional System on Community Health," *Journal of Urban Health: Bulletin of the New York Academy of Medicine* 78, no. 2 (June 1, 2001), pp. 214–35, doi.org.

26. "Incarceration and Health: A Family Medicine Perspective (Position Paper)," AAFP, April 2017, www.aafp.org; "Incarceration," Office of Disease Prevention and Health Promotion, 2020, wayback.archive-it.org/5774/20220414161135/https://www.healthypeople.gov/2020/topics -objectives/topic/social-determinants-health/interventions-resources/incarceration.

27. Doris J James and Lauren E Glaze, "Bureau of Justice Statistics Special Report: Mental Health Problems of Prison and Jail Inmates," U.S. Department of Justice, Office of Justice Programs, September 2006, www.bjs.gov.

28. "How Many Individuals with Serious Mental Illness Are in Jails and Prisons?" Treatment Advocacy Center, November 2014, https://web.archive.org/web/20230124194957/https:// www.treatmentadvocacycenter.org/storage/documents/backgrounders/how%20many%20 individuals%20with%20serious%20mental%20illness%20are%20in%20jails%20and%20 prisons%20final.pdf.

29. "Incarceration and Health: A Family Medicine Perspective (Position Paper)," AAFP.

30. Brie A. Williams, et al., "Addressing the Aging Crisis in U.S. Criminal Justice Health Care," *Journal of the American Geriatrics Society* 60, no. 6 (May 29, 2012), pp. 1150–56, doi.org.

31. Marsha McLeod, "The Private Option," *The Atlantic*, September 12, 2019, www.theatlantic .com.

32. Shalev, "From Public to Private Care the Historical Trajectory of Medical Services in a New York City Jail."

33. "Corizon Launches from Correctional Healthcare Merger," Corizon Health, June 3, 2011, web.archive.org/web/20191018201409/http://www.corizonhealth.com/Corizon-News /Corizon-Launches-From-Correctional-Healthcare-Merger1; "Correctional Medical Services Inc," Better Business Bureau, 2020, www.bbb.org/us/mo/saint-louis/profile/health /correctional-medical-services-inc-0734-110159644; "About," MHM Services, n.d., web.archive .org/web/20190910210729/http://www.mhm-services.com/about.html.

34. "California Forensic Medical Group Inc.: Company Profile and News," Bloomberg, n.d., www.bloomberg.com.

35. "Our Company," PrimeCare Medical, Inc., n.d., www.primecaremedical.com/about-us.

36. "About Us," NaphCare, n.d., www.naphcare.com/about.

37. "About," Wexford Health Sources, n.d., www.wexfordhealth.com/about.

38. "Correct Care Solutions LLC Company Profile and News," Bloomberg, n.d., www.bloomberg.com.

39. "Armor Correctional Health Services, Inc.," Dun & Bradstreet, 2020, www.dnb.com.

40. "Corizon Launches from Correctional Healthcare Merger," Corizon Health.

41. Matt Clarke, "Neither Fines nor Lawsuits Deter Corizon from Delivering Substandard Health Care," *Prison Legal News*, March 3, 2020, www.prisonlegalnews.org.

42. "Centene Corp," Investigate: A Project of the American Friends Service Committee, October 18, 2018, investigate.afsc.org.

43. "Centene to Acquire MHM Services to Expand National Footprint in Correctional Healthcare Sector," *PR Newswire*, February 26, 2018, www.prnewswire.com.

44. McLeod, "The Private Option."

45. Jim Baker, "HIG Capital's and Wellpath's Correctional Healthcare Investment Risks," Private Equity Stakeholder Project, June 2019, pestakeholder.org.

46. "Wellpath," PrivCo;, n.d., system.privco.com.

47. Ibid.; "Divisions," Wellpath, n.d., https://wellpathcare.com/divisions.

48. "YesCare, Corp.," PrivCo, system.privco.com/company/yes-care; "Leading Healthcare Group Forms YesCare, Debuting New Vision and Leadership," Business Wire, May 16, 2022, www.businesswire.com.

49. J.D. Schmidt, "See No Evil, Hear No Evil, Treat No Evil: Centurion and the Curse of For-Profit Prison Healthcare," *Prison Legal News*, January 1, 2024, www.prisonlegalnews.org/news; "Centurion Health Revenue and Competitors," GrowJo, n.d., growjo.com/company/Centurion_Health; "About Us," Centurion Health, n.d., teamcenturion.com/about-us.

50. "NaphCare, Inc.," PrivCo, n.d., system.privco.com/company/naphcare-inc; "About Us," Naphcare, n.d., www.naphcare.com/about; Stephanie Rebman, "Birmingham Company Lands Contract for Health Services in Atlanta Jail System," Bizjournals.com, January 22, 2018, www.bizjournals.com.

51. "Wexford Health Sources, Inc.," PrivCo, n.d., system.privco.com.

52. "Prison Health Care: Costs and Quality: How and Why States Strive for High-Performing Systems," The Pew Charitable Trusts.

53. Ibid.

54. Jimmy Jenkins, "Whistleblower Says Corizon Health Administrators Directed Him to Cheat Arizona Prison Monitors," KJZZ, January 23, 2019, kjzz.org.

55. Joseph Darius Jaafari, "He Went into Jail with a Toothache; He Ended up on Life Support—and in Debt," WITF, March 18, 2020, www.witf.org.

56. "Declaration of Charles Pugh, M.D., in Support of Plaintiffs Memorandum in Opposition to Motion for Summary Judgment by Defendants Corizon et al.," January 30, 2015, www.documentcloud.org.

57. Szep, et al., "Special Report: U.S. Jails Are Outsourcing Medical Care—and the Death Toll Is Rising."

58. Ibid.

59. Ibid.

60. Ibid.

61. Karishma A. Chari, Alan E. Simon, and Carol J. Defrances, "National Survey of Prison Health Care: Selected Findings," National Health Statistics Reports, July 28, 2016, www.cdc.gov.

62. "Telemedicine Behind Bars," *Prison Legal News*, December 15, 2013, www.prisonlegalnews.org.

63. "Telemedicine Breaks Out of Prisons to Widespread Use During Pandemic," *AP News*, June 8, 2020, apnews.com.

64. Woodrow Augustus Myers Jr., MD, "A Letter to D.C. Council Chairman Phil Mendelson," Corizon Correctional Healthcare, March 18, 2015, web.archive.org/web/20190620070513/http://www.corizonhealth.com/Corizon-News/a-letter-to-d.c.-council-chairman-phil-mendelson.

65. "FAQs," Wellpath, n.d., web.archive.org/web/20210624154020/https://wellpathcare.com/about/faqs/; Philip G. Peters, "Twenty Years of Evidence on the Outcomes of Malpractice Claims," *Clinical Orthopaedics and Related Research* 467, no. 2 (December 2, 2008), pp. 352–57, doi.org.

66. Christopher Zoukis, "Seventh Circuit: Two-Month Delay in Ordering Biopsy Not Deliberate Indifference," *Prison Legal News*, July 28, 2017, www.prisonlegalnews.org.

67. Nicole Einbinder and Dakin Campbell, "Hidden Investors Took Over Corizon Health, a Leading Prison Healthcare Company. Then They Deployed the Texas Two-Step," *Business Insider*, August 21, 2023, www.businessinsider.com.

68. Joel E. Barthelemy, "Correctional Healthcare Is Changing and Here's Why," GlobalMed, October 27, 2021.

69. Ingrid A. Binswanger, et al., "Release from Prison—a High Risk of Death for Former Inmates," *New England Journal of Medicine* 356, no. 2 (January 11, 2007), pp. 157–65, doi.org.

70. Doris J. James and Lauren E. Glaze, "Highlights Mental Health Problems of Prison and Jail Inmates," U.S. Department of Justice, Office of Justice Programs, Bureau of Justice Statistics Special Report, December 14, 2006, bjs.gov.

71. Jennifer Bronson and Marcus Berzofsky, "Indicators of Mental Health Problems Reported by Prisoners and Jail Inmates, 2011–12," U.S. Department of Justice, Office of Justice Programs, Bureau of Justice Statistics Special Report, June 2017, www.bjs.gov.

72. Michael Ollove, "Amid Shortage of Psychiatric Beds, Mentally Ill Face Long Waits for Treatment," Pew Charitable Trusts, August 2, 2016, www.pewtrusts.org.

73. Leah Pope, "Racial Disparities in Mental Health and Criminal Justice," National Alliance on Mental Illness, July 24, 2019, www.nami.org.

74. "Arrests by Offense, Age, and Gender," Office of Juvenile Justice and Delinquency Prevention, 2018, www.ojjdp.gov.

75. Jennifer Bronson, et al., "Drug Use, Dependence, and Abuse Among State Prisoners and Jail," U.S. Department of Justice, Office of Justice Programs, Bureau of Justice Statistics Special Report, June 2017, www.bjs.gov.

76. Zoe Greenberg and Sharona Coutts, "Punished for Addiction: Women Prisoners Dying from Lack of Treatment," Rewire News Group, April 1, 2015, rewirenewsgroup.com.

77. Margaret Noonan, Harley Rohloff, and Scott Ginder, "Mortality in Local Jails and State Prisons, 2000–2013—Statistical Tables," U.S. Department of Justice, Office of Justice Programs. Bureau of Justice Statistics, August 2015, www.bjs.gov.

78. Kevin Fiscella, et al., "Alcohol and Opiate Withdrawal in U.S. Jails," *American Journal of Public Health* 94, no. 9 (September 1, 2004), pp. 1522–24, www.ncbi.nlm.nih.gov.

79. "State Prison Health Care Spending: An Examination."

80. "2019 ACA Boston Program Book: 149th Congress of Correction," American Correctional Association, 2019, user-3imepyw.cld.bz/ACA-Program-Books.

81. Greenberd and Coutts, "Punished for Addiction."

82. Kirk Heilbrun and Christopher M. King, "Forced Medication and Competency to Stand Trial: Clinical, Legal, and Ethical Issues," *Psychiatric Times*, April 29, 2017, www.psychiatrictimes .com.

83. Noonan, "Mortality in Local Jails and State Prisons, 2000–2013—Statistical Tables."

84. Greenberg and Coutts, "Punished for Addiction."

85. Binswanger, et al., "Release from Prison—a High Risk of Death for Former Inmates."

86. Sawyer, "The Steep Cost of Medical Co-Pays in Prison Puts Health at Risk."

87. Wendy Sawyer, "How Much Do Incarcerated People Earn in Each State?" Prison Policy Initiative, April 10, 2017, www.prisonpolicy.org.

88. Sawyer, "The Steep Cost of Medical Co-Pays in Prison Puts Health at Risk."

89. Ibid.

90. Ibid.

91. "Texas Department of Criminal Justice Annual Health Care Services Fee," Texas Department of Criminal Justice, March 2019, www.tdcj.texas.gov.

92. Matthew Clarke, "Texas: $100 Medical Copay for Prisoners Generates Less Revenue than Expected," *Prison Legal News*, February 4, 2015, www.prisonlegalnews.org.

93. Sawyer, "The Steep Cost of Medical Co-Pays in Prison Puts Health at Risk."

94. Michelle Andrews, "Prisons and Jails Forcing Inmates to Cover Some Medical Care Costs," *Kaiser Health News*, September 29, 2015, khn.org, Jaafari, "He Went into Jail with a Toothache; He Ended up on Life Support—and in Debt."

95. Worth Rises visit to Mecklenburg County Jail.

96. Jim Newton, "Cruel and Unusual: UCLA Law Exposes Fatal Flaws in U.S. Prisons During COVID-19," UCLA Newsroom, May 4, 2021, newsroom.ucla.edu/magazine.

97. Audrey McNamara, "Health Care Provider Severs Ties with Mississippi Prisons After Jay Z and Yo Gotti Lawsuit," CBS News, August 1, 2020, www.cbsnews.com.

98. See "Drug Policy Action's Measure 110 Prevails, Making Oregon the First U.S. State to Decriminalize All Drugs and Expand Access to Addiction and Health Services," Drug Policy Alliance, November 3, 2020, web.archive.org.

Transportation

1. Eli Hager and Alysia Santo, "Inside the Deadly World of Private Prisoner Transport," The Marshall Project, July 6, 2016, www.themarshallproject.org.

2. Christian Mason, Tod W. Burke, and Stephen S. Owen, "On the Road Again: The Dangers of Transporting Ailing Inmates," *Corrections Today*, November/December 2013, web.archive .org/web/20210324095119/https://www.aca.org/ACA_PROD_IMIS/docs/ochc/Mason_Burke _Owen_Nov-DecCT13.pdf.

3. Hager and Santo, "Inside the Deadly World of Private Prisoner Transport."

4. "Budget Overview Fiscal Year 2023 Congressional Justification," Department of Homeland Security, 2023, www.dhs.gov.

5. "Hidden in Plain Sight: ICE Air and the Machinery of Mass Deportation," Center for Human Rights, April 23, 2019, jsis.washington.edu.

6. *Kentucky v. Dennison*, 65 U.S. 66 (1860).

7. *Puerto Rico v. Brandstad*, 483 U.S. 219 (1987).

8. "Opposing Comment for Docket No. MCF 21067," Human Rights Defense Center, 2016, www.humanrightsdefensecenter.org; Alex Friedman, "For-Profit Transportation Companies: Taking Prisoners, and the Public, for a Ride," *Prison Legal News*, September 15, 2006, www .prisonlegalnews.org.

9. Friedman, "For-Profit Transportation Companies."

10. "Home," Inmate Services Corporation, n.d., www.inmate-services.com.

11. Nomaan Merchant and Angeliki Kastanis, "Deported Immigrants Get Their Last Flight on 'ICE Air,'" *AP News*, December 17, 2018, apnews.com.

12. Jeffrey Kaye, "For Immigration Crackdown Proponent, Deportations Mean Business," *HuffPost*, May 29, 2010, www.huffpost.com.

13. Ibid.

14. "U.S. Customs and Border Protection: Contracting for Transportation and Guard Services for Detainees," U.S. Government Accountability Office, October 17, 2016, www.gao.gov.

15. Grahame Gibson, "G4S North America," Group 4 Securicor, n.d., www.g4s.com/
-/media/g4s/corporate/files/financial-presentations/2004/2008_g4s_north_america
_presentation_may_2008.

16. Colleen Robertson, "GTI Operations Tacoma ICE Processing Center," The GEO Group,
May 25, 2015, www.geogroup.com.

17. "Fact Sheet: Facts and Figures," U.S. Marshals Service, February 25, 2020, www
.usmarshals.gov.

18. Hager and Santo, "Inside the Deadly World of Private Prisoner Transport"; "Safety, Timeli-
ness, and Efficiency: Transporting Roughly 30,000 Inmates for Over 1,200 Government Agencies Per Year," Prisoner Transport Services, 2020, prisonertransport.net.

19. "Budget Overview Fiscal Year 2023 Congressional Justification."

20. Catherine E. Shoichet and Curt Merrill, "The Airline No One Wants to Fly: How U.S. Deportation Flights Work," CNN, January 17, 2018, www.cnn.com.

21. "Budget Overview Fiscal Year 2023 Congressional Justification."

22. Hager and Santo, "Inside the Deadly World of Private Prisoner Transport."

23. Website homepage, Prisoner Transportation Services, n.d., prisonertransport.net.

24. Ally Jarmanning, "Sen. Warren Asks DOJ Inspector General to Investigate Private Prison
Transport Companies," WBUR, October 9, 2019, www.wbur.org.

25. "Which Sectors of America's Immigrant Detention System Are Run by Private Companies?" In the Public Interest, n.d., www.inthepublicinterest.org.

26. "Frequently Asked Questions," TransCor America, n.d., transcor.com/faq.

27. "Secure Transportation," The GEO Group, n.d., www.geogroup.com.

28. Ibid.

29. "G4S 2018 Annual Report," G4S, 2018, www.g4s.com.

30. "Hidden in Plain Sight," Center for Human Rights.

31. Merchant and Kastanis, "Deported Immigrants Get Their Last Flight on 'ICE Air.'"

32. USAspending.gov, 2018–2023, www.usaspending.gov.

33. Merchant and Kastanis, "Deported Immigrants Get Their Last Flight on 'ICE Air.'"

34. Justin Rohrlich, "The Sole Airline Willing to Fly 'High-Risk' Deportations Is Price-Gouging
ICE," *Quartz*, December 5, 2019, qz.com.

35. Hager and Santo, "Inside the Deadly World of Private Prisoner Transport."

36. Eli Hager and Alysia Santo, "Death on a Prison Bus: Extradition Companies' Safety
Improvements Lag," *New York Times*, March 23, 2017, www.nytimes.com.

37. Alysia Santo and Eli Hager, "A Man Died in a Private Prison Van. The Company Says: Not
Our Problem," The Marshall Project, March 29, 2019, www.themarshallproject.org.

38. Hager and Santo, "Inside the Deadly World of Private Prisoner Transport."

39. Hager and Santo, "A Man Died in a Private Prison Van."

40. "Investigation Reveals Pattern of Prisoner Abuse in Private Prison Transport Industry," Equal Justice Initiative, July 27, 2016, eji.org.

41. Hager and Santo, "A Man Died in a Private Prison Van."

42. Hager and Santo, "Inside the Deadly World of Private Prisoner Transport."

43. Ibid.

44. Tracy Jan, "Privately Run Prisoner Transport Company Kept Detainee Shackled for 18 Days in Human Waste, Lawsuit Alleges," *Washington Post*, April 24, 2018, www.washingtonpost.com.

45. Hager and Santo, "A Man Died in a Private Prison Van."

46. Hager and Santo, "Inside the Deadly World of Private Prisoner Transport."

47. Ibid.

48. "Opposing Comment for Docket No. MCF 21067."

49. Jaden Rhea, "Highway to Hell: The Privatized Prison Transportation Industry and the Long Road to Reform," *West Virginia Law Review*, 2017, researchrepository.wvu.edu.

50. Joe Buglewicz, "The Horrible Things I Saw Driving a Van Packed with Prisoners," The Marshall Project, July 8, 2016. www.themarshallproject.org.

51. Hager and Santo, "World of Private Prisoner Transport."

52. "Private Prisoner Transport Company Pays Damages in Lawsuit Over Sexual Assault and Death Threats Against Woman," American Civil Liberties Union (ACLU), March 14, 2003, www.aclu.org.

53. Ibid.

54. Ibid.

55. Jeanna's Act, 114 Stat. 2784 (2000), www.congress.gov.

56. Hager and Santo, "Inside the Deadly World of Private Prisoner Transport."

57. "34 U.S. Code § 60103—Federal Regulation of Prisoner Transport Companies," LII / Legal Information Institute, December 21, 2000, www.law.cornell.edu.

58. "Senators Warren and Booker, Rep. Deutch Call for Greater Oversight of Private Prisoner Transport Companies," U.S. Senator Elizabeth Warren of Massachusetts, October 8, 2019, www.warren.senate.gov/oversight/letters.

59. Floricel Liborio Ramos, "ICE Put Me in a Hot Van with No Windows or Water. I Thought I Would Die," ACLU of Northern CA, July 9, 2018, www.aclunc.org.

60. "Refugees, Asylum-seekers and Migrants," Amnesty International, 2016, www.amnesty.org; Duncan Leatherdale, "Why Do People Risk Their Lives to Get to the UK?" BBC News, October 23, 2019, www.bbc.com.

61. Jeremy Scahill, "Intercepted Podcast: Killing Asylum: How Decades of U.S. Policy Ravaged Central America," *The Intercept*, November 28, 2018, theintercept.com.

62. Matthew Clarke, "Private Prisoner Transport Firm Closes After Escape; Problems Continue to Plague Industry," *Prison Legal News*, May 3, 2019, www.prisonlegalnews.org.

63. Nick Miroff, "ICE Air: Shackled Deportees, Air Freshener and Cheers. America's One-Way Trip Out," *Washington Post*, August 10, 2019, www.washingtonpost.com.

64. Shashank Bengali, "They Gambled, and Lost: Dozens of Migrants Braved Thousands of Miles of Jungles, Seas and Bandits to Reach the U.S. Then They Were Sent Home," *Los Angeles Times*, December 24, 2016, www.latimes.com.

65. Bianca Bruno, "ICE Contractor Faces Suit Over 'Inhumane' Van Ride," *Courthouse News*, May 22, 2019, www.courthousenews.com.

66. "Hidden in Plain Sight," Center for Human Rights.

67. Bruno, "ICE Contractor Faces Suit."

68. Jacey Fortin, "U.S. Put 92 Somalis on a Deportation Flight, Then Brought Them Back," *New York Times*, December 9, 2017, www.nytimes.com.

69. "Hidden in Plain Sight," Center for Human Rights.

Community Corrections

1. Nicolás Medina Mora, "Meet the Bail Bond Queen," *BuzzFeed News*, January 9, 2015, www.buzzfeednews.com.

2. Timothy Schnacke, Michael Jones, and Claire Brooker, "The History of Bail and Pretrial Release," Pretrial Justice Institute, September 23, 2010, cdpsdocs.state.co.us.

3. Ibid.

4. Ibid.

5. Hans Zeisel, "Bail Revisited," University of Chicago Law School, 1979, chicagounbound.uchicago.edu.

6. Alison M. Smith, "U.S. Constitutional Limits on State Money-Bail Practices for Criminal Defendants," Congressional Research Service, February 26, 2019, fas.org.

7. Warren Miller, "The Bail Reform Act of 1966: Need for Reform in 1969," *Catholic University Law Review* 19, no. 1 (1969), scholarship.law.edu.

8. Schnacke, Jones, and Brooker, "The History of Bail."

9. Ryan Labrecque, "Probation in the United States: A Historical and Modern Perspective," Portland State University, 2017, pdxscholar.library.pdx.edu.

10. "Probation and Pretrial Services History," United States Courts, n.d., www.uscourts.gov.

11. Labrecque, "Probation in the United States."

12. Christine S. Schloss and Leanne F. Alarid, "Standards in the Privatization of Probation Services," *Criminal Justice Review* 32, no. 3 (September 1, 2007), pp. 233–45, doi.org.

13. Terry Carter, "Privatized Probation Becomes a Spiral of Added Fees and Jail Time," *ABA Journal*, October 1, 2014, www.abajournal.com/magazine.

14. Lewis Wallace, "Welcome to Georgia, the Epicenter of the Private Probation Racket," *The Outline*, August 17, 2017, theoutline.com.

15. "Dialogue—Issue 37: Parole in the United States: People and Policies in Transition," The Dui Hua Foundation, November 29, 2009, duihua.org.

16. "Probation and Parole: History, Goals, and Decision-Making: Origins of Probation and Parole," American Law Library, n.d., law.jrank.org.

17. Schloss and Alarid, "Standards in the Privatization."

18. Timothy Williams, "'It Didn't Work': States That Ended Parole for Violent Crimes Are Thinking Again," *New York Times*, February 13, 2020, www.nytimes.com.

19. "Dialogue—Issue 37: Parole in the United States: People and Policies in Transition," The Dui Hua Foundation.

20. Todd Bussert, et al., "New Time Limits on Federal Halfway Houses," *Criminal Justice* 21, no.1 (2006), www.frostbussert.com.

21. Lauren-Brooke Eisen, "The Complex History of the Controversial 1994 Crime Bill," Brennan Center for Justice, April 4, 2016, www.brennancenter.org.

22. Emma Anderson, "NPR Choice Page," NPR, May 24, 2014, www.npr.org.

23. Robert Gable, "The Ankle Bracelet Is History: An Informal Review of the Birth and Death of a Monitoring Technology," *Journal of Offender Monitoring*, 2015, www.researchgate.net.

24. Ibid.

25. Sarah Stillman, "Get Out of Jail, Inc.," *New Yorker*, June 16, 2016, www.newyorker.com.

26. "GEO Group Statement on Federal Legislation on Prison Reform (The FIRST STEP Act)," The GEO Group, November 9, 2019, wearegeo.com.

27. E. Ann Carson and Rich Kluckow, "Correctional Populations in the United States, 2021—Statistical Tables," U.S. Dept. of Justice, Office of Justice Programs, Bureau of Justice Statistics, February 2023, bjs.ojp.gov.

28. Zhen Zeng, "Jail Inmates in 2018," U.S. Dept. of Justice, Office of Justice Programs, Bureau of Justice Statistics, March 2020, www.bjs.gov.

29. "Pretrial Release of Felony Defendants, 1992: National Pretrial Reporting Program," U.S. Dept. of Justice, Office of Justice Programs, Bureau of Justice Statistics, November 1994, www.bjs.gov.

30. Traci Schlesinger, "Racial Disparities in Pretrial Diversion," *Race and Justice*, no. 3 (April 5, 2013), pp. 210–38, doi.org; Jennifer A. Tallon, Melissa Labriola, and Joseph Spadafore, "Creating Off-Ramps: A National Review of Police-Led Diversion Programs," Center for Court Innovation, 2018.

31. Emily Leslie and Nolan G. Pope, "The Unintended Impact of Pretrial Detention on Case Outcomes: Evidence from New York City Arraignments," *Journal of Law and Economics* 60, no. 3 (August 2017), pp. 529–57, doi.org.

32. Patrick Liu, Ryan Nunn, and Jay Shambaugh, "The Hamilton Project: The Economics of Bail and Pretrial Detention," Hamilton Project, December 2018, www.hamiltonproject.org.

33. Danielle Kaeble, "Probation and Parole in the United States, 2021," U.S. Dept. of Justice, Office of Justice Programs, Bureau of Justice Statistics, February 2023, bjs.ojp.gov.

34. Jones, "Correctional Control 2018"; Danielle Kaeble, "Probation and Parole in the United States, 2021"; "Frequently Asked Questions About Federal Halfway Houses and Home Confinement," Families Against Mandatory Minimums, n.d., famm.org.

35. Jess Zhang, Jacob Kang-Brown, and Ari Kotler, "People on Electronic Monitoring," Vera Institute of Justice, January 2024, www.vera.org.

36. Ibid.

37. "The GEO Group, Inc., 2022 Annual Report," The GEO Group, February 2023, investors. geogroup.com.

38. Zhang, Kang-Brown, and Kotler, "People on Electronic Monitoring."

39. "Selling Off Our Freedom: How Insurance Corporations Have Taken Over Our Bail System," American Civil Liberties Union (ACLU), n.d., www.aclu.org.

40. "Bail Bonds, Bail Bond Services," Aladdin Bail Bonds, n.d., www.aladdinbailbonds.com; Jennifer Van Grove and Brittany Meiling, "Bail Agents Face Death Sentence in California," *Baltimore Sun*, September 3, 2018, www.baltimoresun.com.

41. Adolfo Flores, "Immigrants Desperate to Get Out of U.S. Detention Can Get Trapped by Debt," *BuzzFeed News*, July 23, 2016, www.buzzfeednews.com.

42. "Selling Off Our Freedom," ACLU.

43. Rebecca Burns, "Diversion Programs Say They Offer a Path Away from Court, but Critics Say the Tolls Are Hefty," *ProPublica*, November 3, 2013, www.propublica.org; Lee Romney, "Private Diversion Programs Are Failing Those Who Need Help the Most," *Reveal*, May 31, 2017, www.revealnews.org.

44. Marianne Møllmann and Christine Mehta, "Neither Justice Nor Treatment: Drug Courts in the United States," Physicians for Human Rights, June 2017, phr.org.

45. "Nonprofit Loses Funding from Florida Department of Children and Families," WKMG, September 22, 2014, www.clickorlando.com.

46. Shoshana Walter, "The Work Cure," *Reveal*, July 7, 2020, revealnews.org.

47. "Judicial Correction Services," Wikipedia, February 27, 2024, en.wikipedia.org/wiki /Judicial_Correction_Services.

48. Beth Schwartzapfel, "Probation-for-Profit Just Got Less Profitable," The Marshall Project, April 14, 2017, www.themarshallproject.org.

49. "CoreCivic Annual Report Form 10-K," CoreCivic, February 14, 2020, ir.corecivic.com; "Probation/Case Management," Recovery Monitoring Solutions, n.d., recoveryms.com.

50. "The GEO Group, Inc., 2022 Annual Report."

51. Lucas High, "Boulder's BI Incorporated Has Earned More Than Half-Billion Dollars from ICE Contracts," *Boulder Daily Camera*, July 13, 2018, www.dailycamera.com.

52. "The GEO Group 2022 Annual Report."

53. Esther Poveda, et al., "Company That Bails Out Immigrants Is Accused of Abusive and Fraudulent Tactics," *Univision*, April 30, 2018, www.univision.com.

54. "New Attenti GPS Device for Criminal Justice Agencies First to Include Wi-Fi Tracking and Communication," PRNewswire, August 15, 2019, www.prnewswire.com/news-releases; "SCRAM Systems," SCRAM Systems, n.d., www.scramsystems.com; Eric Markowitz, "Electronic Monitoring Has Become the New Debtors Prison," *Prison Legal News*, March 3, 2016, www.prisonlegalnews.org.

55. Kara Gotsch and Vinay Basti, "Capitalizing on Mass Incarceration: U.S. Growth in Private Prisons," The Sentencing Project, August 2, 2018, www.sentencingproject.org.

56. *The Banks That Finance Private Prison Companies*, In the Public Interest, November 17, 2016, www.inthepublicinterest.org.

57. "The GEO Group Announces $360 Million Acquisition of Community Education Centers," *Businesswire*, February 22, 2017, www.businesswire.com.

58. "The GEO Group 2022 Annual Report."

59. "CCA Announces Acquisition of Avalon Correctional Services, Inc.," GlobeNewswire News Room, October 29, 2015, www.globenewswire.com/news; "CCA Acquires Correctional Management, Inc.," GlobeNewswire News Room, April 11, 2016, www.globenewswire.com.

60. "CoreCivic 2022 Annual Report Form 10-K," CoreCivic, ir.corecivic.com.

61. Jacob Silverman, "How Bail Work," *How Stuff Works*, February 5, 2007, money.howstuffworks.com/bail.

62. "Selling Off Our Freedom," ACLU.

63. Schnacke, Jones, and Brooker, "The History of Bail."

64. Jessica Brand and Jessica Pishko, "Bail Reform: Explained," The Appeal, June 14, 2018, theappeal.org.

65. "Presumed Innocent for a Price: The Impact of Cash Bail Across Eight New York Counties," New York Civil Liberties Union, March 2018, www.nyclu.org.

66. "Moving Beyond Money: A Primer on Bail Reform," Harvard Law School Criminal Justice Policy Program, October 2016, cjpp.law.harvard.edu.

67. Emily Yoffe, "Innocence Is Irrelevant in the Age of the Plea Bargain," *The Atlantic*, August 5, 2017, www.theatlantic.com.

68. Bernadette Rabuy and Daniel Kopf, "Detaining the Poor: How Money Bail Perpetuates an Endless Cycle of Poverty and Jail Time," Prison Policy Initiative, May 10, 2016, www.prisonpolicy.org.

69. Peter Wagner, "Following the Money of Mass Incarceration," Prison Policy Initiative, January 25, 2017, www.prisonpolicy.org.

70. Louis Jacobson, "Are U.S., Philippines the Only Two Countries with Cash Bail?" *PolitiFact*, October 9, 2018, www.politifact.com/california/statements.

71. Liu, Nunn, and Shambaugh, "The Hamilton Project."

72. "Selling Off Our Freedom," ACLU.

73. Rhonda Cook, "Connections Matter in Ga. Private Probation Industry," *Corrections1*, January 20, 2014, www.corrections1.com.

74. Jazmine Ulloa, "California's Historic Overhaul of Cash Bail Is Now on Hold, Pending a 2020 Referendum," *Los Angeles Times,* January 17, 2019, www.latimes.com.

75. Alysia Santo, "Bail Reformers Aren't Waiting for Bail Reform," The Marshall Project, August 24, 2016, www.themarshallproject.org.

76. Jessi Stone, "Bail Bond Industry a Strong Lobby in Raleigh," Justice Policy Institute, August 29, 2018, www.justicepolicy.org.

77. "Our Results," Brooklyn Community Bail Fund, 2016, brooklynbailfund.org/our-results.

78. Stephanie Wylie and Ames Grawert, "2023 Criminal Justice Reform in New York State," Brennan Center for Justice, July 20, 2023, www.brennancenter.org.

79. "Cash Bail Changes—2023 SAFE-T Act," Illinois Legal Aid Online, n.d., www.illinoislegalaid.org.

80. Micah Hauser, "The High Price of Freedom for Migrants in Detention," *New Yorker*, March 12, 2019, www.newyorker.com.

81. Poveda, "Company That Bails Out."

82. Burns, "Diversion Programs."

83. Ibid.

84. Julia Lurie, "A Disturbing New Phase of the Opioid Crisis: How Rehab Recruiters Are Luring Recovering Addicts into a Deadly Cycle," *Mother Jones*, April 2019, www.motherjones.com.

85. "How Florida Ignited the Heroin Epidemic," *Palm Beach Post*, 2018, heroin.palmbeachpost.com.

86. Jeremy Roebuck, "Once Touted as a Recovery Success Story, Philly Rehab Owner Admits He Illegally Profited from Others' Addictions," *Philadelphia Inquirer,* June 26, 2019, www.inquirer.com.

87. Colton Wooten, "My Years in the Florida Shuffle of Drug Addiction," *New Yorker*, October 14, 2019, www.newyorker.com.

88. Leah Wang, "Punishment Beyond Prisons 2023: Incarceration and Supervision by State," Prison Policy Initiative, May 2023, www.prisonpolicy.org.

89. "Confined and Costly," CSG Justice Center, June 18, 2019, csgjusticecenter.org.

90. Amy Julia Harris and Shoshana Walter, "All Work. No Pay," The Center for Investigative Reporting, 2020, revealnews.org.

91. Wang, "Punishment Beyond Prisons."

92. "Promising Practices in Providing Pretrial Services Functions Within Probation Agencies: A User's Guide," American Probation and Parole Association, June 2010, www.appa-net.org.

93. "Bureau of Justice Statistics (BJS)—FAQ Detail," U.S. Dept. of Justice, Office of Justice Programs, Bureau of Justice Statistics, 2013, www.bjs.gov.

94. Jacobson, Schiraldi, and Hotez, "Executive Session."

95. "Bureau of Justice Statistics (BJS)—FAQ Detail."

96. Jacobson, Schiraldi, and Hotez, "Executive Session."

97. Michael P. Jacobson, Vincent Schiraldi, Reagan Daly, and Emily Hotez, "Less Is More: How Reducing Probation Populations Can Improve Outcomes," *Crime Report,* August 2017, thecri merereport.org.

98. "Confined and Costly," CSG Justice Center.

99. "Profiting from the Poor," Southern Center for Human Rights, July 2008, www.schr.org.

100. "Set Up to Fail," Human Rights Watch, February 20, 2018, www.hrw.org/report.

101. Kira Lerner, "In Oklahoma, Private Companies Run Pretrial Services, Driving People into Debt," The Appeal, June 26, 2019, theappeal.org.

102. Gable, "The Ankle Bracelet."

103. James Kilgore, "Electronic Monitors: How Companies Dream of Locking Us in Our Homes," *In These Times*, April 23, 2018, inthesetimes.com.

104. James Kilgore, "Electronic Monitoring Is Not the Answer," MediaJustice, 2015, mediajus tice.org.

105. Lautaro Grinspan, "Many of Miami's Immigrants Wear Ankle Monitors. Will Technology Betray Them?" *Miami Herald*, August 24, 2019, www.miamiherald.com.

106. "Electronic Monitoring Reduces Recidivism," U.S. Dept. of Justice, Office of Justice Programs, September 2011, www.ncjrs.gov.

107. Sarah Razner, "Fond Du Lac Company Hopes New Tech Will Change Face of Wisconsin Criminal Justice System," *Fond Du Lac Reporter*, July 2, 2019, www.fdlreporter.com.

108. James Kilgore and Emmett Sanders, "Electronic Monitoring Isn't a More Humane Form of Prison. Here's Why," *Wired*, August 4, 2018, www.wired.com.

109. "The SCRAM Tether, How It Works and How It Doesn't," Law Offices of Barton Morris, November 26, 2012, michigancriminalattorney.com.

110. Molly Osberg and Dhruv Mehrotr, "When Your Freedom Depends on an App," *Gizmodo,* April 27, 2020, gizmodo.com.

111. Andrea Armstrong, "A Letter to Jay-Z: Don't Keep This Promise," The Appeal, April 10, 2018, theappeal.org.

112. "How Jay-Z & Other Venture Capitalists Are Creating New Problems in the Name of Social Justice," The Black Youth Project, March 28, 2018.

113. James Kilgore, "Let's Fight for Freedom from Electronic Monitors and E-Carceration," *Truthout*, September 4, 2019, truthout.org.

114. Lauren Sukin, "When Jail Is the Better Option: The Failure of Halfway Houses," The Century Foundation, June 23, 2015, tcf.org.

115. "A Halfway House Nightmare," Cockle Legal Briefs, June 26, 2012, www.cocklelegalbriefs .com.

116. "Frequently Asked Questions," Families Against Mandatory Minimums.

117. Sam Dolnick, "Pennsylvania Study Finds Halfway Houses Don't Reduce Recidivism," *New York Times*, March 24, 2013, nytimes.com.

118. Sam Dolnick, "Finances Plague Company Running Halfway Houses," *New York Times*, July 16, 2012, nytimes.com.

119. Matthew Clarke, "Escapes and Crime at New Jersey's Privately-Run Halfway Houses," *Prison Legal News*, August 24, 2016, prisonlegalnews.org.

120. Sam Dolnick, "As Escapees Stream Out, a Penal Business Thrives," *New York Times*, June 16, 2012, nytimes.com.

121. Dolnick, "Finances Plague Company."

122. Anat Rubin, "A Record of Trouble," The Marshall Project, April 11, 2015, themarshallproject.org.

123. Cecilia Lei, "The Treatment Industrial Complex," *East Bay Express*, February 21, 2018, eastbayexpress.com.

124. Christopher Zoukis, "From Cages to the Community: Prison Profiteers and the Treatment Industrial Complex," *Prison Legal News*, March 6, 2018, prisonlegalnews.org.

125. Carl Takei, "Private Prison Giant CoreCivic's Wants to Corner the Mass Incarceration 'Market' in the States," American Civil Liberties Union (ACLU), November 7, 2017, aclu.org.

126. Deanna R. Hoskins, "The FIRST STEP Act Sets Up a Dangerous Future," *The Hill*, July 20, 2018, thehill.com.

INDEX

Bianca Tylek is the founder and executive director of Worth Rises, a New York–based criminal justice advocacy organization known for its innovative research; federal, state, and local policy work; corporate activism; and a range of other initiatives. She lives in New York City.

PUBLISHING IN THE PUBLIC INTEREST

Thank you for reading this book published by The New Press; we hope you enjoyed it. New Press books and authors play a crucial role in sparking conversations about the key political and social issues of our day.

We hope that you will stay in touch with us. Here are a few ways to keep up to date with our books, events, and the issues we cover:

- Sign up at www.thenewpress.com/subscribe to receive updates on New Press authors and issues and to be notified about local events
- www.facebook.com/newpressbooks
- www.twitter.com/thenewpress
- www.instagram.com/thenewpress

Please consider buying New Press books not only for yourself, but also for friends and family and to donate to schools, libraries, community centers, prison libraries, and other organizations involved with the issues our authors write about.

The New Press is a 501(c)(3) nonprofit organization; if you wish to support our work with a tax-deductible gift please visit www.thenewpress .com/donate or use the QR code below.